The Body
and the Screen

THINKING CINEMA

Series Editors

David Martin-Jones, University of Glasgow, UK
Sarah Cooper, King's College, University of London, UK

Volume 5

The Body and the Screen

Female Subjectivities in Contemporary Women's Cinema

KATE INCE

Bloomsbury Academic
An imprint of Bloomsbury Publishing Inc

B L O O M S B U R Y
NEW YORK · LONDON · OXFORD · NEW DELHI · SYDNEY

Bloomsbury Academic
An imprint of Bloomsbury Publishing Inc

1385 Broadway	50 Bedford Square
New York	London
NY 10018	WC1B 3DP
USA	UK

www.bloomsbury.com

BLOOMSBURY and the Diana logo are trademarks of Bloomsbury Publishing Plc

First published 2017

© Kate Ince, 2017

Library of Congress Cataloging-in-Publication Data
A catalog record for this book is available from the Library of Congress.

ISBN:	HB:	978-1-6235-6292-2
	PB:	978-1-6235-6581-7
	ePDF:	978-1-6235-6626-5
	ePub:	978-1-6235-6520-6

Series: Thinking Cinema

Cover design: Eleanor Rose
Cover image © Still from Fish Tank, 2009, dir: Andrea Arnold © BBC FILMS / THE KOBAL COLLECTION

Typeset by Integra Software Services Pvt. Ltd.
Printed and bound in the United States of America

Contents

Acknowledgements

This book has been over two years in the writing and a lot longer in gestation, and a number of people have contributed to bringing it into being. David Martin Jones patiently encouraged me through the proposal submission process, and he and Sarah Cooper have been supportive and efficient (as well as inspiring) Series Editors whose film-philosophical expertise was particularly appreciated in the final stages of manuscript preparation. A semester of study leave from the University of Birmingham in 2013–14 got writing underway and three months of unpaid leave granted by the School of Languages, Cultures, Art History and Music in 2015–16 enabled me to finish it. Material from a number of previous publications appears in Chapters 3–6, and I am grateful to John Wiley & Sons for allowing me to reuse parts of 'Is Sex Comedy or Tragedy? Directing Desire and Female Auteurship in the Cinema of Catherine Breillat', first published in the *Journal of Aesthetics and Art Criticism* 64: 1 (also the book *Thinking through Cinema*) in 2006, and 'Feminist Phenomenology and the Film World of Agnès Varda' from *Hypatia: A Journal of Feminist Philosophy* 28: 3 (2013). Berghahn Books kindly allowed me to draw on 'Feminist Phenomenology and the Films of Sally Potter', a chapter of *Existentialism and Contemporary Cinema: A Beauvoirian Perspective* (2012), and to include a much modified version of 'Games with the Gaze: Sophie Calle's Postmodern Phototextuality', from the 2005 book *The Art of the Project: Projects and Experiments in Modern French Culture*. Finally, Liverpool University Press kindly gave me permission to reuse parts of 'From Minor to "Major" Cinema? Women's and Feminist Cinema in France in the 2000s' from the 2008 special French cinema issue of the *Australian Journal of French Studies* titled '(Retro)projections: French Cinema in the Twenty-First Century'.

A number of people have provided companionship and essential discussion while the book has taken shape, the first of whom were Lucy Bolton, Codruta Morari and Greg Tuck on a panel presented at the 2010 SCMS conference in Los Angeles. Queen Mary University, London, is a place I visited frequently between 2009 and 2014: two invitations from Lucy Bolton to two highly stimulating one-day 'Phenomenology and Film' conferences in 2010 and

2013, and another from Ros Murray to speak at her conference on feminist activism and the moving image in 2014 facilitated important conversations with Jenny Chamarette and Libby Saxton as well as with the conferences' organizers and other participants. In 2011 I presented a paper on Merleau-Ponty's feminist critics at the annual Society for French Studies conference on the same campus. Early in 2014, David Sorfa and Dan Yacavone's invitation to give the Edinburgh Film Seminar was an opportunity to get useful feedback on draft material from the book, as was the paper on Claire Denis's *White Material* I gave at the Women's Film and Television History Network conference at UEA in May of that year. The annual *Film-Philosophy* conference has become the most valuable event in my academic calendar since it began in 2008, and co-presenting a panel on feminist philosophy and women film-makers with Anna Backman Rogers, Jenny Chamarette and Ros Murray in 2014 in Glasgow, organized (with particularly impressive ancillary support) by David Martin-Jones, was another opportunity to exchange with like-minded colleagues as well as with my co-panellists. More locally, at the University of Birmingham, the company of Camilla Smith, Liz L'Estrange, Lisa Downing, Charlotte Ross and Stephen Forcer has been the kind that keeps writing going, and the enthusiasm of the students on my Artists' Film and Video module in 2014–15 was particularly appreciated. Locally but off campus, I have particularly valued conversations with Jonathan Rowles. In the later stages of writing, Jenny Chamarette and Jonathan Rowles read draft material for me, and I am immensely grateful for the time they took to do so and for the helpful comments they offered. Any inadequacies in what follows are entirely my responsibility.

Kate Ince, April 2016

List of Figures

1

Female Subjectivity in Philosophy and Theory

If there is no such thing today as femininity, it is because there never was. (Simone de Beauvoir, The Second Sex, *p. 4)*

My criticism of Western philosophy above all has concerned the forgetting of the existence of a subjectivity which is different from masculine subjectivity: a subjectivity in the feminine. (Luce Irigaray, Key Writings, *p. vii)*

The 'female' subject-position is linked to fleshy continuity, rather than to an autonomous and individualized 'soul' or 'mind' that merely inhabits the flesh. (Christine Battersby, The Phenomenal Woman, *p. 10)*

Amid the campaigns about women's and feminist film to which so-called second-wave feminism gave birth in the 1970s, direct attention to the issue of female subjectivity was first drawn by Teresa de Lauretis in her book *Alice Doesn't: Feminism, Semiotics, Cinema* in 1984. Responding to the hugely influential argument of Laura Mulvey's 'Visual Pleasure and Narrative Cinema' (Mulvey 1989a), de Lauretis proposed that 'the present task of women's cinema may be not the destruction of narrative and visual pleasure, but rather the construction of another frame of reference, one in which the measure of desire is no longer just the male subject' (de Lauretis 1984: 8). In this opening chapter of this book I shall concentrate on the issue highlighted by de Lauretis, the construction of a 'frame of reference [...] in which the measure of desire is no longer just the male subject'. This issue will also be central to the six chapters that follow the first two – Body, Look, Speech, Performance, Desire and Freedom – whose close readings of a selection of films directed by French and British women in the 1990s, 2000s and 2010s (a time period chosen deliberately to post-date second-wave feminism) examine core elements of (female) subjectivity. The second chapter of this book will address the question of what has become of feminist film theory over forty years after the publication of seminal essays such as Mulvey's and Claire Johnston's 'Women's Cinema as Counter-Cinema' (Johnston 1999), assessing whether it can be said still to exist, how it has both developed with and diverged from trends in film theory more generally, and – crucially – what kinds of theories have assumed the mantle borne by Freudian and Lacanian psychoanalysis in its undisputed heyday of the 1970s and 1980s. By focusing in this first chapter on what leading feminist philosophers have written about the 'problem' of the female subject, I shall introduce the parameters of the readings of films undertaken in Chapters 3–8.

When de Lauretis proposed that women film-makers might do well to shift their attention from the reformulation of film form to 'the construction of another frame of reference', she was in fact reposing a question that had preoccupied feminist philosophers and critics of art forms other than film since well before the 1980s, namely, how should female subjectivity be theorized? The notion of subjectivity established in the seventeenth century and reinforced by Enlightenment philosophy, particularly that of Immanuel Kant, was of a supposedly gender-neutral unitary and universal subject that turned out 'to be implicitly a male subject whose "neutrality" is conceptually dependent on the "shadow" conception of the female subject' (Gatens 1991: 5). While the male subject was constructed 'as self-contained and as an owner of his person and capacities' (Gatens 1991: 5), as able 'to separate itself from and dominate nature' (Gatens 1991: 5) and as possessed of a sexually neutral mind that merely inhabited its body without being connected to it in any explicable way, the female subject is constructed as follows:

[constructed as] prone to disorder and passion, as economically and politically dependent on men, and these constructions are justified by reference to women's nature. She 'makes no sense by herself' and her subjectivity assumes a lack which males complete. She is indistinguishable from a wife/mother. (Gatens 1991: 5)

Gatens' summary of the two kinds of human subjects enfolded within the supposedly unitary Enlightenment concept of subjectivity shows that women's identity was conceived entirely on the basis of its complementarity with men's: female subjectivity was dependent on male subjectivity for its definition. It was also considered to be stable and fixed (women's 'nature') and to be disembodied – because no philosophical account of embodied subjectivity existed. All these presumptions have been challenged by feminist philosophy and theory of the mid- and late-twentieth century, and I shall set out the form these challenges have taken and suggest that certain elements have come to the fore in contemporary thinking about the subjectivity of women. The writers and thinkers who have challenged the Enlightenment model of female subjectivity most forcefully are Simone de Beauvoir and Luce Irigaray, but I shall draw too on the work of Christine Battersby, Sonia Kruks, Judith Butler and Iris Marion Young.

In constructing this overview of recent theories of female subjectivity, I shall not draw on the Freudian and Lacanian accounts of femininity that have been so influential in psychoanalytically oriented feminism and feminist film theory. This is no casual omission, my reasons for it lying (as intimated above) in the arguments I shall develop in Chapter 2 about the failure of psychoanalytic feminist film theory to offer a satisfactory account of female subjectivity – one that integrates embodiment and is sufficiently historically flexible to take account of non-white and other-than-heterosexual female identities. I shall suggest in Chapter 2 that a strand of feminist film-philosophical writing that arose in the early 1990s, just as feminist cine-psychoanalysis began to wane, offers the best prospects for future feminist approaches to film, its rejection of the Cartesian mind/body dualism and openness to minority identities making 'it' (actually a range of approaches) superior to cine-psychoanalytic theorizing of screen women. First, however, I shall set out the understandings of female subjectivity offered by Simone de Beauvoir, Luce Irigaray and Christine Battersby.

Simone de Beauvoir and the embodied, situated female subject

In *The Second Sex*, published in French in 1949, Beauvoir set out her existentialist version of the Enlightenment construction of female subjectivity: 'She is determined and differentiated with reference to man, and not he with reference to her; she is the incidental, the inessential as opposed to the essential. He is the Subject, he is the Absolute – she is the Other' (Beauvoir 1988: 16).[1] In introducing the topic of *The Second Sex* in these terms, Beauvoir was of course setting out the problem rather than condoning the status of woman as Other to man – although her groundbreaking book did not attempt to dismantle the conceptual framework that rendered women Other as secondary to the male norm, its extensive anthropological, historical, biological and sociological investigations into women's lived experience shifted her existentialist thinking onto more materialist ground than Jean-Paul Sartre's. While the second part of the first volume of *The Second Sex* reviews women's history from prehistoric times up to the decade in which Beauvoir was writing, the second volume examines the stages of a woman's life in turn, paying attention to sexuality, education, sexual initiation, sexual orientation, marriage, motherhood and old age. By detailing bodily experiences specific to women such as menstruation, the female experience of sexual relations, gestation, childbirth and the menopause, Beauvoir literally 'fleshed out' a study of female subjectivity that had until then seen only insufficiency in women's social roles as wives and mothers. Her accounts of female bodily experience were rarely positive, with a woman's experience of her body during menstruation described as that of 'an obscure alien thing' (Beauvoir 1988: 61), the implantation of the egg in the uterus at gestation referred to as 'a more profound alienation' (Beauvoir 1988: 62), childbirth considered 'painful and dangerous' (Beauvoir 1988: 62) and nursing 'a tiring service' (all quoted in own translations by Moi 1994: 165). But by co-existing in a single compendious volume these accounts constituted something no woman philosopher had previously achieved, the description of 'subjectivity and women's experience as lived and felt in the flesh' (Young 2005: 7). These are the words with which Iris Marion Young glosses the term 'body experience' in the title of her book *On Female Body Experience*, distinguishing her mode of enquiry (also Beauvoir's) from the social-scientific approach which 'takes bodies as objects or things to observe, study or explain'.[2] In *The Second Sex* Beauvoir had placed the female body at the centre of her investigation of

---

[1] The translation of *The Second Sex* I have used here (Beauvoir 1988) is the one by H.M Parshley first published in 1953 and reissued numerous times up to the 2000s, since in this instance it seems to me superior to the rendering by Constance Borde and Sheila Malovany Chevallier in their recent translation (Beauvoir 2009), from which the great majority of my quotations from *The Second Sex* are drawn.

[2] Young began writing about themes of female embodiment in the 1970s and recalls in the introduction to her book that at that time, 'existential phenomenology was the primary approach available to American philosophers for such a project' and that her earliest essay in the field, 'Throwing Like a Girl', 'relies specifically on the theories of Maurice Merleau-Ponty and Simone de Beauvoir' (Young 2005: 7). She notes the widespread critical reaction from a subsequent generation of French thinkers (Foucault, Derrida, Kristeva, Deleuze and others) to the 'naive

sexually differentiated existence by asserting that the body 'is not a *thing*, it is a situation: it is our grasp on the world and the outline for our projects' (Beauvoir 2009: 46). She described this position simply as 'that of Heidegger, Sartre and Merleau-Ponty' (Beauvoir 2009: 46) without highlighting or even acknowledging that her focus was on the female body, an original departure in political philosophy. But the framework of human identity she employed in *The Second Sex* did follow the readmission to philosophical thought of the notion of lived bodily experience proposed by Edmund Husserl, the founder of phenomenology, early in the twentieth century, and shared a great deal with the phenomenology of perception recently published by her and Sartre's friend Maurice Merleau-Ponty, a different development of Husserl's work from Sartre's in *Being and Nothingness*, published two years earlier. Since this framework is essential to understanding Beauvoir's 'theory' of embodied female subjectivity, I shall make a short digression at this point to explain what it was, via the work of feminist political philosopher Sonia Kruks.

In *Situation and Human Existence: Freedom, Subjectivity and Society* (Kruks 1990), Kruks expounds the notion of situated, social human existence that underpins the 1940s work of Sartre, Beauvoir and Merleau-Ponty. She states of Beauvoir:

> Her work implied that the notion of subjectivity must be rethought in terms of the significance of the body and the weight of social institutions for human situation. Beauvoir herself never explicitly developed the reformulations that her analysis implied. But Merleau-Ponty, whose work I next examine, did. In Merleau-Ponty's writings of the 1940s we find a radical reformulation of the notion of the subject. The subject is no longer the possessor of private, individual consciousness, but is an 'impure' subject. The situated subject is an opening, through the body and perceptual experience, on to a common being and is always an intersubjectivity. (Kruks 1990: 17)

Enlarging on situated subjectivity, Kruks traces the profoundly social, intersubjective nature of Merleau-Ponty's thinking about subjectivity to the concept of 'incarnation' developed by French philosopher Gabriel Marcel in the 1930s, noting that incarnation (embodiment) was for Merleau-Ponty the reason why 'the philosopher is always a situated participant in reality

humanism' of existential phenomenology's conceptions of consciousness and subjectivity, but observes also how 'some Anglo-American philosophers and social theorists who for many years aligned themselves with these French postmodern thinkers have in recent years become more interested in the French phenomenologists' and how Merleau-Ponty's philosophy seems to be gaining renewed interest (Young 2005: 8).

rather than a detached "spectator" of it' (Kruks 1990: 116). The notion of the 'impure' subject Kruks finds in Merleau-Ponty overcame (deconstructed, perhaps), Sartre's distinction between the in-itself and the for-itself, replacing the mind/body dualism that had dominated philosophy since Descartes with an understanding of consciousness as embodied, and envisaging 'man' (sic) as a body-subject rather than a pure, individual consciousness. The body, Merleau-Ponty stated, 'forms between the pure subject and the object *a third genus of being*' in which 'the subject loses its purity and its transparency' (Merleau-Ponty 2002: 408, quoted in Kruks 1990: 117): for Kruks, Merleau-Ponty 'never abandons the notion of the subject as the centre of effective action, but overcomes Cartesian/Sartrian individualism by elaborating this notion of an "impure" subject' (Kruks 1990: 117).[3] In Kruks's view, the publication of *Phenomenology of Perception* in 1945 established Merleau-Ponty as the pre-eminent philosopher of the body and embodiment, but what she insists is often overlooked (I would say perhaps because his philosophical writings contain few examples from everyday life of the kind often plucked from Sartre's *Being and Nothingness* to illustrate the latter's existential phenomenological thought) is that the body-subject he discusses is thoroughly socially situated. Beauvoir reviewed *Phenomenology of Perception* for the first issue of *Les Temps modernes* in 1945, and her review (Beauvoir 2004: 159–164) endorses its framework of human identity every bit as much as it does Sartre's very different, dualist and (arguably) predominantly metaphysical understanding of socially situated subjectivity.

Crucial to Kruks's purpose in *Situation and Human Existence*, which deals with the thought of Merleau-Ponty, Beauvoir and Sartre in the same volume, is to demonstrate how Beauvoir's 1940s thought owed at least as much to Merleau-Ponty as to Sartre, contrary to the picture painted by historians of existentialism up to the 1980s. How aware Beauvoir was of this commonality is hard to estimate, since she always declared herself an adherent of Sartre's framework of human identity, and would side – seemingly for reasons of personal loyalty than on philosophical grounds – with Sartre rather than Merleau-Ponty in the *querelle* that broke out between the two philosophers in the early 1950s. What Kruks's work has led the way in exposing is that Beauvoir's philosophical writings of the 1940s – *Pyrrhus and Cineas, The Ethics of Ambiguity* and *The Second Sex*, along with her novels *She Came to Stay* and *The Blood of Others* – evince an understanding of situatedness and embodiment that is closer to Merleau-Ponty than to Sartre. In turning to the subject of 'woman' for *The Second Sex*, Beauvoir continued to use her own

---

[3]The extent to which the mind/body dualism remains or is modified in Sartre's *Being and Nothingness*, the founding volume of 1940s existentialism, was and remains a debated issue.

version of the existential-phenomenological framework of human identity developed by Merleau-Ponty, Sartre and others, but underestimated in so doing the originality of her focus on women's social situation(s) and female embodiment. It was by means of this move that she was inaugurating the branch of political philosophy now known as feminist phenomenology, and although returning from Kruks's work to Beauvoir has closed the digression signalled above, the introduction of feminist phenomenology necessitates a second one, in order to situate the recently born interdisciplinary field of feminist phenomenology and explain its relevance to this book.

Although Beauvoir should be considered the founder of feminist phenomenology as a discrete branch of philosophical enquiry, it is only with the writings of scholars such as Iris Young, whose essay 'Throwing Like a Girl: A Phenomenology of Feminine Body Comportment, Motility, and Spatiality' first appeared in 1980, that the sub-field has come to be recognized as one. The first book on it in English was Linda Fisher and Lester Embree's co-edited *Feminist Phenomenology*, which was based on a symposium held in 1994, and the 2000s and 2010s have seen a steady growth of publication in the area and the formation of a Society for Interdisciplinary Feminist Phenomenology at the University of Oregon. Feminist phenomenology is probably better regarded as an interdisciplinary field of enquiry close to feminist theory than as a branch of political philosophy, despite relying to a considerable extent on the work of Husserl and Merleau-Ponty, and this is so because of one key element of Merleau-Ponty's philosophy in his *Phenomenology of Perception* – that the perceiving body theorized there is a universally *human* body with an apparently unsexed (ungendered or 'neutral') status. In other words, Merleau-Ponty does not take sexual and other forms of embodied difference into account, whereas feminist commentators have argued and continue to argue that there has never been such a thing as a neutral, universal, 'unmarked' body. Beauvoir's extensive discussions of female embodiment in *The Second Sex* depart from, supplement and implicitly question Merleau-Ponty's understanding of embodied subjectivity rather than directly critiquing it, and it was only in 1981, with Judith Butler's essay 'Sexual Ideology and Phenomenological Description: A Feminist Critique of Merleau-Ponty's *Phenomenology of Perception*', that the *ideological* universality and neutrality of the perceiving body according to Merleau-Ponty was first criticized. In this essay Butler focuses on the part that sexuality (rather than gender or sexuate identity) plays in Merleau-Ponty's understanding of embodiment, according to which sexuality is coextensive with existence. This, Butler notes, 'appears to offer feminist theory a view of sexuality freed of naturalistic ideology ... [and to open] the way for a fuller description of sexuality and sexual diversity' (Butler 1989: 85). But these are possibilities Merleau-

Ponty himself fails to develop: Merleau-Ponty's descriptions of sexuality 'turn out to contain tacit normative assumptions about the heterosexual character of sexuality' (Butler 1989: 86). 'Viewed as an expression of sexual ideology', says Butler, '*The Phenomenology of Perception* reveals the cultural construction of the masculine subject as a strangely disembodied voyeur whose sexuality is strangely non-corporeal' (Butler 1989: 93); in other words, the ideological character of Merleau-Ponty's phenomenology arises, in Butler's reading, precisely from the attempt to describe concrete, lived experience while maintaining a subject unqualified by sex, race, age or other specificities.

Since Beauvoir and her existentialist contemporaries did not anticipate the future fruitfulness of her investigation of female embodiment for feminist philosophy, its importance went unnoticed for some considerable time. Another, subsequent reason for this delay was the coincidence of second-wave feminism of the 1960s and 1970s with the beginnings of contemporary gender theory, initiated by the concepts of gender identity and gender role advanced by John Money in the 1950s and the publication of Robert Stoller's *Sex and Gender* in 1968. By the end of the 1970s the social sciences had adopted the psycho-sociological distinction between biological 'sex' and sociocultural 'gender', and because of the apparent conformity of this constructivist mode of theorizing sex/gender identity with Beauvoir's statement in *The Second Sex* that 'One is not born, but rather becomes, woman' (Beauvoir 2009: 293), Beauvoir started to be viewed as forming part of the constructivist 'camp', particularly when Judith Butler devoted two of her early essays to the implications of 'Beauvoir's now-famous formulation' (Butler 2004: 23).[4] According to Butler in the second of these essays, 'Beauvoir does not claim to be describing a theory of gender identity or gender acquisition in *The Second Sex*, and yet her formulation of gender as *project* seems to invite speculation on just such a theory' (Butler 2004: 23), a speculation Butler immediately goes on to deliver.

A compendium of the ways in which thinking about female subjectivity was advanced by the immense surge in feminist writing and thinking that took place in the 1960s and 1970s is too large a task to embark upon here. It is beyond dispute, though, that the contribution to second-wave feminism of the French feminists dubbed 'post-structuralist' by Anglophone accounts, Hélène Cixous, Julia Kristeva and Luce Irigaray, brought female bodily experience to the forefront of feminist thought more decisively than the publication of *The*

---

[4]'Sex and Gender in Simone de Beauvoir's *Second Sex*', *Yale French Studies* 72 (1986) and 'Variations on Sex and Gender: Beauvoir, Wittig and Foucault', first published in Seyla Benhabib and Drucilla Cornell (eds), *Feminism as Critique: Essays on the Politics of Gender in Late-Capitalist Societies*, Cambridge: Polity Press 1987, reprinted in Sara Salih with Judith Butler (eds), *The Judith Butler Reader*, Blackwell Publishing 2004, 21–38.

Second Sex had done twenty-five years earlier. Beauvoir was of course still active at this time, and involved in diverse political activities, joining the French women's movement in November 1971 (Moi 1994: 285n8) and participating in the campaign to legalize abortion in France that would eventually be successful in 1975. However, it was in Cixous's manifesto 'The Laugh of the Medusa' [1975] and Irigaray's essay 'This Sex Which Is Not One' [1977] that *écriture féminine* was theorized as a way to 'write the body', a feminine and feminist aesthetic that was the first concerted attempt to establish embodied female subjectivity in discourse. Few if any links were observed between Cixous's and Irigaray's writings and the materialist account of embodied subjectivity Beauvoir had offered in *The Second Sex*,[5] certainly in part because of the extent to which Cixous and Irigaray engaged with psychoanalysis, which *The Second Sex* had rejected. For as long as post-structuralist and postmodern feminisms and their understanding of the subject as decentred, fragmented or absent altogether held sway in academia, their pre-eminence throughout the 1980s extended by the publication of Butler's *Gender Trouble* in 1990 and *Bodies That Matter* in 1993, Beauvoir's place in feminist theory seemed uncertain.

It was not, however, to remain so indefinitely. At the same time as Butler published the two essays suggesting that Beauvoir's non-essentialist approach to female identity should be revisited by contemporary theorists of gender, a series of articles by American feminist theorists appeared that rejected postmodernism's usefulness for feminism outright, on account of its depoliticizing influence (Kruks 1992: 89–90). Scholarship on Beauvoir, which had been predominantly French until 1980, became Anglophone, with seventeen of the twenty-one books on her published between 1980 and 1992 in English (Moi 1994: 182), a shift that coincided with a new wave of North American work re-evaluating the existential phenomenology of Sartre and Merleau-Ponty. In 1992, an article by Kruks that restated and developed arguments from *Situation and Human Existence* explicitly proposed Beauvoir's understanding of the body as situation as an alternative to the polarized conceptions of subjectivity offered by Enlightenment thought and postmodern theory:

> Fortunately, we do not have to choose between the un-happy alternatives of an Enlightenment subject (i.e., an autonomous or self-constituting consciousness) on the one hand and the attempt, as Michel Foucault pithily

---

[5]As Toril Moi observed in 1994, 'Perhaps the greatest paradox of all is the fact that feminists inspired by the so-called French feminist theory developed in the 1970s tend either to ignore Beauvoir, or to dismiss her as a theoretical dinosaur....The absence of Beauvoir's name in Cixous's ['The Laugh of the Medusa'] is all the more startling since her essay first appeared in the special 1975 issue of *L'Arc* devoted precisely to Simone de Beauvoir' (Moi 1994: 182).

put it, 'to get rid of the subject itself' on the other ([1977] 1980, 117). In the work of Beauvoir, I want to argue, we find a nuanced conception of the subject that cannot be characterized as either Enlightenment or postmodern: rather, it is a conception of the subject as situated. (Kruks 1992: 92)

This nuanced conception of the subject was Beauvoir's version of the existential phenomenological conception of the subject, as it was only Beauvoir's version of it in *The Second Sex* that had admitted sexual difference to its problematic, through her multidisciplinary investigation into women's lived experience. Even as scholars and students of feminism adjusted to the 'queer turn' of contemporary gender theory taken by the work of Butler and numerous other queer theorists, Toril Moi, who had begun research on Beauvoir in 1988, published *Simone de Beauvoir: The Making of an Intellectual Woman* (1994), a book she described as a 'personal genealogy' of Beauvoir and just one of a series of books re-evaluating her to appear in the 1990s, in the wake of her death in 1986. In 1999, Moi added her voice to Kruks's 1992 call for feminists to adopt Beauvoir's 'nuanced conception' of the situated subject, with the following declaration:

In this paper I too am trying to work out a theory of the sexually different body. Unlike the poststructuralist theorists of sex and gender, however, I have come to the conclusion that no amount of rethinking of the concepts of sex and gender will produce a good theory of the body or subjectivity. The distinction between sex and gender is simply irrelevant to the task of producing a concrete, historical understanding of what it means to be a woman (or a man) in a given society. No feminist had produced a better theory of the embodied, sexually different human being than Simone de Beauvoir in *The Second Sex*... Lacan returned to Freud; it is time for feminist theorists to return to Beauvoir. (Moi 1999: 4–5)[6]

What Beauvoir's account of the female subject in *The Second Sex* offered feminism, in Moi's view, was above all its historical openness and its concreteness, which she did not find in the work of 'the poststructuralist theorists of sex and gender' (op. cit.) who she identifies (just before the above quotation) as Judith Butler and Donna Haraway. Despite agreeing with feminism's original reasons for adopting the sex/gender distinction (to counter

[6]The title of this essay and Moi's book 'What Is a Woman?' is taken from the first page of *The Second Sex* and had already been used by Sara Heinämaa in an article Moi refers to approvingly as she makes this rallying-call, for its critique of the tendency to project the sex/gender distinction on to Beauvoir, 'What is a woman? Butler and Beauvoir on the foundations of the sexual difference', *Hypatia* 12: 1 (1997), 20–39.

biological determinism) and recognizing that the opposition had done and could often still do useful work, the main project of her essay, Moi stated, was 'to show that there is at least one case in which the distinction does no useful work at all, and that is when it comes to producing a good theory of subjectivity' (Moi 1999: 6).

It is out of sympathy with Moi's opening statements in *What Is a Woman?* and agreement with Kruks, Moi and Young's preference for a theory of the subject as situated through her embodiment that I am presenting Beauvoir here as the originator of the 'theory' (the understanding) of the embodied and situated female subject. Butler, despite a training in phenomenology and the thoroughgoing materiality of the gendered body she develops in *Bodies that Matter*, is actually prevented from offering any theory of subjectivity at all by the rejection of any metaphysics of identity implied by her theory of performativity. As Christine Battersby states in *The Phenomenal Woman*, 'Butler exhorts feminists to adopt a philosophical position that is beyond all identity' (Battersby 1998: 103). For Butler, any identity politics is in thrall to the metaphysics of substance progressively rewritten in modern times by Nietzsche, Heidegger and Derrida. Battersby goes so far as to claim that she 'use[s] the inadequacies of a metaphysics of substance to undermine *any* metaphysics – and the notion of a "feminine" identity, in particular' (Battersby 1998: 104). Another way to put this is to say that the undercutting of all notions of identity inherent in Butler's political project of queer performativity makes it impossible for her to theorize female subjectivity. Despite Butler's initial appropriation of Beauvoir's apparently constructivist approach to identity for the performative theory of gender(s) set out in *Gender Trouble*, she does not maintain and build on the approach to embodied subjectivity Beauvoir adopts in *The Second Sex* at all, and pursues a quite separate feminist political project from the group of theorists around Kruks. In my view, the re-evaluation and revival of Beauvoir's political thinking since the 1980s that I have outlined above testifies to both the strength and flexibility of her thinking about embodied, situated female subjectivity.

Luce Irigaray and the relational, ethical female subject

As noted above, Irigaray first came to prominence as a theorist of *écriture féminine* at the same time as Cixous and Kristeva, when several of her essays including 'This Sex Which Is Not One' were translated into English along with the work of a number of other French feminists (Marks and de

Courtivron 1981).[7] Despite this initial reception by literary theory, her training in psychoanalysis, and her research and publications on the gendered use of language and on religion, Irigaray's most important work has been as a philosopher of the *féminin* (either 'feminine' or 'female' in English, the French *femelle* being reserved for female non-human animals).[8] Irigaray's work ranges across the entire tradition of Western metaphysics up to and including Lacan in an effort to recover and reconstruct a feminine Other that she sees as having been repressed by patriarchy and phallocentric culture. As well as devoting books to Nietzsche, Heidegger and Merleau-Ponty, she has written essays on Emmanuel Levinas and engaged with the deconstructive philosophy of Derrida. The term Derrida coined to describe the masculine bias of logocentric philosophy from Plato to the twentieth century, 'phallogocentrism', is a useful one to employ in relation to her work, since like Derrida, she understands Western metaphysical philosophy to be an unbroken line of masculine logic. (This explains why some of her writings call for a return to pre-Socratic philosophy and pre-Platonic cultures, seen as pre-dating the repression of the feminine enacted from then on.) Unlike Derrida, however, Irigaray views the Western metaphysical tradition as a symbolic and discursive economy that is open to change.

Female subjectivity, and the question of how to recover it from a tradition dominated by the masculine subject, has figured in Irigaray's writings from the start: the first chapter of the central section of her doctoral dissertation and first book *Speculum of the Other Woman* (1974) is entitled 'Any theory of the "subject" will always have been appropriated by the "masculine"' (Irigaray 1985: 133–146). Irigaray emphasizes woman's status as Other to the male subject in the same way as Beauvoir does, but adopts a more critical approach to it: in Rachel Jones's words, 'Whereas for de Beauvoir, the problem is woman's identification with the Other, for Irigaray, the problem is that woman has not been recognized as "other" enough' (Jones 2011: 29). Or as Irigaray herself puts it, '[t]he exploitation of women is based upon sexual difference, and can only be resolved by sexual difference' (Irigaray 1990 in Whitford 1991: 32). In Irigaray's use of the term, 'sexual difference' describes not the traditional binary opposition between a mutually complementary 'masculine' and 'feminine', but the as-yet incomplete project of evaluating sexual difference

---

[7]Despite the fact that she focused much more on speech than on writing, Irigaray's inclusion in Elaine Marks's and Isabelle de Courtivron's *New French Feminisms* volume emphasized the similarity she bore to Cixous and Kristeva as a theorist of language, rather than her significant differences from them.

[8]This double sense of *féminin* is encapsulated in the title of Margaret Whitford's pioneering study *Luce Irigaray. Philosophy in the Feminine* (Whitford 1991).

affirmatively *as* difference and 'defining the values belonging to a sex-specific genre' (Whitford 1991: 33). For Irigaray, a different, sex-specific identity is the goal women should pursue, rather than equality with men, and this identity – a feature of her philosophy distinguishing her from all feminist theorists of the sex/gender distinction – is both based on women's bodily differences from men *and* cultural. Irigaray's commentary on Beauvoir's famous formulation in *The Second Sex* 'One is not born, but rather becomes, woman' (Beauvoir 2009: 293) is 'I was born woman, but I still have to become the woman who I am by birth. In other words: I am a woman by nature but I must develop the culture appropriate to this woman' (Irigaray 2008a: 155–156)

If *féminin* is one term in Irigaray's writings that supports her project of sociocultural transformation by blurring the biological and cultural dimensions of sexual identity in this way, another important such term is *sexué*, which French-English dictionaries suggest should be conveyed either by 'sexual' or by 'dimorphic' (a biological term referring to distinct types within a species), but which Irigaray's English translators have rendered by the neologism 'sexuate'. The standard use of *sexué* in French is for plants and animals, so by employing it in relation to human beings as well as culture and cultural projects such as sex-specific rights, Irigaray emphasizes a continuity – one she straightforwardly terms 'life' – between human and non-human life forms. As Jones puts it,

> the 'sexuate' refers neither to a mode of being determined by biological sex nor to a cultural overlay of gendered meanings inscribed on a 'tabula rasa' of passively receptive matter. The 'sexuate' does not separate the becomings that shape our bodily being from the production of social and cultural meanings or behavioural dispositions. Rather, it signals the way that sexual difference is articulated through our different modes of being and becoming, that is, in bodily, social, linguistic, aesthetic, erotic and political forms. (Jones 2011: 9)

In the Preface to her *Key Writings* volume, Irigaray cites sexuate difference as being both 'precisely what Western culture has abolished' (Irigaray 2004: ix) and as meaning 'that man and woman do not belong to one and the same subjectivity, that subjectivity itself is neither neutral nor universal' (Irigaray 2004: xii). For Irigaray, subjectivity in the feminine, profoundly bodily by virtue of sexuate difference, is to be thought through and enacted at all levels – erotic, social, linguistic, political and aesthetic.

According to Tamsin Lorraine, it is possible to distinguish three types of feminine other in the critique of Freud Irigaray makes in *Speculum*, 'the feminine as specular other', 'the feminine co-opted by the masculine' and 'the feminine on her own' (Lorraine 1999: 25–33). Of these, only the third type will avoid women's traditional destiny of 'play[ing] a supporting role in a sexually differentiated economy of subjectivity which privileges masculine subjects' (Lorraine 1999: 30). For Irigaray, it is because she has no way to represent her own (maternal) origins – unlike the masculine subject whose origins are resolved in Freud's framework by the substitution of a partner/wife for his Oedipal relationship with his mother – that the feminine other 'has a different relationship to representation and to cultural symbolic systems' (Lorraine 1999: 30). Under patriarchy, these symbolic systems do not support her, because as a wife and mother a woman is supporting the gender-hierarchical masculine economy of subjectivity: symbolic representation of women's vertical bonds with their own mothers and horizontal bonds with other women would support an alternative economy that did not entail the sacrifice of mother–daughter relationships to marital ties, an economy that could sustain female subjectivity.

The place of psychoanalysis in Irigaray's thought is complex, since despite detailed critiques of Freud and Lacan and the outlining of an imaginary that exists in masculine and feminine forms, she frequently appeals too to a non-sex-specific notion of the imaginary that echoes Lacan's concept of the imaginary order. She also echoes Lacan's notion of the symbolic order, but consistently rejects any understanding of this as phallocentric by offering alternative symbolic morphologies based on the female body, such as the lips/labia that may be oral or vaginal. As Lorraine summarizes, her rejection of phallocentrism also implies a rejection of any Oedipally derived conception of subjectivity:

> That is, one need not be an oedipalized subject to be any kind of subject at all, and indeed [Irigaray's] work indicates that there may already be another kind of subject lurking in the wings. This subject that is currently not much more than the shadow of the oedipal subject operates according to a different kind of economy. (Lorraine 1999: 42)

Intersubjectivity, or relationality, is fundamental to Irigaray's understanding of how this different economy of sexuate subjectivity should work. The essays on male philosophers that make up *An Ethics of Sexual Difference* (Irigaray 1993a) frequently criticize what she terms the ego-logical or auto-telic character of the male subject, the poverty and secondary status of the relationships with others that follow from a logic of identity as self-identity (identity to the same). Irigaray posits relational identity against self-identity: the altered economy of subjectivity she envisages comprises non-self-identical subjectivities open to, and dependent upon, others. This is a much more ethical order of subjectivity than the patriarchal one – and concretely so, in that these relations of dependency are acknowledged in the social practices of civil society. After spending time working with Italian women and members of the Italian Communist Party on such practices in the 1980s, Irigaray published a series of books including *I Love to You: Sketch for a Felicity Within History* (Irigaray 1996), a project she describes as follows in an interview she gave in 1996:

> In *I Love to You*, I try to define the possibility of the intersubjective relationship itself…The fact that I approached the problem beginning with the political level is not an accident. It is on this level that masculine philosophers have at times spoken of the relations between individuals. But it was a question then of relations between individuals in the socio-cultural organization of the world of between-men: the city, the nation, even the religious group. It was never a question – except in an abstract manner? – of the relation between two individuals here and now present one to the other, even, in fact, in the context of marriage…Personally, I consider that the civil relation must be founded upon a real rapport between two concrete individuals…. *I Love to You* corresponds to a small treatise on political philosophy that aims towards a democratic organization of civil community. It is amusing to find that while theorists of the same problem claim to found the community on money, on goods, on the army, and so on, I start from love between a man and a woman capable of surmounting instinct, or immediate attraction, in order to cement, by their desire, a living civil community. (Irigaray 2008: 13–14)

A civil order cemented by desire may sound utopian, perhaps echoing the vision of a non-repressive society put forward by Herbert Marcuse in *Eros and Civilization* (1955), but Irigaray is not celebrating the energy and creative power Marcuse attributed to sexual instincts so much as proposing that relationships of desire and kinship be the foundation of civil society, and insisting that respect for (sexuate) otherness obtain at all levels of that society. Relational subjectivity implies a respect for the world as well as for the identity of the other person and takes different forms for men and for women:

> Men *and* women must modify their relational identity. Certainly, women 'spontaneously' privilege the relation between subjects and men the relation to objects. The feminine subject constructs itself through a relation to the other, the masculine subject through the manufacture of objects and worlds starting from which it is possible for him to exchange with the other. Let us say that woman must learn to put some objectivity

susceptible to being shared between *I* and *you*: this relation must not remain, for her, at the level of need and of subjective immediacy, otherwise the *you* risks disappearing as *you*. The man, on the other hand, needs to rediscover the other as subject beyond his universe of objects. (Irigaray 2008: 14)

In the books of essays that followed *I Love to You*, *Democracy Begins Between Two* (Irigaray 2000b) and *To Be Two* (Irigaray 2000a), Irigaray developed this notion of sexually differentiated relational identity in more explicitly political terms, and the intersubjective and dialogic character of her teaching practice began to be evident in the publications that resulted from it.[9]

The substitution of relational identity for self-identity already implies ethics, and Irigaray's concept of relational identity strongly resembles the relationship of Subject and Other found in the ethics of Levinas, whose Subject is grounded in being, like Merleau-Ponty's body-subject and Heidegger's *Dasein*, yet made ethical in so far as it ex - ists – is drawn out of being – by means of the demand of the Other. Levinas's Subject, like Irigaray's, is ethical rather than logical, relational rather than self-same, his thought turning metaphysics inside out so that ethics rather than ontology is 'first philosophy'. Despite their shared emphasis on ethics, however, Irigaray's two essays on Levinas, 'The Fecundity of the Caress' (Irigaray 1993b) and 'Questions to Emmanuel Levinas: On the Divinity of Love' (Irigaray 1991a), lambast him for ignoring sexual difference and the possibility of female subjectivity altogether, in so far as the figures of femininity in his work – particularly in the 'Phenomenology of Eros' section of *Totality and Infinity* – all occur 'on the side of the Other'. For Levinas, Irigaray states, 'The feminine is apprehended not in relation to itself, but from the point of view of man, and through a purely erotic strategy, a strategy moreover which is dictated by masculine pleasure [*jouissance*]' (Irigaray 1991a: 178). Or as Dave Boothroyd puts it, 'in Irigaray's view, Levinas fails to think the relationship between sexual difference and the origin of the ethical, and his philosophy ultimately fails to break with the masculine-neutral' (Boothroyd 2013: 61). Boothroyd's chapter on Irigaray in his *Ethical Subjects in Contemporary Culture* gets to the heart of Irigaray's critique of Levinas in a way few other commentators have done, so I shall draw on it here in order to bring out her critique and how it relates to female subjectivity.

---

[9]For example, Luce Irigaray, *Dialogues. Around Her Work*, special issue of *Paragraph* 25:3 (November 2002), 22–31, *Conversations. Luce Irigaray* (London and New York: Continuum 2008) and *Luce Irigaray. Teaching* (London and New York: Continuum 2008).

What exactly is meant by 'the relationship between sexual difference and the origin of the ethical' and how does Irigaray herself think it? Common to Irigaray's and Levinas's ethics is the emergence of the ethical out of the threshold of contact between bodies: the lived, material body is as central to Levinasian subjectivity as it is to Merleau-Ponty's, Beauvoir's and Irigaray's subjects. Irigaray's figure of the oral or vaginal lips/labia employed in *This Sex Which Is Not One* has been widely commented on and is the principal cause of the accusations of biological essentialism levelled at her, but in Boothroyd's view, '[h]er discourse interprets the anatomical body whilst weaving in phenomenological aspects of the lived body to produce what could be described as a metaphorised lived-anatomy of female sexuality' (Boothroyd 2013: 58). Although the priority Levinas gives to ethics over ontology moves his philosophy away from phenomenology, his account of the Subject, which in *Totality and Infinity* is called the Same, is thoroughly phenomenological and can be seen as an aspect of his thought that Irigaray draws on directly 'in order to develop her own account of how sensate life at the level of touch, contact and Eros constitutes the materiality of the ethical relation to the Other' (Boothroyd 2013: 61). Irigaray is both indebted to Levinas and critiques him for the egology of his erotics – the confinement of fecundity to the father–son relationship, whereas fecundity in her sense of the term takes place between male and female lovers, the latter bearing the active descriptor '*amante*' rather than Levinas's passive '*aimée*'. By setting her figure of the lips that constantly touch each other against Levinas's notion of the caress, which by Levinas's own admission 'does not touch the other' (Irigaray 1991a: 179), she is able to claim that 'Levinas's account misses the morphology of sexual difference as this figures in erotic contact, with the result that he neither accounts for this difference within the sexual contact of touching bodies, nor addresses the important matter of how touching differs in the cases of male-female, male-male and female-female contacts' (Boothroyd 2013: 62). Boothroyd states nevertheless that an indebtedness to Levinas can be seen in Irigaray's attempt 'to identify the ethical significance of sensual contact with the body of the Other' (Boothroyd 2013: 63): her critique of Levinas is Levinasian to the extent that she stages and retains 'an ethical understanding of the tactility of contact'. This is why Boothroyd can conclude that Irigaray's 'encounter with Levinas's thinking is selective in terms of the specific points of contact it makes with his corpus' (Boothroyd 2013: 61).

In Boothroyd's chapter on Irigaray from which I have been quoting, he coins the term 'labial feminism' to describe the sexing of the ethical subject that pervades her philosophy. Developed in the most concentrated manner in *An Ethics of Sexual Difference* and subsequent essays such as 'Questions to Emmanuel Levinas', this labial feminism never abandons the critique of the feminine as specular other set out in *Speculum* or the material, multiform character of 'woman' poetically set forth in the essays of *This Sex Which Is Not One*. Irigaray's figure of the two lips conveys a female subjectivity that is always already '"two", defined by an internal difference' (Boothroyd 2013: 50). She pursues the recovery of female subjectivity from a tradition dominated by the masculine subject without ever endorsing the qualities of unity and visibility that govern phallocentric culture, writing deconstructively in so far as any reversal of the hierarchical masculine/feminine opposition is avoided, and 'woman' is never set up as a totality. Where psychoanalysis only theorizes the feminine on the basis of lack, as a damaged (castrated) whole male Subject, Irigaray's female subject

> does not set herself up as one, as a 'single' female unit. She is not closed up or around one single truth or essence. The essence of a truth remains foreign to her…she does not oppose a feminine truth to a masculine truth…Because this would once again amount to playing the – man's – game of castration…the female sex takes place by embracing itself, by endlessly sharing and exchanging its Lips, its edges, its borders… (Irigaray 1991b in Boothroyd 2013: 59)

Insisting on the symbolization of the two-lipped female sex rather than the totalizing and unitary discourse of the masculine-neutral, Irigaray weaves a discourse 'in' the feminine, a sexuate discourse that constructs 'woman' from the anatomical female body while also drawing on aspects of the lived body of phenomenology.

Christine Battersby and the fluid, fleshy female subject

Irigaray is one feminist theorist for whom female subjectivity is characterized by fluidity,[10] but another philosopher who has focused on developing the notion is Christine Battersby, in *The Phenomenal Woman: Feminist Metaphysics and the Patterns of Identity*. The main concern of Battersby's

---

[10]Liquidity and fluidity are aspects of the feminine Irigaray theorizes particularly in the essay 'The "Mechanics" of Fluids' in *This Sex Which Is Not One*, in *Elemental Passions*, from which Boothroyd quotes the question 'Why is setting oneself up as a solid more worthwhile than flowing as a liquid from between the two Lips?' (Irigaray 1992 in Boothroyd 2013: 59), and in several of the essays in *The Ethics of Sexual Difference*.

book is, she states, 'to ask what happens to the notion of identity if we treat the embodied female as the norm for models of the self' (Battersby 1998: 38). This is a project she is quick to distinguish from any positing of 'an "other" form of subjectivity which is that of the "feminine" or "female" subject' (Battersby 1998: 2), a formulation that clearly alludes to Irigaray.

Despite her preference for the concepts of 'self' and 'subject-position' over 'subjectivity', taking the embodied female as a norm around which to build a feminist metaphysics evidently allies Battersby to some extent with both Beauvoir and Irigaray on the issue of female embodiment. She distinguishes her analysis of the female from Beauvoir's by pointing to the Cartesian dualism that can sometimes be detected in Beauvoir's writing, in the tension or opposition between the embodied and the authentic, 'free' self as it projects itself towards the future (Battersby 1998: 36). Pointing to the 'horrid' terms in which Beauvoir often describes female body experiences in *The Second Sex* ('the clinging, slimy, flabby, sticky, fleshy "in-itself"' (Battersby 1998)), she declares an affinity with Irigaray rather than Beauvoir in wanting 'a more positive thinking of that sticky boundary between self and other' (Battersby 1998), a *rapprochement* pointing to the emphasis on fluid female subjectivity in Irigaray's earlier work. Battersby's critical attention to Beauvoir's dualist moments is entirely fair, but her description of them as evidence of an 'obsessive desire for a freedom that is only exercised through the negation of flesh' (Battersby 1998) is extreme and goes against the majority of recent readings of Beauvoir: it emphasizes the Sartreanism of her 1940s writings before *The Second Sex* rather than the reciprocal influence Beauvoir and Merleau-Ponty exerted upon one another before and during this period. Battersby is kinder to Beauvoir (as well as to Sartre) when she acknowledges that, 'via the slogan "existence precedes essence"', their existentialism 'made it possible to think the essence of the human more fluidly' (Battersby 1998: 35), like the account of a 'fluid essence' she sets out in *The Phenomenal Woman*.

In exploring the notion of a fluid essence, Battersby is countering a certain tradition of Western metaphysics that she emphasizes is often taken to be the only one – the Aristotelian tradition, in which being is prioritized over becoming. 'For Aristotle', she states, 'the essence of a thing is linked to its "substance" or "being" (*ousia*), and to the timeless and necessary element in the species or genus which persists across change' (Battersby 1998: 25), whereas 'other notions of essence are available in the history of philosophy that would help us think the specificities of being female without reifying feminine experience or female lifestyles into a monolithic unity' (Battersby 1998). Alternative notions of essence indicate alternative currents within a Western metaphysics often assumed to be monolithic because of how, in the wake of Aristotle's analysis of *ousia*, '[M]etaphysics became synonymous with [...] the study of "being", "substance", "time", "space", "cause", "essence" and "identity"' (Battersby 1998: 5). Drawing attention to how other philosophers before her have also rejected the Aristotelian metaphysical tradition, Battersby sets out how two sorts of metaphysics became distinguishable in the Enlightenment era of Kant, a 'speculative' or noumenal metaphysics equivalent to Aristotle's analyses of being, and – the kind her book goes on to develop – a 'descriptive metaphysics' focused more on existence than essence. Descriptive metaphysics, which she later also terms a 'metaphysics of immanence' or a 'metaphysics of becoming' (Battersby 1998: 11), is a tradition that may be called post-Kantian (Battersby 1998: 5). Battersby's redescriptions of the concepts of self and subject-position attempt to think a type of persisting subject which is not fixed in its essence or permanent in its substance, but which arises out of stable patternings within the 'patterns of identity' of a feminist metaphysics. 'Persistence of a "subject" or "object" over time', she writes, 'can also emerge from within intersecting force-fields, dependence and flow' (Battersby 1998: 12). The female self Battersby attempts to think is rather than a 'thing' or a 'substance', 'more like an "event" that is "born" in the space and time of interactive forces' (Battersby 1998: 8).

It is soon evident in *The Phenomenal Woman* that Battersby's overarching topic is female identity rather than female subjectivity, a difference of terminology she doubtless opts for because even the concept of subjectivity risks privileging substance, stasis and the self-same over force fields, fluidity and relationality. Female identity – she justifies her use of 'female' rather than 'feminine' by recalling that in the English language, it 'involves a reference to embodiment, in a way that to be "feminine" does not' (Battersby 1998: 9)[11] – does not suggest singularity in the same way as female subjectivity does. By using the term 'female subject-position' she avoids placing a limit on the infinite variety of positions occupied by women as social subjects and forces us to think the paradox of 'positions' that are sticky and fleshy rather than cleanly delineated from one another. The fleshy contiguity of self and other Battersby insists upon in fact follows directly from the embodied female self she is taking as a norm, because of natality – the capacity of the female body to give birth, regardless of whether a particular woman does so or not. Natality is the first of five features of the female subject-position Battersby sets out, 'as an abstract category of embodied (female) selves' (Battersby

---

[11]Here Battersby distinguishes her terminology from the ambiguity between 'feminine' and 'female' found in the French *féminin* and positively exploited by Irigaray, despite the two philosophers' shared emphasis on fluid and relational modes of identity.

1998: 7), at the start of *The Phenomenal Woman*.[12] Taking the body that births as a norm forces a rethinking of the concept of identity that has dominated the tradition of the metaphysics of substance, the tradition to which the male subject – the 'autonomous and individualized "soul" or "mind" that merely inhabits the flesh' (Battersby 1998: 10) – serves as linch pin. Putting a body that can birth at the centre of this rethinking of identity transforms our habitual understanding of 'self', 'other' and self-other relations by 'constru[ing] identity in terms of living forces and birth, not as a "state" of matter that is dead' (Battersby 1998: 8). For the new notion of self derived from the phenomenal, birthing woman, 'the "other" is within, as well as without' (Battersby 1998: 9).

Battersby's focus on natality and the birthing female body is also arrived at, differently, in Irigaray's thought, via her critique of the Levinasian mode of fecundity attributed (in 'The Phenomenology of Eros') to the father–son relation, a paternal genealogy. Against this, and in tune with her longstanding emphasis on the symbolization of maternal and feminine genealogies, 'Irigaray presents her own account of *maternity* as a non-instrumental model of the body-to-body relation between mother and child in *birthing*; birthing is the model of the *feminine* relation to the Other par excellence' (Boothroyd 2013: 63). Importantly, this figure of birthing is not limited to actual sexual reproduction: for Irigaray, 'fecundity between lovers in Eros … does not depend, as it does for Levinas, on its "offspring" for its ethical significance' (Boothroyd 2013). Birthing in Irigaray's work models an ethical relation in the feminine between lovers or between mother and child, whereas Battersby claims no ethical significance for this relationality. Battersby's feminist metaphysics is a quite different enterprise from Irigaray's feminist ethics, but as I hope has now become evident, the appeal of both philosophers to fluidity, relationality and the fleshiness of the birthing female body establishes firm points of contact between their writings on female identity and female subjectivity, respectively.

Embodied and ethical female subjectivity

Where relational identity or intersubjectivity is concerned, a potential complementarity between the thought of Beauvoir and Irigaray is that although Beauvoir wrote the only volume of existentialist ethics, *An Ethics*

---

[12]The remaining four features are the ontological dependence of each self upon others as modelled by the dependence of the foetus on the mother, the emergence of two distinct but not opposed or contradictory selves (e.g. mother and child) out of the embodied self, fleshy continuity and 'monstrosity', meant in the sense that the female subject-position 'has direct links with the anomalous, the monstrous, the inconsistent and the paradoxical' (Battersby 1998: 11). Battersby is using these 'antinomies' of the female subject-position 'to think identity anew' (Battersby 1998: 2).

of Ambiguity, she did not make relationships between women a topic of her philosophical writings. (Irigaray, by contrast, emphasizes mother–daughter relationships and relationships between women generally throughout her work.) Battersby states explicitly that her feminist metaphysics is not an ethics, respecting the traditional compartmentalized branches of academic philosophy, but its emphasis on fleshiness and birthing invites a drawing-out of the ethical implications of her thinking. Apart from these points of comparison, Beauvoir, Irigaray and Battersby arrived at the understandings of female subjectivity set out above in very contrasting historical and philosophical contexts, and to attempt to bring their accounts together further would probably not serve any useful purpose. There are, nonetheless, two overarching aspects of female subjectivity that stand out across the accounts of the three philosophers: embodiment, in its various modes of situation, fleshiness and natality, and ethicality – of intersubjectivity as it figures in Beauvoir's thought, relationality as it is emphasized by Irigaray and fluidity as underlined by Irigaray and Battersby. It is embodiment and the ethical that will guide my approach to female subjectivity in this book's readings of films, and I would for this reason, in order to complete exposition of the considerations that will guide my readings of films in Chapters 3–8, now like to give a little more consideration to an ethic I think is shared by the trio of feminist philosophers considered in this opening chapter – an ethic I shall call a 'feminist ethic of embodiment'.

Since they began in the 1990s, the debates of the humanities' 'ethical turn' have been contributed to by a number of contemporary philosophers and theorists, principal among them Alain Badiou (in his *Ethics* (2003)), Judith Butler (in *Giving an Account of Oneself* (2005) and *Frames of War* (2009)) and Slavoj Žižek (in 'Neighbours and Other Monsters: A Plea for Ethical Violence' (2005)). Boothroyd traces parts of these debates in *Ethical Subjects in Contemporary Culture*, and Mari Ruti's recent volume *Between Levinas and Lacan: Self, Other, Ethics* (2015) considers them in detail, but one of the first books to summarize the respective approaches of their main contributors was Downing and Saxton's *Film and Ethics: Foreclosed Encounters*, in 2010. Like Ruti, Downing and Saxton characterize the ethics of most of the philosophers they consider as either an ethics of self or of the other, and although Levinas, Derrida and Badiou are considered individually (Lacan and Žižek are bracketed together for understandable reasons), no women or feminist philosophers are mentioned by name. Feminist ethics is treated in two short paragraphs extending to only just over half a page, and neither Irigaray nor the extensive work in analytic feminist ethics pioneered by Alison Jaggar is given any consideration, even if it is fairly pointed out that in film theory, it would be possible to conduct a properly ethical revisit of Mulvey's 'Visual Pleasure and

Narrative Cinema' 'and the numerous responses, redresses, correctives and derivations it spawned, since it addresses head-on the relationship between subject and other, and a dynamic of pleasurable possession that may be embraced or rejected' (Downing and Saxton 2009: 6–7).

An array of possible approaches exists to the study of ethics and film, which is a relatively new and burgeoning field in film studies.[13] The joint study of ethics and film suggests consideration of both the content of film narratives and, perhaps particularly, of questions of spectatorship: to what extent does the screening of violent or obscene material charge the viewer (not to mention the film-maker and distributor of the film or DVD) with a responsibility for his/her act of viewing? Extreme content figures to some extent in some of the films to be discussed in this book, in the form of explicit sex acts, but in order to bring out the ethically embodied female subjectivity that is my principal focus, I shall concentrate more on the ethics of sexual difference suggested both in the films' narratives and by the acts of directing and viewing them.

A major aim of this book is to argue that female and feminist philosophers should be included in the 'canon' of philosopher-theorists now being put into dialogue with film. But where in the range of contemporary approaches to ethics contested by the philosophers referred to above does the notion of a feminist ethic of embodiment fit? If we accept Rosi Braidotti's confirmation of the generally held view that the impulse behind the humanities' 'ethical turn' is 'an offshoot of the crisis of the rational subject that has shaken the phallogocentric system to its very foundations' (Braidotti 1994: 125), and that we are therefore [in 1994] 'faced with a fundamental dissonance between on the one hand the discourse of the crisis of the logos and of its feminine, and on the other the project of feminism in terms of sexual difference' (Braidotti 1994), an approach has to be found to this 'fundamental dissonance'. My contention is that feminist phenomenology can supply such an approach, precisely because it brings the ambivalently logocentric understanding of subjectivity found in existential phenomenology together with a field of political thought – feminism – that having survived engagements with poststructuralism and postmodernism in the 1970s, 1980s and 1990s, now comprises a highly diverse, sophisticated and flexible set of strategies. In its

---

[13]Two of the first publications in this field were Sarah Cooper's *Selfless Cinema? Ethics and French Documentary* (Cooper 2006) and Catherine Wheatley's *Michael Haneke's Cinema: The Ethic of the Image* (Wheatley 2009). These have been followed more recently by Jinhee Choi and Mattias Frey's co-edited *Ethical Dimensions of Film Theory, Practice, and Spectatorship* (Choi and Frey 2014), Robert Sinnerbrink's *Cinematic Ethics: Exploring Ethical Experience through Film* (Sinnerbrink 2016) and David Martin-Jones's edited section of *Film-Philosophy* 20: 1 (2016), 'Film-Philosophy and a World of Cinemas' (Martin-Jones ed. 2016).

Husserlian form, phenomenology was understood to entail a foundational and universal understanding of subjectivity – something I hope it is already clear that this book will not endorse; I engage with phenomenology only as it has been approached by feminist philosophers (Beauvoir, Kruks, Young), and feminist phenomenology, although it began in earnest with Beauvoir's *The Second Sex* in 1949, has only developed in the 1990s and twenty-first century, the same period from which the films discussed in this book are drawn. Feminist phenomenology is a new sub- or trans-discipline of the critical humanities rather than any kind of 'return' to the universalist phenomenology practised by Husserl, and the feminist ethic of embodiment I am proposing to accompany it resembles the critical and historical ethics investigated by Michel Foucault at the end of his life more closely than any ethics one might find in or derive from 'classical' phenomenology. It is intriguing to note that Foucault only turned to 'the question of ethics' in the wake of Sartre's death in 1980, and therefore at a moment when existential phenomenology (which had long since ceased to dominate French intellectual life) had finally lost its leading and most tenacious public spokesperson. The ethics at which Sartre had hinted in the closing pages of *Being and Nothingness* in 1943 had never been written, although the notes for it would be posthumously published in 1983, as *Notebook for an Ethics*. Foucault's late works propose an ethics at just this juncture, one set out in the second and third volumes of *The History of Sexuality*, a number of interviews and lectures subsequently collected into single volumes, and his last three series of lectures at the Collège de France. Foucault also began actively to entertain the notion of freedom at this time, and although the ethics proposed by these late works of his bears no real resemblance to the existentialist ethics Beauvoir had essayed and Sartre had never completed, it does resemble them in making an appeal to freedom – as a practice and a value rather than as a concept, the same mode in which it was reconsidered by Kruks and other feminist political philosophers in the 1980s and 1990s. There is more than a passing resemblance between the practical, social mode of freedom Kruks uncovers in Beauvoir's writings in *Retrieving Experience* (to be detailed in Chapter 8) and the ethics of/as freedom Foucault describes in 'The Ethics of Concern for the Self as a Practice of Freedom' (Foucault 1989: 432–449). And not only does Foucault's *ethos* of freedom correspond very closely to the reciprocal investment of freedoms to be found in Beauvoir's existentialist ethics of the 1940s; it is of a piece with the understanding of identity as relational found in the more politically focused work of Irigaray.

As Lisa Downing observes, Foucault's announcement in the early 1980s of his interest in 'a genealogy of how the subject constituted *itself* as subject' (Martin et al. 1988: 4) – the feminist version of which is what has concerned me in this chapter – was accompanied by a description of this genealogy as 'an ethical enquiry into "the freedom of people" that would counter the traditional ethics of humanism with an *ethos* closer to the Greek care for the self' (Downing 2008: 101). 'What I am afraid of about humanism is that it presents a certain form of our ethics as a universal model for any kind of freedom' (Foucault quoted in Downing 2008: 101). Foucault's identity as a critical rather than a traditional philosopher (if he is to be described as a philosopher at all) is palpable in these statements: decisively historical and anti-universalist, he emphasizes the diversity of possible practices of freedom rather than (in Sartrean style) appealing to freedom as a concept that can found a theory of the subject. Different forms of freedom are an issue I shall return to in Chapter 8, but it is already evident, I hope, that the practices of freedom undertaken by embodied female subjects enfold the kind of feminist ethic of embodiment I am proposing should accompany the feminist phenomenological understanding of subjectivity I shall draw on throughout this book.

The treatment of subjectivity in Foucault's late texts is an area of controversy among scholars of his work because it is perceived by some of them to differ markedly from his approach in earlier ones. Downing suggests in relation to this point that '[t]he agency of the subject is certainly seen to be greater here than in studies of the operation of disciplinary power, such as *Discipline and Punish* and *The Will to Knowledge*. However, the subject does not operate *autonomously* but *relatedly*' (Downing 2008: 97) – a mode of operation that matches the ethical and relational identity Irigaray was developing in the lectures of *An Ethics of Sexual Difference* in the early 1980s. If the agency of the subject is seen to be greater in Foucault's late texts than in his earlier ones, then this might be attributed, as with the *ethos* and practice of freedom, to the return of certain existential phenomenological emphases in the final stage of Foucault's career – bodily agency being central to the existential phenomenological understanding of subjectivity. And some compatibility can be observed between Foucault's and Irigaray's ethics: Battersby, interestingly, looks to a combination of Irigaray and Foucault to articulate what she terms the singularity of the female subject-position, arguing that Foucault's work is necessary to counterbalance an account of the history of Western philosophy and culture that in Irigaray's account is 'too homogeneous' (Battersby 2011: 136), a 'monolithic view' of the past that 'plays down the achievements of past and present women artists, writers and also philosophers' (Battersby 2011). Foucault certainly supplies historicity to an account of the history of philosophy that can sometimes make it seem that everything remains to be done, but Irigaray's ethics of sexuate difference insists on an enunciation in the feminine that is entirely lacking from Foucault's ethics.

Approaching ethical and embodied female subjectivities in film

The extent to which the thought of Beauvoir, Irigaray and Battersby has been applied to film varies considerably: only one recent study (Boulé and Tidd 2012) has considered Beauvoir's phenomenological and existentialist writings in relation to film, whereas a number of articles and two books (Bainbridge 2007, Bolton 2011) have explored the potential significance of Irigaray's work for the filmic medium, and none at all (as far as I am aware) have undertaken to do the same with Battersby's feminist metaphysics. No single study has yet undertaken to scrutinize *embodied* female subjectivity in film, either as it is represented or as it may be reinforced or constituted by the act of viewing such representations. How to theorize female spectatorship has been one of the chief lines of enquiry of feminist film studies, and is not a question I shall emphasize in this book, but I shall consider in the next chapter how taking account of the embodiment of the spectator (along with the embodied status of on-screen characters and of the film's director) essentially modifies any approach to female spectatorship. All the films to be discussed in this book are directed by women, and they all also focus on one or more female protagonists who in some instances is the director herself or a fictionalized version of her. The films, therefore, all feature what might be called a 'primary look' between women that precedes the viewer's look at the film, and this look may be understood as a duality within femaleness corresponding to its openness beyond what Derrida or Irigaray terms 'the economy of the proper' – the realm of self-identity. In the medium of film, this relationship is always visual, but it is not limited to the visual dimension, and exploring other domains in which it operates, such as narrative and the 'syntax' of a film's construction of time, cinematography and editing, is a task I shall be attentive to. Before embarking on so doing, however, the approach I am adopting should be contextualized, historically and theoretically, within the field of feminist film studies as it has developed since the 1970s.

2

Feminist Film Studies and Women's Cinema after Psychoanalysis

Feminist film theory originated in a decade when film theory was dominated by the combination of Lacanian psychoanalysis, semiotics and Althusserian Marxism. The confluence of these paradigms in the journal *Screen* in the 1970s suggests that as they became less influential or were critiqued, feminists needed to ask where else they should look to in order to underpin to their challenges to patriarchally dominated film form and film industries. The history of David Bordwell and Noël Carroll's assaults on the combination of theoretical approaches they caricatured as 'Theory' with a capital T and 'Grand Theory' is well known,[1] and their alternatives to it were not the only ones proposed to the rapidly changing field of film theory and film philosophy in the 1990s. One was the gradual emergence of the sub-discipline of film *philosophy* as distinct from film *theory*, largely an Anglophone enterprise, although also taken up in continental Europe under the names of (among others) *cinéphilosophie* and *Kinophilosophie*. Another was the publication of Vivian Sobchack's *The Address of the Eye: A Phenomenology of Film Experience* (1992), which introduced a fully formed model for the embodied experience of film viewing to the field of film theory and film philosophy, and which I shall discuss in this chapter along with a 1990 article by Gaylyn Studlar that recommended ways in which feminist film theory might appropriate phenomenological insights.

Sobchack's fully developed phenomenological model of film viewing and Studlar's article may together be seen, I would suggest, as the initial

---

[1] See in particular Carroll (1988) and Bordwell and Carroll (1996).

meeting of feminist film studies with what is now called film-philosophy, the inauguration of a mode of feminist film-philosophy that has recently begun to flourish and that is insufficiently acknowledged by some of the leading male writers in the field. An example of this occurs in the mapping of the expanding set of relationships between philosophy and film studies Robert Sinnerbrink undertakes in *New Philosophies of Film: Thinking Images*. Sinnerbrink classifies these relationships into three currents: the *'cultural-historicist* current that incorporates cultural studies, media theory, post-colonialism and diverse historical and cross-cultural approaches; the *cognitivist-naturalist* paradigm, which includes "post-Theory", cognitivism, analytic philosophy and, more recently, neuroscience and evolutionary biology' (Sinnerbrink 2011: 4), and what he calls film-philosophy, 'a distinctive approach, the founding figures of which I take to be Cavell and Deleuze' (Sinnerbrink 2011: 4). Sinnerbrink includes gender studies and queer theory in his cultural-historicist current, but makes no mention of feminist film studies as a separate set of approaches with its own distinct history: it seems to me that the feminist philosophy of film as an enterprise distinct from gender- and queer-theoretical work on film was launched by Sobchack, Studlar and the film critics who began to look to phenomenological philosophy in the early 1990s. I shall trace the birth, growth and diversification of feminist philosophy of film later in this chapter, after revisiting the main developments in feminist film theory since the mid-1980s.[2] Since I am doing this with the question of female subjectivity in mind, I shall dwell on issues of subjectivity and authorship as much as film form, spectatorship or the cultural register of women's film-making, which may probably fairly be described as the most important issues for feminist film theorists of the 1980s and 1990s.

From 'Woman' to women:
The work of Teresa de Lauretis

Towards the end of Noël Carroll's introduction to the scathing critique of 'contemporary film theory' (shorthand for 'film theory that proceeds within a semiological framework... amplified by Marxism and psychoanalysis'

---

[2]Most feminist film theory of the 1970s was only indirectly concerned with the question of female subjectivity, and possibly for good reasons, since as Sue Thornham demonstrates in *What If I Had Been the Hero?*, women's film-making of the decade comprised just as many documentaries and explicitly political projects as it did fictional feature films, and to the women who conceived of and shot these films, their own bodily subjectivity was probably not in question.

(Carroll 1988: 1)) set out in *Mystifying Movies: Fads and Fallacies in Contemporary Film Theory*, Carroll comments on the omission from his introduction of the topic of feminism. Acknowledging that he has learned 'a great deal' (Carroll 1988: 7) from feminists working 'in the area that is sometimes called the study of the image of women in film' (Carroll 1988: 7), Carroll also allows that the development of a theory of the female subject (which it is 'certainly true' that some feminist theorists are developing (Carroll 1988: 8)) amounts to a 'fundamental' alteration to the premises of contemporary film theory. Although he does not think this fundamental alteration is worth making, because it is not worth rebuilding the mistaken framework he holds contemporary film theory to be (Carroll 1988: 8), it is telling that in 1988, before his and Bordwell's terms for the film theory prevailing in US academia hardened into Theory and Grand Theory (the terms used in *Post-Theory: Reconstructing Film Studies*), Carroll feels that he should mention feminism and does not know where to place it. He is not generous enough to name the feminist theorists then developing an account of the female subject, but one of them must surely be Teresa de Lauretis, whose call for such a theory I quoted at the start of Chapter 1. In *Alice Doesn't: Feminism, Semiotics, Cinema* (1984) and *Technologies of Gender* (1987), de Lauretis decisively reoriented the emphasis of Mulvey and Johnston's 1970s work away from 'woman' as spectacle and object of the look towards *women* as 'real historical beings … whose material existence is nonetheless certain' (de Lauretis 1984: 5). As Shohini Chaudhuri states, this reorientation marked the onset of a new phase of feminist film theory 'which seeks to reclaim female agency within dominant discourses rather than merely viewing those discourses as oppressive' (Chaudhuri 2006: 62). 'Through the Looking-Glass', the first essay in *Alice Doesn't*, argued that in their different ways, both psychoanalysis and semiology 'deny women the status of subjects and producers of culture' (de Lauretis 1984: 8). Explicitly critiquing Christian Metz's turn from the semiological to the psychoanalytic signifier in *The Imaginary Signifier*,[3] de Lauretis concluded that

> the psychoanalytic vision of cinema, in spite of Metz's effort, still poses woman as telos and origin of a phallic desire, as dream woman forever pursued and forever held at a distance, seen and invisible on another scene. (de Lauretis 1984: 25)

Although the importance of psychoanalysis for the study of cinema and of film should be acknowledged, because '[i]t has served to dislodge

---

[3]Metz (1982).

cinematic theory from the scientistic, even mechanistic enterprise of a structural semiology and urged upon it the instance of the subject' (de Lauretis 1984: 30), de Lauretis seemed to be arguing that this work had been achieved, and that it was time to turn to a non-psychoanalytic materialist theory of subjectivity.

The Beauvoirean materialist understanding of female subjectivity I outlined in Chapter 1 may have been available to feminist film theorists of the 1980s, but as I suggested there, it did not occur to them to avail themselves of it, for two understandable reasons: first, it did not constitute a fully fledged theory of how female subjectivity functioned in society at large or in the reading and viewing of cultural texts, and second, it had apparently been superseded by the new French feminisms of Cixous, Irigaray and Kristeva. (In striking contrast to the hostility to continental philosophy and critical theory exhibited by Carroll and Bordwell, US feminists of the 1980s were highly receptive to these theorists.[4]) In the poststructuralist climate prevailing in US academia at this time, the obvious theorist for de Lauretis to turn to for her materialist theory of subjectivity was Foucault, whose approaches to sexuality as constructed in discourses and practices and to the body as a site of power relations were being enthusiastically taken up by Anglophone feminists worldwide.[5] And de Lauretis does this to some extent, particularly in the chapter of *Alice Doesn't* titled 'Now and Nowhere', a reading of Nicolas Roeg's *Bad Timing* (1980). In other chapters of the book such as 'Desire in Narrative', she continues, rather puzzlingly given what she writes in the introduction about psychoanalysis denying women the status of subjects and producers of culture (de Lauretis 1984: 8), to draw on psychoanalytic theory. Her continuing call on such theory takes the guises of 'Freud's story of femininity, Heath's account of narrative cinema as Oedipal drama, and Metz's notion of identification' (de Lauretis 1984: 10), elements of cine-psychoanalytic thinking she calls 'points of departure for a more adequate and specific understanding of the subjective processes involved in female spectatorship' (de Lauretis 1984: 10). She justifies this recourse to psychoanalysis by saying that the feminist work on film required at the moment she is writing is

> not anti-narrative or anti-Oedipal; quite the opposite. It is narrative and Oedipal with a vengeance, for it seeks to stress the duplicity of that scenario and the specific contradiction of the female subject in it, the

---

[4]See, for example, Fraser and Bartky (1992).
[5]Irene Diamond and Lee Quinby's (1988) was the first book in this area, although it included essays published previously and was rapidly followed by volumes such as Jana Sawicki's (1991), McNay's (1992) and Ramazanoglu's (1993).

contradiction by which historical women must work with and against Oedipus. (de Lauretis 1984: 157)

The readings generated by this quasi-deconstructive approach in 'Desire in Narrative' are entirely convincing, but in my view this is the point at which de Lauretis fails decisively to embrace the notion of agency she sees women as having been denied by semiology and psychoanalysis. By asking 'in what ways does narrative work to engender the subject in the movement of its discourse, as it defines positions of meaning, identification and desire?' (de Lauretis 1984: 10), she both attributes an overly deterministic power to narrative and retains too many of the terms of psychoanalytic feminist work on film. The female subject does not need to be constructed *ex nihilo*, as had been pointed out by critics of Mulvey's omission of the female spectator from 'Visual Pleasure and Narrative Cinema'.[6] She exists outside the cinema and brings subjectivity to it, even if that subjectivity then undergoes alteration as a consequence of her viewing. The interaction of narrative, desire and subjectivity remains as important a set of questions for feminist film studies in the 2010s as it was in the 1980s, and will return in my readings of films in Chapters 3–8, and in my conclusion.

Intensive scholarship on Beauvoirean phenomenology was going on in the wake of her death in 1986, but if it did not occur either to any feminist film critics or to any Beauvoir scholars that bringing their respective areas of interest together might be of mutual benefit, it may also have been because of the distance between them: Beauvoir had written only one essay of any substance on the cinema, although she had shared Sartre's interest in the phenomenology of vision, through the motif of disclosure (*dévoilement*) she discusses in *The Ethics of Ambiguity*.[7] Jenny Chamarette has recently pointed out that Constance Penley envisaged the possibility of bringing phenomenology together with the study of film in 1989 (Penley 1989: 37, quoted in Chamarette 2016, forthcoming), but Penley was pessimistic about 'phenomenology's capacity to deal with the "unconscious" of the film, or to analyse and actively critique the implicitly political aspects of film and cinema' (Chamarette 2016, forthcoming). It would be the 1990s before feminist film scholars began to draw on the accounts of bodily agency and intentionality offered by phenomenology, and I shall turn to Sobchack's *The Address of the Eye: A Phenomenology of Film Experience* in a moment, but first I want to return to de Lauretis, in order to highlight two particular points

---

[6] Doane (1999) and Rich (1999: 45).
[7] *Brigitte Bardot and the Lolita Syndrome* (Beauvoir 1962) was first published in *Esquire* magazine in 1959.

in her work of the late 1980s that seem to me important for subsequent developments in feminist film studies.

De Lauretis begins the essay 'Rethinking Women's Cinema' by observing the same contradictory forces at work in feminist theory of the mid-1980s as in film feminisms of the previous decade, 'a tension toward the positivity of politics, or affirmative action in (sic) behalf of women as social subjects, on one front, and the negativity inherent in the radical critique of bourgeois, patriarchal culture, on the other' (de Lauretis 1987: 127). Dismissing any search for a feminine aesthetic (an issue that had found no consensus in the 1970s) as a legitimation of 'the hidden agendas of a culture we badly need to change' (de Lauretis 1984: 131), she proposes instead a de-aestheticization of images of women in the cinema. Referring to Lizzie Borden's 1983 film Born in Flames, and Anne Friedberg's observation that the images of women in it are 'unaestheticized', possessing a documentary quality that makes this de-aestheticization seem deliberate (de Lauretis 1984: 144), de Lauretis concludes that paradoxically, 'the deconstruction or the destructuring, if not destruction, of the very thing to be represented' (the female body) may be the best route to constructing the female social subject in cinematic representation. I am highlighting this proposal of de Lauretis's at this point both because of its striking anticipation of many of the techniques to be essayed by women film-makers in the years that followed and because adopting this stance towards an aesthetic or aestheticized bodily subjectivity suggests at least a preliminary ethical suspicion of the aesthetics of gender representation in the cinema.

The second point arises from de Lauretis's work as a queer theorist, and concerns relationships between women in the cinema, in their different roles of director, spectator and character. A reconceptualization of the notion of sexual difference to mean, rather than the difference between men and women, 'the differences between and among women, including differences that are "not strictly sexual" as well as those directly concerned with sexuality itself' (Chaudhuri 2006: 82) was already apparent in the arguments of Alice Doesn't and 'Rethinking Women's Cinema' about constructing screen women as social subjects, and in her queer theoretical work de Lauretis developed this into the notion of the 'eccentric subject' – the lesbian subject who is 'eccentric' to the institution of heterosexuality. Her emphasis on lesbian specificity came up against a more fluid understanding of the differences between heterosexual women and lesbians put forward by Jackie Stacey in an article published in Screen in 1987, concerning the films Desperately Seeking Susan (1985) and All About Eve (1950) (Stacey 1987). Although neither of these could be termed 'lesbian films', Stacey argued that 'they offer female spectators certain pleasures associated with women's active sexual desires' (Chaudhuri 2006: 83). De Lauretis's response was to maintain that the desiring dynamics between women in both films were not at all sexual: the relationships depicted were, in the psychoanalytic vocabulary she used, identificatory (to do with ego- or narcissistic libido) rather than desiring (to do with object-libido). In Chaudhuri's summary, '[i]t is the difference between wanting *to be* or *be like* the other woman (a form of identification) and wanting to *have* her (sexual desire)' (Chaudhuri 2006: 83). But Stacey's article had already questioned psychoanalytic film theory's 'rigid distinction between *either* desire *or* identification' (Stacey 1987: 464; Chaudhuri 2006: 83), and by reasserting this binarism and lesbian specificity de Lauretis was insisting on just the kind of *in*flexibility in relationships between women that she had opposed in 'Rethinking Women's Cinema' and other earlier essays.

The point of drawing attention to this disagreement between de Lauretis and Stacey is not to needle de Lauretis once again for continuing to appeal to psychoanalytic concepts whose inadequacies she often signals awareness of, but to highlight just how fraught the question of differences between and among women was at this juncture in feminist theory generally. In the so-called 'postmodern' feminism that had become hegemonic in the academy, differences of race, class and sexuality had become as essential to feminist theoretical models of reading, viewing and social and political action as sexual/gender difference in its everyday sense of 'difference(s) between women and men'. The emphasis on female/feminine genealogies in the work of Irigaray, which would increase in her more explicitly political 1990s writings, did not begin to be taken up by Anglophone feminists until the publication of Whitford's book on her in 1991. The question of the symbolic status of relationships between women pinpointed by Irigaray's female genealogies does of course relate to *relationships* between women rather than social or other differences between them; however, Irigaray's emphasis on symbolizing what had always resisted symbolization was entirely in tune with de Lauretis's call to *make visible* differences left out of account by focusing on an aesthetic image of Woman. Interestingly, de Lauretis herself gave an address at the University of Utrecht around this time titled 'Feminist genealogies: a personal itinerary' (de Lauretis 1993), and in 1990, Mary Ann Doane critiqued apparatus theory's unfailing recourse to the abstraction of historical female subjectivities, suggesting that feminist theory's task now 'must be not that of remembering women, remembering real women, immediately accessible – but of producing remembering women. Women with memories and hence histories' (Doane 1990). Overall, however, attempts to build relationships or differences *between* women into feminist methodologies had made little headway by the early 1990s.

Phenomenology, film, feminism:
Vivian Sobchack and Gaylyn Studlar and
early feminist film-philosophy

Like David Bordwell and Noël Carroll's attacks on 'contemporary film theory', Sobchack's ground-breaking formulation of a Merleau-Pontyan model of the film experience was envisaged as an intervention into a field still dominated, in the early 1990s, by Lacanian psychoanalysis and neo-Marxism. Unlike Bordwell and Carroll, however, Sobchack makes it clear in the Preface to *The Address of the Eye* that she sees this phase in film theory as having effectively dynamized the 'rigorous structuralism' (Sobchack 1992: xiii) that had presided over film as well as many other fields of studies in the humanities in the 1960s. She is aware that her appeal to a notion of 'experience' might seem to be a retrograde move, reminiscent of the 'sloppy liberal humanism' (Sobchack 1992: xiv) that had preceded structuralism, and very aware too of phenomenology's 'precontemporary sins' of idealism, essentialism and ahistoricism (Sobchack 1992: xiv). She makes no mention in *The Address of the Eye* of Judith Butler's critique of Merleau-Ponty, but draws to a considerable extent on Iris Young's combination of Merleau-Ponty's and Beauvoir's existential phenomenology in 'Throwing Like a Girl' in the section of her book entitled 'Whose Body? A Brief Meditation on Sexual Difference and Other Bodily Discriminations'. She also suggests in her Preface that the female authorship of her book is not incidental: to say that it is not an 'overtly feminist' work (Sobchack 1992: xv) implies that it is somewhat feminist in orientation. In addressing the issue of bodily differences, she emphasizes how Merleau-Ponty's notion of the lived-body is 'excessive and ambiguous in its materiality, its polymorphism, and its production of existential meaning' (Sobchack 1992: 144), and can, therefore, never be described in its entirety by its sex/gender or race: 'the lived-body is never merely or wholly male or female, white or black' (Sobchack 1992: 144). Other bodily features she names as open to phenomenological description are class, age and disease, and she insists that the marks that binarily distinguish these and all bodies from 'the invisible and "natural" ground that is the unmarked term and the cultural dominant' (Sobchack 1992: 145) do literally 'dis-figure' or 'de-face' the 'lived-body as a whole'. I shall return to this issue later in this chapter.

As already mentioned, a second publication of the early 1990s that proposed the possible usefulness of phenomenology for feminist film studies was an article by Gaylyn Studlar in the *Quarterly Review of Film and Video* (Studlar 1990). Acknowledging phenomenology's rootedness in the male philosophical tradition and its 'egologically centered approach' (Studlar 1990: 70), Studlar, who focuses on the phenomenology of Husserl and Merleau-Ponty rather than that of Heidegger, Sartre or Beauvoir, suggests that feminism should try to appropriate phenomenology '[b]ecause phenomenology raises issues that intersect with key concerns in feminist film theory: the apprehension of spectatorial subjectivity and the production of meaning through the text/spectator encounter' (Studlar 1990: 71). Although the 'preconceived political agenda' of feminist methodologies may appear completely at odds with the 'presuppositionless method' (Studlar 1990: 71) of Husserlian phenomenology, certain of Husserl's commentators hold phenomenological method to be more flexible than Husserl's own writings imply. And Merleau-Ponty's notion of the 'enworld' – the thoroughgoing immersion of a body-subject in its world – counters the bracketing-off from the world that takes place in Husserl's transcendental reduction. For Merleau-Ponty, embodied perception *connects* the subject powerfully to its world and makes it possible to envisage a film 'as an imposing force on the subject's *Lebenswelt*' (Studlar 1990: 72). In the final part of her article, Studlar critiques existing psychoanalytic models of female spectatorship for not 'do[ing] justice to the complexities of female experience with the cinema' (Studlar 1990: 74), citing the debate over Linda Williams's 'more sociological approach to female spectatorship' (Studlar 1990: 74) that had taken place around the film *Stella Dallas* in *Cinema Journal* in 1984–5, and had raised very much the same issues as de Lauretis's 'Rethinking Women's Cinema'. According to Studlar, this debate had tended (like de Lauretis herself) to overemphasize the construction of the female spectator by the film 'text', rendering her 'passively receptive' and 'transhistorical' (Studlar 1990: 74) and exacerbating the difficulty of any resistance she might put up to the appropriation of her image. In psychoanalytic theories of spectatorship, Studlar concludes that the female spectator 'emerges as nothing more than a subjectified object' (ibid.).[8]

---

[8]The shift from 'subjectified object' to subject that Studlar implies could be brought about by moving away from a psychoanalytic approach to spectatorship finds an exact parallel in the 'change not of perspective but of problematic' observed by Foucault's interviewer in 'The Ethics of the Concern for Self', a shift in Foucault's thinking from 'a "passive" to an "active", a politically active subject' (Foucault 1989: 440). When Foucault answers the interviewer's charge that he had until this point 'forbidden' people to talk to him about 'the subject in general' (Foucault 1989: 440), he nuances the charge by saying that he had not forbidden people to speak to him about anything, but that he had rejected 'the idea of starting out with a theory of the subject – as is done, for example, in phenomenology or existentialism' (Foucault 1989: 440). 'I had to reject a priori theories of the subject in order to analyse the relationships that may exist between the constitution of the subject or different forms of the subject and games of truth, practices of power, etc.' (Foucault 1989: 440). I undertook this book project faced with just such a vacuum, although the only pre-existing theories I opted to reject are those of the Freudo-Lacanian kind (as this chapter explains), no other fully formed ones being available. But as I hope is now becoming evident, a shift from 'subjectified object' to subject is brought about by substituting feminist phenomenological approaches to female cinematic subjectivity for psychoanalytic feminist film theory.

The questions Studlar proposes as arising from the *Stella Dallas* debate and 'women's relationship to the cinematic process' in general (Studlar 1990: 75) are rather different from those I am working with while constructing this overview of feminist film studies, but I entirely concur with her suggestions that a phenomenological social theory of women's cinematic experience 'would provide an alternative to the conceptual narrowness and theoretical abstractionism of many psychoanalytic accounts of female subjectivity' (Studlar 1990: 75) and that 'the freedom of intentionality in women's spectatorship' is a 'sorely neglected possibility' (Studlar 1990: 75). 'A feminist appropriation of phenomenology to film also holds a promise', Studlar insists, 'the promise of opening our sensibilities to perceiving not inevitabilities but the multivalent actualities of our experience as women who can *see*' (Studlar 1990: 77). As I suggested at the start of this chapter, Sobchack's and Studlar's introduction of phenomenology to (feminist) film theory and philosophy can be seen as a vital moment in feminist film studies, the beginning of a mode of feminist film-philosophy that would not really flourish until the 2000s and 2010s, and whose development I shall trace further after reviewing other trends in feminist film studies of the 1990s and early twenty-first century.

Diversification and stagnation: Feminist film studies 1990–2005

One reason why psychoanalysis remained so influential in film feminisms into the 1990s was the quantity of research being undertaken in feminist psychoanalysis more broadly, an important volume such as Teresa Brennan's edited *Between Feminism and Psychoanalysis* appearing as late as 1989. Judith Mayne's *The Woman at the Keyhole* and *Cinema and Spectatorship* came out in 1990 and 1993, while important studies into gendered representation in particular film genres such as Carol J. Clover's *Men, Women and Chainsaws* and Barbara Creed's *The Monstrous Feminine: Film, Feminism, Psychoanalysis* appeared in 1992 and 1993, respectively. As already noted, feminist film studies was quick to extend its purview to queer theoretical issues such as lesbian spectatorship, through the work of scholars such as de Lauretis and Mayne. Psychoanalysis was relied upon less by the feminist scholars who turned their attention to race in the cinema in the late 1980s and early 1990s, who drew instead on the class-based framework of cultural studies (McCabe 2004: 52–56). Black feminists such as Jacqueline Bobo and bell hooks viewed existing feminist work on spectatorship as limited to white, middle-class women viewers, and although they employed the concept of the gaze, tended to draw attention not only to how black women might appropriate it, but to the objectification and violence it could inflict and to how dominant structures of looking might be resisted (McCabe 2004: 52–53). Bobo conducted ethnographic studies of black women's viewing practices and responses to cultural texts that began to remedy the complete lack of research in this area up to this point (McCabe 2004: 53).

A summary of the state of film feminisms in 2004 is offered by Janet McCabe in her conclusion to *Feminist Film Studies: Writing the Woman into Cinema*, and despite recognizing the quantity of important work done and the institutionalization of feminist film studies as an academic area by the 1990s, McCabe concurs with the negative assessment made by B. Ruby Rich in *Chick Flicks: Theories and Memories of the Feminist Film Movement* (Rich 1998): 'What sprang up in the 1970s and was institutionalised in the 1980s has been stagnating in the 1990s, its vigour bypassed by queer culture, on the one hand, multiculturalism on the other, and cultural studies in general' (Rich 1998: 5, quoted in McCabe 2004: 110). McCabe picks out female subjectivity as the concept feminist film theory had failed to address convincingly (managing only to confirm the 'ahistorical, abstracted female subject' (McCabe 2004: 111) it had started out with) and identifies 'restrictive definitions of sexual difference' (McCabe 2004: 111) as what had led it into the 'intellectual cul-de-sac' (McCabe 2004: 111) it had arrived in. A less decisive assessment of the state of affairs in the early 2000s is offered by a special issue of *Signs* titled 'Beyond the Gaze: Recent Approaches to Film Feminisms' (McHugh and Sobchack 2004). Laura Mulvey, Annette Kuhn, Mary Ann Doane, E. Ann Kaplan, Judith Mayne, Linda Williams and Jane M. Gaines are among the contributors to this issue, but while Doane and Williams write tellingly about how they no longer see themselves as contributors to the field of film feminisms, Kuhn is surprisingly complacent about the state of feminist film and media studies, asserting that 'many of the battles have been won' (McHugh and Sobchack 2004: 1221). She is also oddly attached to finding an answer to a particular question of film semiotics posed by Metz in *The Imaginary Signifier* thirty years earlier (McHugh and Sobchack 2004: 1225). While the non-nostalgic 'rethinking' of feminist film theory of the 1970s undertaken by Mulvey in her article anticipates the reflections on time and history she would develop more fully in *Death 24× A Second* (2006), the reflections of E. Ann Kaplan respond more directly than those of most other contributors to the questions asked by the issue's editors: 1. Does feminist film theory still exist as such? 2. What are the histories of film feminisms that have not been told? 3. Does psychoanalytic theory still have something to offer feminist inquiry into the affect and effects of media? 4. How might feminist film theory avoid parochialism and address an ever-expanding media culture? (McHugh and Sobchack 2004: 1205–1206). Kaplan is the only contributor to observe that the displacement of psychoanalytic theory into trauma theory and memory studies that had begun to happen across the humanities had yet to be significantly engaged with by film feminisms (although she was doing so in her own work), and describes the current state of cine-psychoanalysis as 'destabilized' (McHugh and Sobchack 2004: 1240) but far from over. This is probably the moment to note that despite the title of this chapter, I am not at all opposed to the continuing use of psychoanalytic theory in the broader field of contemporary film and media studies, only to psychoanalytic theories of femininity and sexual difference, because they failed so signally to provide film feminisms with the positive approaches to subjectivity and agency they badly needed much earlier in their eventful international history. Interestingly, no consensus about this emerges from the 2004 *Signs* issue, even if the editors' third question appears rather leading (justifiably, I would say) in this regard. What does emerge clearly from the issue is a broad appreciation of the enormous diversification in (feminist) film studies brought about by the growth in television and new media studies, the conversion to digital, and increasing cross-fertilization between film studies, queer theory, critical race theory and other strands of cultural studies.

One issue which can probably be said to have escaped the sense of crisis and fragmentation that increasingly overtook film theory in the 1990s is authorship and the question of the *auteur*, which underwent something of a revival during the decade. As I have detailed elsewhere (Ince 2008), this applied to film authorship in general as well as female film authorship, which did not really become a focus of interest at all until Kaja Silverman took it up in 'The Female Authorial Voice' (Silverman 1988), although it had been central to Claire Johnston's 'Women's Cinema as Counter-cinema' in 1973. As Mayne observes in *The Woman at the Keyhole*, women's authorship was important not only because of women's different and much lower level of representation in film industries than men, but because 'the articulation of female authorship threatens to upset the erasure of "women" which is central to the articulation of "woman" in the cinema' (Mayne 1990: 97) – the same tension between a plurality of different female subjectivities and an idealized image of Woman that had marked debates in the 1980s.

In a valuable overview of feminist work on female authorship first published in 2001, Catherine Grant reviews Silverman's and Mayne's treatments of the topic in 1988 and 1990, then moves on to examine studies of single women directors such as Mayne's book on Dorothy Arzner (Mayne 1994). These began to appear in significant numbers in the 1990s, encouraged by new publishing enterprises such as Manchester University Press's 'French Film Directors' series, which included volumes on Agnès Varda (by Alison

Smith), Diane Kurys (by Carrie Tarr) and Coline Serreau (by Brigitte Rollet) among its first publications. The kind of female agency that had so often been lacking in theories of the female spectator was readily identifiable in most of these studies, Grant noting 'a reasonably confident return to considering various aspects of directorial "authors" as agents: female subjects who have direct and reflexive, if obviously not completely "intentional" or determining relationships to the cultural products they help to produce, as well as to their reception'.[9] In another essay that first appeared in the early 2000s, Angela Martin proposed Agnès Varda's concept of *cinécriture* as a means of allowing feminist critics to talk about women's *auteur* film-making without engaging at all closely with *auteur* theory in the depoliticized mode it had increasingly assumed after the 1960s (Martin 2008: 132–4). The sense in which '*auteur* cinema' designates films of a particular cultural register (a close equivalent to 'art-house') had been extended in the 1990s by analysis of the commerce of auteurism first undertaken by Timothy Corrigan (Corrigan 1991), and with directors' names now effectively functioning as brands to market their films, auteurism became repoliticized in a different manner, one about which many women directors were just as ambivalent as they had been about its former connotations. A decisive move to jettison the term *auteur* while encouraging and embracing 'new directions in authorial film practice' was made by Rosanna Maule in *Beyond Auteurism* (Maule 2008), where she argues, like Grant in 'Secret Agents', that it remains valid to consider single directors as case studies, because 'it is still a relevant category in the critical evaluation of films, and more importantly, it is tied to a specific mode of film production and marketing' (Maule 2008: 15). To replace the tired term *auteur* cinema, Maule suggests 'author cinema', which although inelegant, has the distinct advantage of drawing attention to the director herself, her location and her politics, rather than the style of her film-making. I shall offer some further comments on *auteurism* and authorship in the final section of this chapter, in relation to the films to be discussed in Chapters 3–8.

Feminist film-philosophy II: Constable, Bainbridge, Bolton and Chamarette

The books of these four scholars, all of whom work in the UK and to whose energies and contributions to the field of film-philosophy I am variously indebted, represent a new current in film feminisms. While Constable, Bainbridge and Bolton draw only on feminist philosophers, Chamarette's

---

[9] www.catherinegrant.wordpress.com/secret_agents (accessed 18 November 2015).

study, *Phenomenology and the Future of Film: Rethinking Subjectivity Beyond French Cinema*, really belongs in the lineage of phenomenological studies of film begun by Sobchack and significantly added to in the 2000s by Laura Marks in *The Skin of the Film: Intercultural Cinema, Embodiment and the Senses* (2000) and *Touch: Sensuous Theory and Multisensory Media* (2003) and by Jennifer Barker in *The Tactile Eye: Touch and the Cinematic Experience* (2009). Chamarette's study is a much more extensive exploration of embodied cinematic subjectivity than this book aspires to be, drawing particularly on the phenomenology of Merleau-Ponty, but is not primarily a feminist project. It merits a mention here, though, because of the rich readings it offers of arguably gendered dynamics in the films, video art and installation works of Agnès Varda and Chantal Akerman.

Catherine Constable's *Thinking in Images: Film Theory, Feminist Philosophy and Marlene Dietrich* inaugurated this new UK-based current of feminist film-philosophizing while presenting itself more as a contribution to the crisis-ridden field of film theory, and employs an innovative blend of the philosophies of Irigaray and Michelle LeDoeuff in relation to three films of the 1930s Sternberg-Dietrich cycle. Constable's double focus on Marlene Dietrich, a 'strong' and sexually ambivalent performer who often also played such characters, and on the rhetorical force of images in cinematic discourse, demonstrates how the trope of female stardom can disrupt and force the reorganization of elements of patriarchal narrative and representation. Bainbridge's and Bolton's studies of the importance of Irigaray's work for film studies take distinct approaches, Bainbridge focusing on the possibility of a feminine cinematic 'language' in a number of films directed by women, and Bolton on how a comparison of three contemporary films paired with classic counterparts brings out changes that have taken place in the representation of female subjectivity over the intervening period. Bainbridge's study reserves a place for psychoanalysis – or at least for a notion of fantasy partly derived from it – in her highly effective deployment of some of Irigaray's key ideas, but although she is evidently interested in female subjectivity as it functions both within the narratives of her chosen films and authorially, she maintains quite a formalistic style of analysis that she emphasizes is directed not only at the films' narratives, 'but also [their] formal strategies and mechanisms and [their] contexts of production, direction and reception' (Bainbridge 2007: 184). Bolton's study is particularly successful in the blend it brings about of Irigaray's philosophy with 'sensuous' theory – which I shall engage with further over her reading of Lynne Ramsay's *Morvern Callar* (2002), in Chapter 7. It is less secure, it seems to me, in its deployment of philosophical vocabulary, particularly for female subjectivity 'itself', since after explaining early in her introduction that she has used the word 'consciousness' *rather* than 'subjectivity' in her book's title 'in order to avoid some of the political and cultural connotations associated with the word "subjectivity", arising out of Althusser (1971) or Foucault (1991)'[10] (Bolton 2011: 3), she goes on to use the two terms apparently interchangeably. What Bolton says she means by 'consciousness' is 'the characters' inner lives, their thoughts, desires, fears and emotions, and the introspective contemplation of these (Bolton 2011: 3), and this type of female/feminine interiority is indeed an aspect of Irigaray's thought brought out in a number of Bolton's readings of films and reinforced in her conclusion, but to use 'consciousness' to refer to it would seem to align her at least to some extent with either a phenomenological or a cognitivist approach to film analysis, neither of which is discussed. *Film and Female Consciousness* conveys amply and excitingly the 'positive vision of [women's] possibility and activity' (Bolton 2011: 202) Bolton finds in Irigaray's writings, but to focus on 'a trend in contemporary filmmaking towards the depiction of women with interior lives' (Bolton 2011: 203) while defining 'subjectivity' as 'the individual, mental perspective of a character, which can be represented by a point-of-view shot that is either literal or subjective' (Bolton 2011: 3) is to juxtapose invisibility with filmic 'syntax' without explaining how the latter can convey the former – although it often seems in Bolton's readings that this is by means of the type of spectatorial identification familiar from psychoanalytic feminist film theory, Irigaray's endorsement of which seems doubtful. As a set of studies that evidently break away from a psychoanalytic approach either to film narrative or to subjectivity, that probe filmic syntax and that explore women's film authorship to different degrees, however, these four books break more new ground than had been covered in the entire previous decade of feminist film studies and represent a type of philosophical enquiry into film to which I intend this book to add.

Female subjectivities in film: Towards a method

Questionable though it may be to discuss the subjectivities of female characters as if they were contained within the narratives in which they perform, rather than being variable constructs of image and sound that exist between directors and viewers, I shall do this to a considerable extent, in order to bring out agentic, embodied action on the part of women that I think has been insufficiently observed in existing feminist film criticism. Applied feminist phenomenology takes differences between male and female modes

---

[10]If this means the Althusserian Marxism that was part of the so-called Grand Theory, then why is Foucault mentioned?

of moving and relating to space as the starting point for its enquiry into differentiated embodiment: body comportment, motility and spatiality are among its chief concerns (Young 1989). Since a feminist phenomenological approach to film must start from and focus on screen women as embodied subjects of their own experience and desire, this suggests, together with the phenomenological tenet affirmed by Sobchack that 'thick' description is the best foundation for subsequent analysis, that description of the bodies and movements of the female protagonists of film must be the foundation of any critical activity that will do justice to their *sub*jectivity. This principle will shape the style of film analysis I undertake in Chapters 3–8: it may often read as descriptive, but should rather be understood as a descriptive mode of analysis that constitutes, if not a fully fledged methodology, then a flexible and heuristic method.

Guiding my readings will be an attention not just to the situation and agency of the female character(s) in question, to the bodily and emotional experiences and intersubjective encounters that shape her 'progress' through the film, but to the dynamics of feminine intersubjectivity detectable between director and character, and between character and viewer. In 'Visual Pleasure and Narrative Cinema', Mulvey famously drew attention to the three looks of narrative cinema, proposing that desiring psychic identification between the looks of male character, director and camera produced (in a Hollywood cinema dominated by male directors) a 'male gaze'. (She revised this model several years later, in 'Afterthoughts on "Visual Pleasure and Narrative Cinema" (Mulvey 1989b) to explain that women spectators were not entirely excluded from the cinema, as they could identify with this masculine viewing position in a restless, 'transvestite' manner.) It would be foolish to imitate this model along binarily sexually differentiated lines, since that would double rather than alleviate the exclusions brought about by a binary concept of sexual difference, and reemploy a psychoanalytic notion of secondary identification whose film-theoretical insufficiencies – in particular the exclusion of embodiment – have been amply demonstrated by phenomenologically oriented writings on film (Sobchack 2004). But the open, 'overflowing' character of female subjectivity sketched out in Chapter 1, described by Irigaray as its twoness and ethical relationality and by Battersby as its sticky fleshiness, suggests that it is important to focus on female subjectivities in relationship in film narratives and viewing situations, paying particular attention to a feminine intersubjectivity understood as the dynamic between two female *subjects* rather than as any kind of subject-object relationship. This is of course exactly what Irigaray's concept of female/feminine genealogies refers to, making a brief reminder timely of what she argues is at stake in the recovery and construction of such 'vertical' and 'horizontal' relationships between women.

In the essay 'The Forgotten Mystery of Female Genealogies', one of Irigaray's most extended reflections on this issue (Irigaray 1989), she affirms that (re-)creating links between women is a sine qua non for bringing about the ethics of sexual difference that underlies every part of her philosophy. Following the reading of Sophocles's *Antigone* made in the chapter of *The Ethics of Sexual Difference* devoted to Hegel, she again turns to Greek myth to illustrate how such an ethics has been suppressed by patriarchal philosophy and culture. Just as Antigone's punishment for defying civil law by giving her brother a proper burial was to be 'walled up in a cave on the border of the world of citizens' (Irigaray 1993a: 107, quoted in Jones 2011: 210), Korè-Persephone, the daughter of Demeter, is abducted by the God of the underworld and imprisoned beneath the earth, in retaliation for which her mother Demeter makes the earth sterile. There are several different versions of this myth, but all of them illustrate the direct suppression of the vertical type of female genealogy between a mother and a daughter by a set of men between whom an alliance is sealed *by this very act* (here, the abduction of Persephone, 'arranged' by her father Jupiter to supply Hades, the God of the underworld, with a wife). For Irigaray, in other words, there is nothing incidental about the suppression and invisibility of female genealogies under patriarchy, which comes about as a direct result of the formation of power relationships between men. Although she does often point to the impossibility, within a Freudian or Lacanian narrative of psychosexual development, of a daughter connecting to her maternal origins (because psychoanalysis represents the mother–daughter relationship as unmediated and 'fusional'), the cause of their separation from one another is not the danger of a fusional loss of identity, but the overlaying of a maternal genealogy by a paternal one:

> So psychoanalysis teaches us that the father must take the mother's place in order to allow the establishment of a distance between mother and daughter. This is false. The mother-son relationship is fusional because without reciprocity, the son does not know how to situate himself in relation to his mother. He cannot conceive within himself: he can only artificially identify with his conceiver. To separate himself from his mother, a man therefore needs the mediation of all sorts of objects, including transcendental ones – gods, Truth. (Irigaray 1989: 121–122, my translation)

A woman, on the other hand, can coexist peacefully with her mother without needing specific objects to mediate their relationship, which is always-already mediated by her capacity to conceive of herself *in* her mother, as well as by the earth, language and other environmental elements (Irigaray 1989).

mediation

As Jones summarizes:

> Such genealogies would allow women to relate directly to one another without mediation via the desires of (or for) a male subject. Instead, they would register both the differences between mothers and daughters (in terms of their respective positions in a generative order) and their likeness (their shared sex). In turn, this would allow women to relate to their origins in their own sex without simply identifying themselves with a maternal function. (Jones 2011: 210)

The (re)construction of horizontal and vertical relationships between women is not some kind of correction of psychoanalytic phallocentrism, but a founding step in the creation of a new type of civil order, and essential to an Irigarayan politics and ethics. Irigaray's ethics of *sexuate* difference can only be realized in the context of a civil order where women can relate to one another as subjects regardless of their status in society and the family (married or single, a mother or not), and where their relationships with one another are mediated in visible and audible form (images and words) rather than sublimated into symbolic social structures.

Given the importance of cultural representations like film and literature in mediating social, civil, family and intimate relationships, surprisingly little attention has been given by recent feminist writings to the steady, incremental change in relationships between women observable in cultural texts of the 1990s and 2000s–2010s. I have chosen the films to be discussed in this book in part because their narratives evolve around a female protagonist who is as important as (usually more important than) any other character. Since all the films, which are probably best described as independent or 'author' cinema rather than as mainstream, experimental or avant-garde productions, are directed by women, feminine intersubjectivity is in a sense a fundamental characteristic they share as cultural representations that *may* reflect existing and *may* influence subsequent civil relationships between women. Is it an exaggeration to describe the making-visible of some of the diverse bonds between women in contemporary societies as ethical work? I hope not, and since I intend my readings to add to understanding of such bonds' interdependency with a new ethical order of female subjectivity prized by the feminist philosophers who have (along with the film-makers) inspired them, I shall maintain this emphasis on ethics throughout the film-based chapters.

Women's cinema in transnational context

As already indicated, the vast majority of the films to be discussed in Chapters 3–8 are French or British, the exception being Marleen Gorris's *Mrs Dalloway*, which was produced jointly in the US, the UK and its director's home country, the Netherlands. While French directors outnumber British ones, a consequence of the many years of teaching and writing about French cinema I spent in a department of French studies up to 2011, the films of Sally Potter, Andrea Arnold and Lynne Ramsay are just as important to my exploration of female subjectivities as those of Catherine Breillat, Agnès Varda or any of the other French directors included (Sophie Calle, Claire Denis, Eva Ionesco, Laetitia Masson and Céline Sciamma). Three directors – Breillat, Potter and Varda – in fact constituted a kind of core or nucleus around which the book took shape, and this was not (as far as I am aware) connected to their nationality at all, but to the force of their respective visions of sexual difference and female embodiment, subjects all three women had discussed with unmistakable passion and commitment in diverse interviews, documentaries and TV/video appearances. The absence of an obvious connection between a film-maker's working context and the film(s) she writes and directs does not, however, mean that no such connection exists, and a brief comparison of the British and French film industries in the 1990s, 2000s and 2010s, therefore, seems called for before I turn to the films themselves.

One indication of the striking difference between how women directors fare in France and Britain, albeit one stemming from an academic approach, is the quantity of critical literature their films generate. Studies of women directors working in France far outnumber writings on their counterparts in Britain, where, despite considerable media attention to the representation of women in the film and television industries (as also exists in the US), books devoted to women's film-making are few and far between – in addition to Sue Harper's *Women in British Cinema: Mad, Bad and Dangerous to Know* (Harper 2000) and Melanie Bell and Melanie Williams' *British Women's Cinema* (Bell and Williams 2010), I draw just on two recent monographs on Sally Potter (Mayer 2009; Fowler 2009). French-language studies of films directed by women in France are also strikingly scarce, there having been no new study in monograph form since Françoise Audé's *Cinéma d'elles 1981–2001*, in 2003. Anglophone studies of French women's cinema are much easier to identify: if Carrie Tarr and Brigitte Rollet's *Cinéma and the Second Sex* (2001) is the only book to examine the overall picture over a substantial historical period, a number of director-based studies of Catherine Breillat, Claire Denis and Agnès Varda have now appeared, along with the books on Kurys, Serreau and others (including Varda, Denis and Breillat) in the Manchester University Press's 'French Film Directors' series mentioned earlier in this chapter. In 2010 I co-organized, with Carrie Tarr, a conference titled 'Women's Film-Making in France 2000–2010', which led to two journal issues updating Tarr's study of the 1980s and 1990s to the end of the first decade of the twentieth century (Tarr 2012; Ince 2013). Since the introductions to these two collections of articles provide statistics that evidence the much higher annual production figures in women directing films in France compared to the UK, I will not reproduce those statistics here, but I will make the additional observation that in the world of film, there are no predictable relationships between industrial/commercial activity, success (critical or other) and public awareness of the ethnographic make-up of the industry. In an era increasingly dominated by the internet and social media, there are a huge number of websites, blogs, and virtual (as well as actual) networks that support women in the film and television industries, and yet no ready evidence that these epiphenomena are positively influencing production levels and the access to training, resources and funding women need in order to direct a film of their own.

To turn to the reception in France and Britain of the films themselves, I have not conducted a thorough reception study of how the films directed by Potter, Ramsay and Arnold fared in France, but they were all released there and gained critical attention particularly marked in the case of Arnold's *Fish Tank*, in competition at the 2009 Cannes film festival, which Ramsay's *Morvern Callar* also was in 2002. While *Fish Tank* was seen by French critics as belonging to the tradition of social realism pioneered by Ken Loach and Mike Leigh rather than as in any sense part of a 'women's cinema', and found considerable favour on this account, Sally Potter's *Orlando* and *The Tango Lesson* do not seem to have impressed the French critical establishment as much as the corresponding Anglophone one, Potter herself taking a lot of criticism for choosing to star and dance in *The Tango Lesson*, alongside the Argentine tango expert Pablo Verón. Despite the definite awareness that exists in France both of the notion of a 'film de femme' and of a director's status as *auteur*, then, any claim of a public consciousness in France of women's cinema in Britain would most definitely be an exaggeration. And in spite of the healthiness in global terms of the percentage of women regularly directing projects in France or that are (mainly) French-funded, it is definitely not true to say, in the case of women's films that perform moderately or very well there, that this guarantees release in the US or UK (the latter usually following the former because of the extent of American control of distribution circuits). So while most (not all) of the films of Catherine Breillat and Agnès Varda have been released in the UK, and Céline Sciamma's *Girlhood* made it to the UK in May 2015, some months after it appeared across continental Europe, neither of the films directed by Eva Ionesco or Laetitia Masson I discuss in Chapter 6 travelled to either of the main countries in the Anglophone market. Ionesco has directed only two features and a short and is probably still better known as an actress, so this may not be surprising, but despite the eight feature films, several shorts, TV films and episodes Masson has to her credit (far more than Arnold or Ramsay), she seems fated only to be known outside France through the festival circuit and the release of a number of her films on DVD.

This cross-cultural overview of the industrial context of women's cinema in Britain and France will be supplemented, in the chapters that follow, by short introductions to the careers of the featured directors, offered when one of that director's films is discussed for the first or only time (Andrea Arnold, Sally Potter, Agnès Varda and Catherine Breillat in Chapter 3; Marleen Gorris in Chapter 5; Eva Ionesco, Sophie Calle and Laetitia Masson in Chapter 6; Lynne Ramsay and Claire Denis in Chapter 7; Céline Sciamma in Chapter 8). In a short conclusion that follows Chapter 8, I shall bring matters together in a manner that will also return to many of the questions raised in the two introductory chapters.

3

Body

In recent years, contemporary gender and queer theory have done at least as much as existential phenomenology to make embodiment a focus of research in cultural studies and the critical humanities. If feminist and queer theorists have led the way in exploring embodied cultural identity in all its myriad forms, though, their explorations have also been stimulated by new emphases in post-poststructuralist philosophy such as phenomenology's encounters with different forms of identity politics.[1] As set out in Chapter 2, early feminist film theory's identification of the viewed female body as the centre of its concerns was both an enormously productive and a problematic move: it enabled the (ethically and politically) undesirable aspects of cultural texts' preoccupation with women's bodies to be identified, but risked – if sufficient attention was not paid to the philosophical underpinnings of these problems – reinforcing the very tendencies it sought to counter. And yet, any call for an end to objectifying images of women in film would carry about as much conviction as calls for a total ban on pornography. The difficulty for film-makers of any gender who want their dramas to give increased 'space', screen time, dialogue and attention to female subjectivity is how to undo and rework the codes that embed male subjectivity into film narratives, substituting for them new forms of cinematography and narrative. My exposition of Beauvoirean feminist phenomenology and of a strand of feminist phenomenological approaches to film has already intimated that I think feminist film studies would gain by adopting perspectives from the interdisciplinary field that feminist phenomenology has become in

---

[1] Ahmed (2006) is probably the main publication to date arising out of phenomenology's interest to queer theoreticians.

recent years. As Sobchack and Studlar warned in the early 1990s, though, no straightforward substitution of the lived woman's body of feminist phenomenology for the fetishized female body of Mulvey's 'Visual Pleasure and Narrative Cinema' is possible, because the lived body of phenomenology can never be described in its entirety by its sex/gender (or race, age or class) (Sobchack 1992: 144). In one of the very few pieces of criticism to make a feminist phenomenological reading of a film directed by a woman, Elena del Rio declares that she is seeking to redress the imbalance created by feminist film theory's long-held tendency to conceive of the body as 'a written and a spoken sign' rather than a 'material entity' (Del Rio 2003: 11). This tendency, in del Rio's view, was '[b]orn of urgent necessity', and did not foresee how it 'would relegate the sensual and bodily aspects of female subjectivity to a practically irrelevant status' (Del Rio 2003: 11). Del Rio affirms that she is not entirely rejecting semiotic and psychoanalytic perspectives, but 'combin[ing] these with a phenomenological approach that identifies bodily action as not only inherently significant, but also indivisible from symbolic and discursive structures' (Del Rio 2003: 12). The readings I shall undertake will resemble del Rio's in detailing the pleasure women take in movement and bodily action, while also considering the meanings offered by their living, acting bodies and the symbolic frameworks within which their agency and physical actions take place.

Dancing in the ghetto: Andrea Arnold's *Fish Tank*

Andrea Arnold first achieved international public attention as a director when her short film *Wasp* (2003) won the Oscar for Best Short Film in 2005. Before *Wasp*, which also garnered multiple other awards, Arnold had directed two shorts titled *Milk* (1998) and *Dog* (2001), and shortly afterwards she made a highly successful move into feature film directing with *Red Road* (2006). *Fish Tank* (2009), which won the 2009 Cannes film festival's Jury prize as well as being nominated for the Palme d'Or, and was subsequently awarded a BAFTA for Best British Film in 2010, established her as one of Britain's leading directorial talents, and one of very few British women directors to have received international recognition.

To anyone on the lookout for innovative filming of the active, mobile female body, the opening shot of *Fish Tank* is electrifying. Mia, the fifteen-year-old girl at the centre of the film's story line, is leaning over to get her breath after an evidently heavy exercise session. The shot is frontal, and although Mia's body – seen in her tank top and jogging bottoms against a blank wall – fills only the bottom half of the frame, the heaving of her shoulders and torso

FW's study of the still, passive women's body

and the sound of her breathing instantly grab and keep our attention. When she stands up and moves over to the window to phone a friend with whom she has argued, only her head and shoulders are filmed, from behind and out of focus, meaning that the only image of her face viewable in this opening scene is riveted to her breathing, exercising body. This opening scene of *Fish Tank* could serve as a model to both women directors and theorist-critics of how to approach the screening of embodied female subjectivity – head-on, with attention to activity, effort and movement, and without fetishistic fragmentation of the female body. It illustrates feminist phenomenological theory in practice, Mia's agency and intentionality prominent in her dancing as it is in all her bodily actions. *is agency dependent on mobility?*

Hip hop dancing, which Mia teaches herself by watching online videos in her local internet shop, is an activity we see her engage in no fewer than eight times in *Fish Tank*. It is important to the film's story line and yet a kind of narrative red herring, since despite successfully getting an audition for a dance job at a local club that is advertising for 'fresh young (female) talent', she walks out of the audition when she realizes that only erotic and flesh-baring dancers are wanted. The idea of using her dance ability to get out of the continued poverty she faces in unemployment (she is about to turn sixteen and has dropped out of school) comes to nought. When Connor, her mother's boyfriend, first sees her practising her steps in the kitchen of the family flat one morning, he remarks that she 'dance[s] like a black', adding when Mia does not reply, 'That's a compliment': her hip hop dancing is vigorous, athletic and as streetwise as she is. The narrative dead end it turns into, however, only increases the aesthetic and formal importance of the numerous dance scenes in *Fish Tank*, which never objectify or glamorize Mia, or subject her to a male gaze. In them, her shoulders are the most that is bared, and she is sometimes seen to make a wrong move or execute one badly. It is not the proficiency or polish of her dancing that is emphasized, but the effort and entirely subjective expression that dancing is for her – an outlet for energies that would otherwise go unused and a way to express her desire for a different life.

When Mia returns to the empty flat later on the film's first afternoon, her concentration on the start of her practice session is disturbed by spotting her mother from the window, leaving her flat dressed for an evening out: the argument they have had shortly beforehand has revived the regular conflict in their dysfunctional relationship. Mia launches into her routine, putting up the hoodie of her grey sweatshirt top to complete her 'bad girl' image. The late afternoon sunlight slanting into the room picks out her hooded head and face, and the noisy, rhythmic music, accelerated camera movements and rainbow patterns of the light combine dizzyingly as she jumps and spins, communicating her sensations vividly to the viewer. The next scene of her

is Mia excellent for us or for herself?

FIGURE 3.1 *Mia at dance practice in* Fish Tank

dancing alone, after she spots the advert for the audition, is much shorter, includes one or two jump cuts, and is framed by shots of her walking to the disused flat and returning home along the landing of her own tower block, as if to emphasize the disciplined regularity with which she rehearses. But when she comes to record a routine on DVD in application for the audition, Mia, wearing smarter jogging bottoms than usual and with her hair down, is filmed from a variety of angles in quick succession, either in full or medium shot, with some rapid pans conveying additional movement inserted into some of these: her dynamism is shared with the viewer by this mobile camerawork. Her rehearsal of the actual audition routine takes place in darkness, and she works it out in silence, filmed by Arnold entirely from behind so that she is silhouetted against the artificial lights outside, with the focus repeatedly alternated between Mia and the view from the window in order to emphasize (it seems) both her dead-end situation and resolve to get out of it. This dance, to Bobby Womack's cover of 'California Dreamin', is slower and more balletic than all her others, showing a quieter and dreamier side to Mia that appeals to Connor when she performs it to him later that evening, at his request. Like the earlier one in the empty flat, the only lighting in this scene is provided by the deep yellow-orange glow of artificial lights outside the sitting room window, so that Mia is sometimes profiled against the glow and Connor, the spectator, is bathed in it. There are no full-body shots of Mia that stand in for Connor's gaze at her dancing, though; instead, close-ups on her face and upper body keep us close to the sensations of movement she is experiencing.

Performing her audition routine is the second time Connor has suggested Mia dance for him, the first having been in the car park of the pub he drives the family (her mother Joanne, Mia and her sister Tyler) to on the kind of outing to the countryside the girls have rarely had. Here, Connor puts music on his car's sound system and challenges Mia to dance by humorously doing so badly himself. Drawn in, Mia moves without skill but with obvious pleasure and an infectious sense of freedom – until she hears Joanne, returning across the car park with the drinks, call 'What the fuck are you doing?' Mia mouths abuse at her mother and strides away barefoot (as she has also been dancing), furious to be interrupted. For Mia, as only Connor notices, dancing is one of the few ways she can enjoy herself at all. Hip hop is usually practised collectively, but she pursues it alone, both because she is too abrasive to engage with people easily and because it occupies her spare time and energy.

Fish Tank's final dance scene, though, brings Mia together with others rather than isolating her. Connor has disappeared from the family's life after his semi-drunken seduction of Mia overcomplicated his relationship with ~~rape?~~ Joanne, and as Mia, who is taking advantage of a lift to Cardiff with her friend Billy in order to stage her inevitable departure from the family home, prepares to leave the flat and Essex, she moves to the doorway of the sitting room and says 'I'm going then'. Her mother, smoking and still teary at losing Connor, is listening to a CD of Mia's she says she likes, and although she answers Mia with the words 'Go on then, fuck off…what are you waiting for?', she then contradicts herself by moving into a dance that is a kind of invitation to Mia to join her – which she does. The two women are utterly contrasted in their looks, Mia dark and dressed in black and Joanne shorter and blonde, but they move in parallel up and down the room, in perfect synchronization that silently acknowledges perhaps the only thing they share – a pleasure in their own physicality and in movement. (We are reminded of Joanne dancing in the kitchen after Connor first stays the night with her.) As they move with effortless adult strides, Tyler joins in by holding on to the back of Mia's waist in order to keep up, and although this dance *à trois* is then made humorous by a shot of the family dog reacting with surprise to this unprecedented show of unity in the home, it evokes a powerful bodily tie binding Joanne to Mia and Tyler that can only be acknowledged wordlessly, in movement and in gesture.

In *Fish Tank*, dance conveys female bodily agency and intentionality in a manner that only a feminist phenomenological analysis can really appreciate: in subsequent chapters I shall discuss other forms of bodily action that work to construct Mia as a paradigmatic 'phenomenological' female protagonist, not on account of her character or because of the authenticity it acquires from the performance of Katie Jarvis, but because of the place Arnold grants to agentic embodied action in *Fish Tank*, and the way she films this. Our participation in Mia's coming-of-age drama would be impossible without the film's scenes of hip hop and slower, more balletic dance movement, and the scene in which she dances with Joanne and Tyler is an even more revelatory glimpse of embodied, existential female subjectivity that profoundly suggests its non-individual structure. The Williams family is broken beyond repair, but the synchronized embodied movement of Joanne and her two daughters expresses a resistant, enduring ethical bond between women in which no man is involved. *is it too easy, long-lasting as this?*

The embodied female subject in *Orlando* and *The Tango Lesson*

Since her debut with the acclaimed short *Thriller* in 1979, Sally Potter has carved out a place for herself as one of Britain's leading independent film-makers, but success has often not come easily: her experimental first feature *The Gold Diggers* (1983) failed to find much appreciation, and she struggled for nine years to be able to complete the highly acclaimed *Orlando* (1992), her adaptation of Virginia Woolf's 1928 *Orlando: A Biography*.[2] According to one familiar narrative of the history of women's film-making, the making of *Orlando* carried Potter from experimentalism and explicitly political reflection on representation towards narrative pleasure, a trajectory followed by numerous other women directors in the 1980s. Whether this narrative is accurate or not, there is no denying the feminist twist Potter gives to Woolf's story of time-travel and gender-bending from the seventeenth to the twentieth centuries.

In *Orlando*, Potter treats her protagonist's travels from the Elizabethan age to the twentieth century in six chapters, 1600 Death, 1610 Love, 1650 Poetry, 1750 Society, 1850 Sex, and finally, Birth (date unspecified). Within these time periods female subjectivity is screened principally through Orlando's physical actions and movement: as man and as woman (when she is not constrained by her clothes), Orlando engages in an enormous

---

[2]As commentators have pointed out, the dispersal of *Orlando*'s action over more than three centuries makes it better described as an 'elegy' than as a fictional biography or a novel: Woolf wrote it above all as a satire on the very grounded and chronological conventions of the literary biography.

range of physical activity, from the straightforward (running back to and through Queen Elizabeth's court in '1600 Death', hastening through the maze until she breaks into a run after indignantly refusing the Archduke Harry's offer of marriage) to the sporting – skating on the frozen river Thames, horse riding with Shelmerdine (Figure 3.2) and motorcycling through London with her daughter. Tilda Swinton's lithe, muscular physique is given every opportunity to run, jump and indulge in these sporting activities: Orlando courts Sasha, the daughter of the Muscovite ambassador to England, as they skate elegantly on the Thames, in contrast to Orlando's clumsy fiancée and the self-important English nobleman who insists on having a cloth laid on the ice for him to walk over, and when Shelmerdine is thrown by his horse and twists his ankle after riding out of the mist, she rides them both to safety. In the brief scene of Orlando's pregnancy, she runs frantically across a twentieth-century battlefield at night, stumbles and falls, but the image cuts to her standing again, and as she moves on, the shelling ebbs away, she rubs her rounded belly, day breaks and she disappears into the quiet mist, communicating a sense of tranquillity and hope. We do not see her give birth, and generally, as a woman, Orlando appears strong, healthy and active rather than passive in her love-making and encounters with other bodies, such as her daughter's.

FIGURE 3.2 *Orlando rides Shelmerdine to safety,* Orlando

FIGURE 3.3 *Orlando rushes into the future,* Orlando

Many critics have admired the dynamism, energy and narrative drive of *Orlando*,[3] but its sexuate character – how and to what extent Orlando's 'voyage of "becoming"' (Pidduck 1997: 172) *is* female, feminine or feminist – has only really been touched on by Julianne Pidduck. Drawing on Teresa de Lauretis's essay 'Desire in narrative' and Mary Ann Doane's extension of a gendered economy of stasis and movement to spatiotemporal patterns of genre, Pidduck proposes that there is 'an explicit play (in both Virginia Woolf's source novel and Potter's film adaptation) upon gendered conventions of movement' (Pidduck 1997: 173). By observing that during *Orlando*'s 'utopian feminist voyage of "becoming"', 'the dry theoretical problem of gendered narrative movement becomes an explicitly collective project of social critique' (Pidduck 1997: 173), Pidduck opens the door to feminist accounts of embodied subjectivity and motility, but quickly shuts it again by turning to Mikhail Bakhtin (whose 'Forms of time and chronotope in the novel' takes no account of sexual difference) for an account of

---

[3] '*Orlando* promises the fulfilment of a metaphysical quest where the question concerns what every being is *in potentia* of becoming' (Degli-Esposti 1996: 82); 'I would even go so far as to say that *Orlando* develops a utopian feminist voyage of "becoming" which can delicately "move", inspire or amuse [its dispersed feminist] audience' (Pidduck 1997: 172).

articulations of time and space within historical literary genres. Although she returns to de Lauretis's 'Desire in narrative' later in her article, she then cites de Lauretis citing a structuralist narrative theorist called Lotman whose fundamental binary opposition is into mobile and immobile character types, again without reference to differentiated embodiment (although de Lauretis herself does add male and female to the theoretical mix). For Pidduck, finding in *Orlando* the unadulterated dynamism that might seem necessary 'to a feminist journey of becoming' 'would be manipulating the text to my own ends' (Pidduck 1997: 185): she points out that Orlando ends his/her historical peregrinations in the same places he began them, and there are all kinds of ways in which his/her actions are not effective and purposeful. In my view these instances of inefficacy pertain mostly to his 150+ years as a man, when as England's ambassador to an unspecified Eastern country, he fails to match the Khan at drinking and to take up arms in battle. If Pidduck rightly points out that Orlando does not *achieve* much for a narrative that extends over more than 350 years (though I am inclined too to argue that independence, motherhood and success as a writer adds up to a lot), then it should probably be remembered that when assessing the gendered qualities of movement and achievement in *Orlando* or any film, different levels of action must be distinguished, at least analytically. My descriptions of the positivity and dynamism of Swinton's movements remain at the level of performance, whereas for feminist phenomenology, different analytically separable levels of action are fused: the body is 'our grasp on the world and the outline of our projects' (Beauvoir 2009: 46). It is precisely to counter the deterministic tendencies that arise from building sexual difference into this philosophy of free, transcendent action – as Beauvoir does in *The Second Sex* by emphasizing women's historical desire and capacities – that it is worth dwelling on the detail of particular visions and narratives of female embodiment.

The treatment of movement and action to be found in *Orlando* is continued in Potter's next film *The Tango Lesson*, in which Potter herself performs numerous dance scenes with her co-star and real-life tango professional Pablo Verón. By directing and starring in *The Tango Lesson*, as Lucy Fischer points out, Potter joins a distinguished list of other women artists – Maya Deren and Yvonne Rainer among them – who have made experimental films highlighting their status as dancers and film-makers (Fischer 2004: 46). Fischer's view that Potter's decision to make a dance film 'links her to the mainstream cinema' seems to me arguable, but she also makes two points wholly supportive of the vision of female embodiment and its capacities, as evident in *The Tango Lesson* as it is in *Orlando*. The first, actually articulated by Beatrice Humbert, is that although tango gives the more spectacular role to the man (vividly illustrated by Pablo's display of wounded narcissism after Sally fails to follow his every move in their one public stage performance), its popularity in Europe at the turn of the twentieth century was in part because it 'opened a venue for women to exhibit sensuality in public...Tango showed and performed the strong changes in gender roles that were under way at the time' (Fischer 2004: 50). The second is the ambivalent status of dance on film as both visual spectacle and athletic physical performance. Potter trained as a dancer as well as a choreographer in the 1970s, in her twenties, but for *The Tango Lesson* had not only to master an entirely new dance form (albeit one she was obviously passionate about), but regain comparable strength, suppleness and technique in her mid-forties, all while directing herself, other actors and the entire film. Her physical achievement alone in *The Tango Lesson* is remarkable, though not without obvious effort and fatigue – in a scene where she returns to her Buenos Aires hotel after a night's dancing to find a sheaf of faxes from producers, Sally is seen soaking her aching feet in a hot bath while she starts to phone replies[4] – and if her dancing is not as spectacular as Pablo Verón's, she nonetheless fulfils her intention 'to show, somehow, what dancing *feels* like, rather than what it *looks* like' (Potter, quoted in Guano 2004: 471). The aim of the very physical project she undertook in making this personal, clearly partly autobiographical, film was not to produce visual spectacle her audience could marvel at from a distance, but to communicate the intensely bodily experience of dancing, from her woman's point of view.

Although displayed more subtly, choreography is employed almost as extensively in *Orlando* as it was to be in *The Tango Lesson*. This reinforces how Potter's experience as a choreographer is to the fore in her adaptation, whose credited choreographer is Jacky Lansley, the dancer with whom Potter cofounded The Limited Dance Company in 1974 (Fowler 2009: 21), and who performed in her previous films *Thriller*, *The Gold Diggers* and *The London Story*. And action and movement are not the only way in which embodied female subjectivity features in *Orlando*, since the idea of the female body as situation put forward by Beauvoir and more recently taken up by Kruks and Young figures enormously in the film's unusual mode of historical drama. As noted above, Potter divides the film into dated chapters titled Death, Love,

---

[4] 'Bruises and Blisters' is the title of Potter's commentary on the film in *Sight and Sound*'s supplement to the 1997 London Film Festival, where she explains that after rehearsing the 'tango for four' she dances with Pablo and her two Buenos Airean teachers towards the end of the film, 'it took two hours to be eased out of my shoes at the end of the day – a doctor in attendance to lance the blisters' (Potter 1997: 7).

attention to transchoming in Orlando's becoming?

Poetry, Society, Sex and Birth: the death is that of Queen Elizabeth I, the love Orlando's for Sasha and the birth that of Orlando's daughter (in one of Potter's few significant changes to Woolf's text, where Orlando's child is a son). The moment of this childhood seems to be a mixture of 1928 (the date of Woolf's book) and the 'present day' of the film (1992), in that Orlando rides a vintage 1928-style motorbike with a sidecar through a recognizable early 1990s London of Canary Wharf and Docklands. Orlando is thus always in a defined historical situation, even if he/she inexplicably advances as an embodied and situated subject through over three centuries while 'hardly ageing a day', as both book and film state.

That Orlando's body is his/her situation is illustrated in two evident ways. First, there is his change of sexed body just before her entry into the society of 1750, upon which follow two scenes emphasizing just how objectified and excluded women of the period were. In one, Orlando wanders idly through the sunny, silent long gallery of her country seat to the sole sound of peacocks calling on the lawns outside, adjusting her movement to prevent her voluminous hooped skirts from knocking over pieces of furniture draped in sunlit white dust-sheets. Since Orlando too is clad in brilliant white, the most striking element of this brief scene is her resemblance to the furniture, and hence, the status of woman as property at this period – a prefiguring of how she will be stripped of her inheritance by a lawsuit that begins in the eighteenth century and concludes in the nineteenth. In the second scene, a literary gathering hosted by a countess at which Jonathan Swift, Alexander Pope and Joseph Addison hold court, 'Orlando is immobilized like one elaborate frosted blue cake on a love seat. Complete with an unlikely sculpted headdress, she becomes a porcelain figurine, hampered equally by costume and convention from moving or responding to the routine snubs of the male "wits"' (Pidduck 1997: 176). The second manner in which *Orlando* situates its protagonist in history, already anticipated in the scenes described above, is the continuously glorious use it makes of lavish costume. But although the film is often included alongside Jane Campion's *The Piano* (Australia/New Zealand/France 1993) and Julie Dash's *Daughters of the Dust* (US 1991) in a list of what was in 2003 called 'the emerging global feminist reappropriation of costume drama' (Imre 2003: 188), the genre category 'costume drama' suggests a realist treatment of a particular era and set of characters never allowed to develop by *Orlando*'s restless progress. Rather, as Patricia Mellencamp argues, 'the performative elements (of gesture, glance, pose, costume) are more telling than the narrative. History becomes something to learn from, move through, and get beyond' (Mellencamp 1995: 283). Orlando the character and *Orlando* the film skip energetically through history, or perhaps fly in the manner characteristic of Hélène Cixous's *écriture féminine*,[5] defying history's gravity and territorializing forces.

By virtue of its transgendering narrative and passage through nearly four centuries, *Orlando* allows – or perhaps we should say, gloriously stages – the comparison of woman's becoming to man's that Beauvoir speaks of in *The Second Sex*. One aspect of the film on which much critical commentary has focused is the contrast between the universalist androgyny of Woolf's text and the queer postmodern reconstruction of a female genealogy in Potter's film: as Roberta Garrett summarizes, 'Woolf's "modernist" project aims to undermine the stability of forms of gender identification, whereas Potter's "postmodern" interpretation posits a "reconstructed" notion of female subjectivity which acts as a locus of resistance to the "master narrative" of British history' (Garrett 1995: 96). The birth of Orlando's daughter and her happiness as a mother despite having been dispossessed of her inheritance would seem to make this digression of film from book unambiguous, and yet Potter has stated that where Orlando's change of sex is concerned, she thought that using the same actor for the male and female character would help the idea of individuality to prevail, and what she has called 'the seamless individuality across the genders' would not be lost (Potter in Degli-Esposti 1996: 88). She may have been wary of making a feminist film – '"feminist" has become a sort of trigger word that closes down thinking rather than opening it up' (Potter in Degli-Esposti 1996: 89) – but ended up with one nonetheless, perhaps because of the thoroughly postmodern sensibility of *Orlando*'s queer, flighty, disrespectful treatment of identity, history and the genre of costume drama.

The Beaches of Agnes and the carnal *cinécriture* of Agnès Varda

In the cinema of Agnès Varda, the grand old lady of French cinema since at least 2008, when she filmed part of her eightieth birthday party, there is plentiful evidence that female subjectivity is always 'lived', that is, embodied and actively animated, even when it remains a viewed object. One of the activities by which we most remember Cléo of *Cléo de 5 à 7* and Mona of *Sans*

---

[5]'For us the point is not to take possession in order to internalize or manipulate, but rather to dash through and to "fly" (*volen*)', 'The Laugh of the Medusa' (Marks and de Courtviron 1981), 258. A translator's note to 'fly' on this page explains how in French, Cixous puns on *voler*'s double meaning of 'to fly' and 'to steal' in this and subsequent sentences.

toit ni loi/Vagabond is their dynamic walking through city and countryside, respectively, which it seems to me we are invited to view as subjective expression rather than in a 'sex-pervasive' manner.[6] The representation of animated, mobile female bodies was, however, comprehensively confirmed by Varda's performance in *Les Plages d'Agnès/The Beaches of Agnes*, openly acknowledged by her to *be* a performance 'of the role of a little old lady... plump and talkative, telling the story of her life' (Romney 2009: 46), where she engages in or narrates numerous very deliberately executed embodied activities. She reports, for example, how at the age of nineteen, for the three-month period between abandoning her training as a curator and beginning evening classes in photography, she carried out the very physical 'manual' labour of rowing for Corsican fishermen as they dealt with their nets, masts and sails. This period, not incidentally also the time of her first significant sexual experiences, has just been echoed in shots of her sailing a small lateen boat across the Mediterranean port of Sète (the location of an early part of the film), then, in a typically wry edit, along the Seine and under the Pont des Arts in Paris. The pleasure Varda takes in practical, embodied activity is signalled here in the very representation of her shuttling back and forth from provincial France – her family had left Belgium for Sète during the Second World War – to Paris, as her film-making career began to take off in the mid-1950s. The most frequent and striking example of symbolic embodiment in *The Beaches of Agnes*, however, is the humorous but entirely knowing device of walking backwards, which Varda does first on the beach at Sète, again on the Pont des Arts, and later in several more of the film's locations. This bodily mime of the process of remembering is Varda's personal contribution to the multiple 'living' installations that feature in her film.[7]

Beaches, timeless spaces according to Varda, are the motif linking the seventy-plus years of memories recounted in *The Beaches of Agnes*, but

---

[6]The term 'sex-pervasive' is deployed to particular effect by Toril Moi (see Moi 1999). Moi links the birth of the sex/gender distinction (which like Iris Young she is critiquing in favour of feminist phenomenology, though only in Beauvoirean mode and less subtly) to the 'pervasive picture of sex' born with modern, Enlightenment feminism. Female anatomy began to be pictured as pervaded by sex/sexuality at this point in history, Moi claims, as Western culture moved from what Thomas Laqueur calls a 'one-sex model' to a 'two-sex model' of sexual difference (i.e., women's reproductive organs began to be viewed as distinct from men's rather than just 'a different arrangement of the same parts'), and biological sex became 'something that seeps out from the ovaries and the testicles and into every cell in the body until it has saturated the whole person' (10, 11). 'It is in the encounter with the pervasive picture of sex that the need for something like the sex/gender distinction is born', Moi states (12). The idea of sex-pervasiveness seems to me to be particularly pertinent to the female walker or *flâneuse*, which even feminist criticism has had difficulty separating from the streetwalker, or prostitute.

[7]On the mix of installations into the film, see Bellour (2009).

by mixing autobiographical narration with installation art and filmic and photographic montage, the film also gathers the diverse geography of her life into one document in a way none of her previous films or exhibitions has done. Varda's preferred locations apart from Sète-La Pointe Courte and the Languedoc – Los Angeles-Venice Beach, Paris's fourteenth *arrondissement* and Rue Daguerre and the Brittany island of Noirmoutier, to which she was introduced by Jacques Demy – each figure in a number of her works. Together, these places constitute a 'world' in the sense meant by existential phenomenology, where the term's meaning differs qualitatively from the concept of an objective physical world described by the natural sciences, although varies somewhat from one thinker to another.[8] A specific sense is already given to 'world' by Merleau-Ponty in his *Phenomenology of Perception*, where perception, rather than being an inner, subjective, mental state as for so much previous philosophy, is described as a mode of being in the world and what links the perspective constituted by each lived body to its 'world', or environment. 'I am conscious of my body *via* the world', says Merleau-Ponty, or, again, 'I am conscious of the world through the medium of my body' (Merleau-Ponty 2002: 94, 95). Most of Merleau-Ponty's aesthetic theory is formulated around painting, which he regards as a thoroughly embodied form of expression, as 'essentially worldly' (Carman 2008: 204). The sense he ascribes to 'world' undergoes further development by the time of his draft and notes for *The Visible and the Invisible*, where body and world come to be seen 'as overlapping sinews in a common "flesh" (*chair*), related ... as kind of "chiasm", an "interweaving" or "interlacing" (*entrelacs*) of threads in a single fabric' (Carman 2008: 79–80). For Merleau-Ponty by the end of his life, therefore, 'to understand a work of art is to understand its involvement in the world' (Carman 2008: 204), where that world is defined as a set of material, fleshy relationships between the artists and the objects and places on which his or her perceptions have been exercised, in the reversible dynamic of perception and expression evident in Merleau-Ponty's early work and expanded in his drafts for *The Visible and the Invisible*. Varda's film-world, accordingly, is the set of locations on which her perceptions have frequently been exercised (by inhabiting them) and of which she has repeatedly composed expressions. 'World', for existential phenomenology and for Varda, is materially imbricated with the body that perceives it, which

---

[8]Husserl refers to the *Lebenswelt*, while one of the most precise formulations of Heidegger's notion of 'world' can be found in *Being and Time*, and is summarized by David Farrell Krell in his introductory note to 'The Origin of the Work of Art' as 'the structural whole of significant relationships that Dasein experiences – with tools, things of nature, and other human beings' (Heidegger 1977: 145).

is why the term is so well suited to the locations Varda has contemplated and conveyed with such caring attention in her cinema; they are so entirely fused with her sensibility that it has become impossible to think of her films without thinking of them.

The majority of Varda's films are powerfully rooted in a particular place, as we have seen, and her film-world is made up of places she has actually inhabited. Her unusually keen vision of her immediate surroundings adds up to more than a 'sense of place' – what is expressed is the part played by a material social environment in the construction of personal identity, a belief Varda explained in 1961: 'I believe that people are made of the places they love or have lived in; I believe that location inhabits and propels us' (Michaud and Bellour 1961: 14). This steady construction over Varda's career of a phenomenological geography or 'world', expression of which culminated in *The Beaches of Agnes*, is one evident way in which she may be seen as a 'lived body' film-maker. Having set out what I mean by Varda's 'film-world', a few selected critical accounts of its character and texture, including some by Varda herself, will illustrate further how this existential phenomenological character pervades her work as a film-maker.

Numerous critics since the 1960s have in fact remarked on the carnality of Varda's *cinécriture*. For Marcel Martin and Jacqueline Nacache reviewing her films up to *Jane B. by Agnès V.* and *Kung-Fu Master*, it is because of 'her pulsating sensibility and its carnal vibration' that Varda's cinema is 'profoundly feminine/female' (profondément *féminin*), though not '*féministe*', which for Martin and Nacache requires a militant or otherwise propagandistic message. René Prédal comments that 'Varda always imposes a natural physical presence that prevents discourse from dematerializing itself by posing problems of skin and hormones right in the middle of intellectual debates'.[9] The most memorable example of Varda's organization of a film around her own body is probably *Daguerréotypes*, the 1975 documentary about the community of 'her' part of Paris's Rue Daguerre, the content of which was decided by the entirely material condition that it takes place within eighty metres of her home, where she was looking after her baby son Mathieu Demy. Varda's use of an electrical cable to measure out the maximum distance her camera could travel points wittily to the centrality of her own maternal body to her film-making, but just as importantly, emphasizes the materiality and materialization of filmic

---

[9]'Is this cinema a *feminist* cinema? No, because apart from the fact that she refrains from any propagandistic intentions, her films are sufficiently *open* to attract attention and sympathy to the female condition while managing not to impose any militant "messages"' (Martin and Nacache 1988: 57; Prédal 1991: 20).

space.[10] The blurring of the boundary between fiction and documentary to be found in so many of Varda's films is inseparable from – and perhaps largely a consequence of – this insistence on the materiality of space, as is her description of herself as a 'witness-auteur' (*auteur-témoin*, in Varda 1975: 36): in *Vagabond*, when she introduces Mona as she emerges from a swim in the sea, Varda's use of her own voice weakens the fiction in favour of a strong dose of documentary by placing herself (anonymously here) in the same film-world as her protagonist. Varda's acute sensibility, the materialization of filmic space and the blurring of the boundaries between fiction and documentary found across her *oeuvre* are further ways in which her film-making comes suggestively close to the intentional expression of the lived body theorized by Merleau-Ponty, as well as confirming the incarnate character of her vision. In the next section I shall develop this question of the incarnate character of Varda's filmic discourse by turning to her acclaimed documentary *Les Glaneurs et la glaneuse/The Gleaners and I* (2000).

Haptic images in *The Gleaners and I*

In *The Skin of the Film: Intercultural Cinema, Embodiment and the Senses* (Marks 2000), Laura Marks draws on a number of sources in order to explore 'haptic visuality', which she defines (following but modifying the Austrian art historian Aloïs Riegl, coiner of the term 'haptic') as vision in which 'the eyes themselves function as organs of touch' (Marks 2000: 162). Whereas optical visuality 'sees things from enough distance to perceive them as distinct forms in deep space', haptic looking 'tends to move over the surface of its object rather than to plunge into illusionistic depth, not to distinguish form so much as to discern texture' (Marks 2000: 162). The haptic image is thus a sensuous image, often a close-up, while haptic perception 'privileges the material presence of the image' (Marks 2000: 163).[11] In developing her notions of haptic visuality and perception, Marks draws to a significant extent on Gilles Deleuze's philosophy of film, but also on the work of Merleau-Ponty, whose

---

[10]'I started with the idea that women are attached to the home. So I attached myself to my home, literally, by imagining a new kind of umbilical cord. I attached an electric cable to the electric meter in my house which, when fully uncoiled, turned out to be 80 metres long. I decided to shoot *Daguerréotypes* within that distance' (Varda 1975: 39–40).

[11]Where French film is concerned, Martine Beugnet has been the closest and most prolific observer of haptic processes in the films of Claire Denis and other contemporary film-makers. See Beugnet (2007, 2006, 2004).

phenomenology of perception emphasizes that the perceiver's relationship with the world is symbiotic and mimetic – that is, that in embodied perception (and for Merleau-Ponty all perception is embodied) there is an enfolding of self and world of which cinema spectatorship can be seen as a special example (Marks 2000: 163). For Marks, 'haptic images are often used in an explicit critique of visual mastery, in the search for the way to bring the image closer to the body and the other senses' (Marks 2000: 151–152). So while she does not accept Merleau-Ponty's phenomenology of perception unquestioningly, its insights about the sensual involvement of our bodies in the world (and in particular, about how the encoding of history in our bodies influences our perception) strongly inform her readings of sense memories in intercultural film.

In Varda's films, haptic visuality first occurs in *Jacquot de Nantes*, the film-portrait of her husband Jacques Demy made as he was dying of AIDS in 1990. Varda's camera tracks slowly and in extreme close-up over Demy's skin in a tender and regretful observation of its condition, still tanned but now flawed by the purple patches of Kaposi's sarcoma. Varda films the male body with particular tenderness in *Jacquot de Nantes* because it is that of her husband: it is of course significant that she comes to haptic visuality in an eroticized relationship and only films her own woman's body in the same unfocused extreme close-up ten years later. Shots that caress Varda's own skin occur at two moments in *The Gleaners and I*:[12] in the first, the camera cuts from a shot of Varda combing the grey roots of her dark chestnut coloured hair to the deeply lined and wrinkled skin of her hands against a car dashboard, as she speaks her rhyming refutation of a famous line about old age from Corneille's *Le Cid*, 'No, no, it's not "O rage", not "O despair", not "O my enemy old age", it might even be "my friend old age", but even so, there's my hair, and there are my hands, which tell me that the end is near.' This haptic shot is returned to and extended in the second moment, also involving the trope of ageing, where the notion of self-portraiture is explicitly introduced by some high-quality postcard-sized reproductions of Rembrandt portraits and self-portraits Varda has brought back from a trip to Tokyo. Here, her camera moves from a detail of a picture of Rembrandt's wife Saskia to her own left hand, tracking down her fingers to the base of her thumb then back up her index finger in a movement that caresses at the same time as it searches. The commentary with which Varda accompanies this shot, 'Saskia, in close-up .... and then, and then my hand in close-up .... which is to say that that is my project, to film one

---

[12]When reflecting on *The Gleaners and I* in *Deux ans après/Two Years On*, Varda has to be alerted to the similarity between these sequences in her two films, having apparently not noticed it.

hand with the other', could hardly echo more closely if she had set out to do so a celebrated passage in Merleau-Ponty's essay 'The Philosopher and His Shadow', in which he describes the meeting of his hands:

> When my right hand touches my left hand, I am aware of [*sens*] it as a "physical thing". But at the same moment, if I wish, an extraordinary event occurs: here is my left hand as well starting to feel my right, *es wird Leib, es empfindet* (Husserl, *Ideen II* p. 145). The physical thing becomes animate. Or more precisely, it remains what it was (the event does not enrich it), but an exploratory power comes to rest upon or dwell in it. Thus I touch myself touching; my body accomplishes "a sort of reflection". In it, through it, there is not just the unidirectional relationship of the one who perceives to what he perceives. The relationship is reversed, the touched hand becomes the touching hand, and I am obliged to say that the sense of touch here is diffused into the body – that the body is a "perceiving thing", a "subject-object" (Husserl, *Ideen II* p. 119 *empfindendes Ding*, p. 124 "*Das subjective Objekt*"). (Merleau-Ponty 1964a, 166)

This two-way 'bodily reflection' anticipates if it does not already formulate the notion of the reversibility of the flesh Merleau-Ponty would set out in *The Visible and the Invisible*, a book he did not live to complete, but was working on when the essay containing this passage was published, in 1960. As noted in the previous section, the fragments of and notes for *The Visible and the Invisible* set out new notions of 'flesh' (*la chair*) and 'intertwining' (*l'entrelacs*) – a reversible material relationship between body and world in which they are not separate entities but 'threads in a single fabric' (Carman 2008: 80).[13] Through the deployment of a haptic gaze, Varda's body – the filming and the filmed body – becomes here the 'feeling thing' and 'subject-object' Merleau-Ponty describes. Subjectivity and objectivity blur and become indistinguishable auto-erotically, in contrast to the erotic blurring at work in *Jacquot de Nantes*. *The Gleaners and I*, inhabited by the enhanced 'exploratory power' of the mini digital camera's movement, develops Merleau-Ponty's 'sort of reflection' of the flesh into a self-portrait

---

[13]A critique of Merleau-Ponty's notions of the intertwining and the chiasmus is made by Irigaray in Part IV of *An Ethics of Sexual Difference*, titled 'The Invisible of the Flesh: A Reading of Merleau-Ponty, The Visible and the Invisible, "The Intertwining – The Chiasm"' (Irigaray 1993a: 151–184), but since this has in turn been convincingly challenged by Judith Butler, who points out that Irigaray's critique is endebted to Merleau-Ponty's conceptualization in ways Irigaray does not acknowledge (Butler 2006) – a very similar response to that of Dave Boothroyd to her critique of Levinas discussed in Chapter 1 – this chapter traces Varda's implicit feminist challenge to Merleau-Ponty rather than adopting Irigaray's explicit feminist critique.

*intimacy w/
proximity to
Jacques: to herself*

of the ageing woman film-maker, a self-portrait in haptic rather than optical space. A further detail of the second of these two moments in *The Gleaners and I* is important – that the hand to which Varda's camera moves from the detail of Rembrandt's portrait of Saskia is obscuring a reproduction of one of Rembrandt's self-portraits that is revealed only when her meditation on the unknown 'horror' of her own ageing flesh is over, and she raises the finger. Even then, what we view is Rembrandt's face rather than his hand: only the next shot, that of a self-portrait by the artist Maurice Utrillo, returns us to an image of an artist's hand, this time that of a man rather than of a woman. Varda's haptic moment of filmic self-portraiture 'as an old lady' (Rosello 2001) displaces Rembrandt's mastery of the conventional painted self-portrait – neatly, modestly and without drawing attention to what it is doing in any way, but displaces it nonetheless. A woman's perception and hands are explicitly privileged at the expense of a man's in this sequence, so that although the viewer's senses may shortly afterwards re-engage with conventional masculine self-portraiture by alighting on Maurice Utrillo's hands, a temporary bracketing-off of the image of the male artist reduces possible sensory engagement to a perceptive perspective gendered female.

A similar kind of suggestively subversive filmic performance can be seen in Varda's assumption of the identity of 'gleaner' in *The Gleaners and I*, where her actions intersect strikingly with the gender-specific and historical phenomenological descriptions of lived-body experience collected by Iris Young. Young's 'Throwing Like a Girl' essay, as I have already noted, 'combines the insights of the theory of the lived body as expressed by Merleau-Ponty and the theory of the situation of women as developed by Beauvoir' (Young 2005: 31), and by collecting, detailing and meditating upon 'modalities of feminine body comportment, manner of moving and relation in space' as she does in this essay, Young has in a way set out a framework for a feminist phenomenological film criticism that can do justice to Varda's performance in *The Gleaners and I*. Gleaning, Varda notes at one moment in her commentary, is 'a modest gesture', but when it comes to identifying herself as the gleaner in the title of her film, it is Jules Breton's proud and solitary female figure rather than Jean-François Millet's three more modest ones she imitates. (The two particular paintings at the origin of Varda's investigation into gleaning are Millet's *Les Glaneuses* of 1857 and Breton's *La Glaneuse* of 1877.) Opposite Breton's painting where it hangs in the museum and art gallery of Arras, and in a mirror image of it, though in the same plane, Varda stands with a large bundle of corn on her right shoulder which she then lets drop and replaces with her digital video camera: this is a humorous moment that is also replete with signification, since Varda's action expresses a preference for a particular use of space while identifying herself in multiple ways, as the admirer and companion of the nineteenth-century peasant women at the origin of her documentary (who were painted by Millet with socially critical intent) as well as a viewing body-subject *at the same time as* being the viewed body-object they are. The lived body as described by Merleau-Ponty and Young is both immanent and transcendent, immanent in its materiality and situation, yet transcendent in how it is lived by a subject as intention and as action. The ambiguous transcendence of the body when lived by a woman that Young illustrates in feminine body comportment, for example in living space as enclosed or confining or when 'stand[ing] in *discontinuous unity* with both itself and its surroundings' (Young 2005: 38), is both acknowledged and resisted by Varda in self-portraiture that works with and through other bodies and representations of bodies, both female and male. This revelation of different modes of body comportment and relationships to space – including on the part of bodies from different social classes – is crucial to *The Gleaners and I*, as are the contradictory modalities of feminine bodily existence Young outlines and claims 'have their root…in the fact that for feminine existence the body frequently is both subject and object for itself at the same time and in reference to the same act' (Young 2005: 38).

The striking correlation between Varda's actions and gestures in *The Gleaners and I* and Young's Merleau-Pontyan and Beauvoirean framework for explaining feminine body comportment illustrates feminist phenomenological theory in action. Unlike the moments in *The Gleaners* where haptic images register the collapse of optical space into haptic space and the sensuous enfolding of Varda's film-maker-body into her perceptual world, it is less Merleau-Ponty's insights about embodied perception than his understanding of the particular, socially situated character of movement and gesture that are relevant here. In *The Skin of the Film*, Marks recognizes that feminist criticism and theory have played an important role in the increasing acceptance of the notion of embodied spectatorship into film criticism, but stops short of theorizing any particular relationship between haptic visuality and sexual difference, stating that although 'the use of haptic images may be a feminist strategy, there is nothing essentially feminine about it' (Marks 2000: 188). Young, by contrast, develops existential phenomenology in an explicitly feminist direction by focusing on female body experience, and by so doing, both returns to and develops the focus on the lived body and women's embodied experience pioneered by Simone de Beauvoir in *The Second Sex*. The haptic visuality that occurs in *The Gleaners and I* is a different, complementary and possibly even stronger confirmation of the identity of 'lived body' film-maker that arises out of the construction of a phenomenological geography or 'world' in Varda's cinema.

Catherine Breillat's *Romance* and the phenomenal birthing body

French director Catherine Breillat has what must be some of the best feminist credentials of any European film-maker of the 1990s and 2000s, having made (by 2013) fourteen features all concerned with women's lives and female sexuality. She is associated particularly with the loose trilogy of films about adolescent girls and their sexuality formed by *Une vraie jeune fille/A Real Young Girl* (1976), *36 fillette/Virgin* (1988) and *A ma soeur!/Fat Girl* (2001), but the majority of her films have a woman or women as their leading protagonists, the only exceptions (where a man or men are equally important focalizers of the narrative) being *Sale comme un ange/Dirty Like an Angel* (1991), and to a lesser extent, *Parfait Amour!/Perfect Love* (1996), *Brève Traversée/Brief Crossing* (2001) and *Anatomie de l'enfer/Anatomy of Hell* (2004). Breillat seemed to make a clear change of direction when she shifted from original auteurist narratives to literary adaptation with *Une vieille maîtresse/The Last Mistress* (2007), a version of Barbey D'Aurevilly's 1851 novel, and went on to make two adaptations of fairy tales in *Barbe bleue/Bluebeard* (2009) and *La Belle endormie/Sleeping Beauty* (2010). She has suggested since, however, that the continuity of *The Last Mistress* with the 'décalogue' of original stories that preceded it is just as noteworthy as its discontinuity,[14] and has subsequently moved away from adaptation again with the autobiographical drama *Abus de faiblesse/Abuse of Weakness* (2013). Dramas of intimate experience are the mainstay of Breillat's cinema, and it is probably not exaggerating to label her first ten films dramas of female subjectivity.

The international controversy caused by *Romance* (1999), which was released just over a year before Virginie Despentes and Coralie Trinh Thi's *Baise-moi* (2000), and whose explicit scenes of oral sex, bondage, masturbation and male erections saw Breillat accused of being a 'porno-auteur' (accusations she put down firmly), also marked the start of her widespread acceptance and fame. (She was able, for example, to use its success to get her previously unseen first film *A Real Young Girl* released.) *Romance* has been admired for the sobriety and cleanliness of its *mise en scène*, which makes bold and striking use of monochrome white sets with periodic splashes of vibrant red, as well as of theatrical locations, both interior

---

[14]This view is borne out by the reading of the film made by Keesey (2009). Breillat borrows the term 'décalogue' from Krzysztof Kieslowski's TV mini-series of one-hour films 'The Decalogue' (1989–90).

(the opulent apartment inhabited by one of her lovers) and exterior (the Roman arena in Arles, and the vast sands of the Camargue at Aigues-Mortes, not far from Marseilles). Its main protagonist Marie (Caroline Ducey) is a young woman whose boyfriend of some months, Paul (Sagamore Stévenin), is now refusing to have sex with her, which leads her to initiate a sequence of sexual encounters with other men. Almost as striking as the film's sober, Japanese-style aesthetic, evident above all in its white, black and red colour palette and presentation of blank surfaces, is the interior monologue voiced by Marie. Through this monologue spectators have access to her intimate, complex and often self-demeaning thoughts and feelings about her body and her desires.

The character of Paul in *Romance* is almost a caricature of patriarchal masculine sexuality, announcing as he drives Marie and his friend Ashley home from a nightclub where he has danced with several unknown women that the thrill of the chase is what befits a man. Paul is unable to bear even a trace of activity or dominance in Marie's sexual behaviour towards him, though proposes marriage to her as soon as it is confirmed she is pregnant with his child, then makes love to her for the only time in the film, delighted that she is serving his desire to reproduce. As Keesey states, 'Paul exhibits a mind/body dualism that manifests itself as a Madonna/whore complex' (Keesey 2009: 119), and this duality also colours – though does not ultimately determine – Marie's exploration of her sexuality with both her first lover Paolo (Rocco Siffredi) and her second, the headmaster of the primary school where she teaches, Robert (François Berléand). A split between head and body marks the imagery of several scenes of *Romance*, most strikingly a semi-pornographic fantasy of Marie's in which the upper half of her body is separated from her pelvis and legs by a guillotine-style contraption built into the wall of a circular room:

> On one side of the divide, the upper half of a white-clad Marie lies in a white maternity ward as her husband-to-be Paul bends tenderly over her bed to give her loving comfort. But protruding through the other side is Marie's lower half, garbed in garters and a flouncy red skirt like a whore, her sex a hole which anonymous, apelike men use to demonstrate their phallic dominance in a scene with red lighting. (Keesey 2009: 124)

Another scene visually constructed around this dichotomy between Marie's face and her sex (in French, 'con') is one in which she is examined, some weeks into her pregnancy, by an entire team of junior doctors she dismisses as 'spotty interns' ('jeunes praticiens boutonneux' (Breillat 1999a: 64)). As each of them slips on a rubber glove before inserting his hand deep into her vagina, the camera shifts from a position that approximates the look of the doctors at the thick dark hair covering her pubic area, to Marie's beautiful face, tightly framed, to a position behind Marie's head – the scene as it appears to her, subjectively. In a brief scene following this one whose location is unclear, but which directly precedes her semi-pornographic fantasy, Marie is seen examining her pubic area and her face alternately in a mirror, and remarks in voiceover, 'Paul's right. This face can't be loved attached to this c***. This c*** cannot belong to this face' (Breillat 1999a: 65). What Keesey sees as a culturally Catholic division of her person into spiritual and sexual parts is exactly, to my mind, what Marie is countering in her liaisons with other men, and by exploring her masochistic impulses in bondage sex with Robert. Overcoming division will lead to the sexual subjectivity Paul silences and represses, but this is a struggle in which Marie does not always have the upper hand.

At the night club where Paul ignores Marie in order to flirt with other women, she is heavily pregnant and about to go into labour, and it is through the act of giving birth that she finally attains a sort of moral equality between – if not the actual integration of – the sexual and spiritual dimensions of her being. The birth of Marie's son Paul, by means of which the son exactly replaces his father, blown up in the simultaneous gas explosion of his flat Marie arranges, is filmed with an extraordinarily graphic directness underlining the brute material power of the female body. In keeping with her modest and rather melancholy character, Marie strains quietly on the delivery table rather than screaming and shouting, but the camera then moves directly from her face to an extreme close-up on the baby's head crowning forth from her vagina, blue and dark-haired against the warm tones of Marie's blood-streaked thighs. The body that follows is 'mauve and spindly like the body of a skinned rabbit, with a Veronese-green umbilical cord' (Breillat 1999a: 73). This birth is an event of erotic bodily power, filmed as graphically as the two intense scenes of BDSM sex in Robert's apartment, but with the force of the birth heightened by its contrast with the slenderness and paleness of Marie's body: a 'phenomenal woman' both in the brute materiality of the birth and poetically. An ultra-quick tableau shot of Marie moments later with the baby in her arms suggests that the birth's eroticism is tinged with death, as she is surrounded by flowers that could easily be funeral bouquets, and the following, final, anti-realist 'oneiric vision' (Breillat 1999a) of the elder Paul's funeral similarly hints at death and perverse sexuality. Motherhood is presented in *Romance* as both an act and a condition of female power, physical and metaphysical, a victorious conclusion to the struggle of Marie's transgressive sexual journey.

In this chapter I have introduced four of the film-makers central to this book – Andrea Arnold, Sally Potter, Agnès Varda and Catherine

Breillat – and offered analysis of *Fish Tank*, *Orlando*, *The Tango Lesson*, *The Beaches of Agnes*, *The Gleaners and I* and *Romance* that shows how a feminist phenomenological approach can bring out the embodied agency, movements and actions of the films' female protagonists better than any other mode of reading. In the next chapter I investigate the woman's look in several female-authored films, returning first to *Orlando* and *The Tango Lesson*, then offering readings of Breillat's *Brief Crossing* and Arnold's *Red Road* that explore both agentic looking by women and a (feminist) existential phenomenological approach to vision.

helpful perhaps to point to other modes, readings already carried out?

4

Look

The partial history of film feminisms traced in Chapter 2 suggested that no balanced assessment of the advantages and disadvantages of 'gaze theory' has ever been undertaken. The very concept of the gaze as formulated by Metz and Mulvey has been disputed by Lacanians, Joan Copjec commenting that the 'commonplace of film theory' holding that 'the gaze is a single cognitive position from which it is not only possible, but necessary, to look' is 'supported partially by a misreading of Lacan' (Brennan 1989: 244). (The renaissance of a mode of Lacanian film theory working more closely with Lacan has recently been seen in the work of Todd McGowan (McGowan 2007).) Although Bordwell and Carroll's critiques of Grand Theory undoubtedly lessened the extent to which the concept of the gaze was drawn on within film studies, it has continued to be widely used in art history and other branches of visual studies, and the notion of a voyeuristic optics continues to be relevant to all sorts of viewing situations and cultural forms, particularly those governed by a dominant and objectifying masculine look. Looking is not inevitably power-laden, however, and psychoanalytic feminist film theory undoubtedly limited its development by overemphasizing the likely identification of women viewers with a passive or masochistic gaze allegedly set up by the film text. In this chapter, I want both to illustrate some active, agentic looking on the part of female characters (no longer a rarity in films directed by women) and to propose some alternative ways of thinking about cinematic looking, both diegetic and extra-diegetic. The illustration of agentic looking by women will take off from a critique of Mulvey's deployment of the active/passive binarism which will imply that women are entirely as capable as men of looking actively, while the particular alternative type of cinematic looking I shall explore is an *ethical* vision suggested by the motif of *dévoilement* ('disclosure') to be found in Beauvoir's *The Ethics of Ambiguity*.

To my mind, the most negative aspect of the concept of the gaze set out by Mulvey in 'Visual Pleasure and Narrative Cinema' – and by this I mean 'most negative for female subjectivity' – was its division into active-sadistic and passive-masochistic forms, the latter crystallized in Mulvey's memorable term 'to-be-looked-at-ness'. Does the Freudian concept of scopophilia (*Schaulust*) on which Mulvey was drawing necessarily impose the passivity and stasis on women that her neologism implies?

Of course, in emphasizing the voyeurism and curiosity of cinematic looking, Metz and Mulvey were identifying a core characteristic of the technology that cinema is and of Western modernity. If the pleasures of investigation and the acquisition of knowledge have been expressed using visual metaphors ever since Plato, then this ocularcentrism – the privileging of vision, technologically assisted or not, over the other senses – can in a way only be perpetuated by film, which has been and continues to be used in the service of science as well as by artists and for entertainment. The early Christian theologian and philosopher Augustine spoke of *concupiscentia ocularum*, or ocular desire, and Mulvey describes this curiosity as 'a desire to know something so strongly that it is experienced like a drive' (Mulvey quoted in Riggs 1997: 224). However, it is not theology or philosophy but psychoanalysis that Mulvey cites as the authority on ocular desire, and in a critique of Mulvey's approach to Hitchcock's *Vertigo*, Marian Keane points out that Mulvey elaborates the concept of scopophilia she employs as the linchpin of her concept of the gaze:

> Mulvey's account [in Mulvey 1989a: 16–17] presents itself as simply a transcription of Freud, but it is not. At no point does Freud claim to have a 'theory of scopophilia' or that scopophilia subjects others to a 'controlling and curious gaze' ... Neither does Freud claim that scopophilia is 'essentially active' ... In both 'Three Essays' and 'Instincts and Their Vicissitudes', Freud singles out scopophilia-exhibitionism and sadism-masochism precisely because 'these are the best-known sexual instincts that appear in an ambivalent manner'. His crucial discovery is that these instincts always appear in pairs ... Mulvey identifies active controlling looks with men and passive looked-at-ness with women, alignments Freud explicitly rejects when he discovers that the active and passive forms of the instincts are always found together in the same human being. (Keane 2009: 237–238)

Referring to the well-known footnote Freud added to his 'Three Essays on the Theory of Sexuality' in 1915, which specified three different uses for the terms 'masculine' and 'feminine', biological, sociological, and 'the sense of activity and passivity', Keane points out that Freud emphasizes that his own description of the libido as 'masculine' draws on the last of these three uses, 'for an instinct is always active even when it has a passive aim in view' (Freud quoted in Keane 2009: 238). If Freud is taken at his word, no reference to a quality possessed by men only should be read into his labelling of the libido as 'masculine' (objectionable though this labelling is to women), and since scopophilia is one of the component instincts of the libido, it makes no sense to divide and polarize the exercise of a desiring look (which is not necessarily 'controlling') into active and passive forms that are then aligned with separate agents, identified by Mulvey as male and female, respectively. If Freud is read on his own terms, then ocular desire must always function in a more ambivalent manner than this: a 'controlling' male gaze is undermined by a passive element that allows its exerciser to be looked at even as he stares lustfully at the object of his desire, and a woman is every bit as capable as a man of looking actively, even if the power relations of her (cinematic or actual) situation hinder rather than assist her self-expression.

Looking is a particularly important activity to Zoë (Natalie Press), the protagonist of Andrea Arnold's *Wasp* (2003), since as the single mother of four young children she cannot afford to feed, she is always looking *after* her children or looking *out* for them. When a chance re-encounter with a man she knew before she had her children, Dave (Danny Dyer), leads to the first offer of a date she has had in years, she pretends the children are those of a friend she is just baby-sitting for and agrees to meet him in a local pub that evening. In so far as her tactic for demonstrating that she is now available again – Dave knew the father of her children – is to conceal them 'in plain sight' outside the pub while she drinks and plays pool with Dave inside, visibility is the trope on which the plot of *Wasp* turns, and this is just as evident in how Arnold films Zoë's and Dave's pleasure in looking at one another as it is in the drama-laden scenes of the children playing unattended outside the pub. Zoë dresses alluringly for the date, in a short skirt and skimpy top that contrast utterly with the nightdress she was wearing as Dave drove past earlier in the day: *Wasp*, like *Fish Tank*, is filmed in the housing estates of Dartford (low-rise rather than high-rise estates like the tower block inhabited by Mia, her mother and sister Tyler), and disputes between neighbours like the argument between one of Zoë's daughters and the neighbour's are settled spontaneously, on the doorstep. So in order to respond to Dave's beep on his car horn to attract her attention, Zoë has to park her three daughters and bare-bottomed baby on a nearby pavement and put both the argument and her unflattering state of dress out of her mind. Concentrating on what Dave has to say is the only way to capitalize on what she instinctively recognizes is a rare opportunity.

Arnold films this first conversation between Zoë and Dave in relatively conventional shot-reverse shot, Zoë leaning towards the car's open passenger window as Dave remains at the wheel. Although emanating from a point to the left of Zoë's left shoulder, the shots of Dave, which begin by framing his head and shoulders, then move in slightly each time the camera returns to him, function as POV shots that convey the pleasure Zoë takes in looking at his healthy, tanned face and arms (he has just left the army), clean white and navy sports shirt, and good-natured grin at her unusual state of dress. He is not 'objectified' in any demeaning sense, and not rendered passive by Zoë's attention (he has pulled over to speak to her, he enquires what has become of Mark, her ex-boyfriend, and he suggests that they get together), but he is undoubtedly the object of her appreciative look, and the object of *Wasp*'s slender narrative. Zoë sees in Dave, who confirms just before he drives away that she is as attractive to him as she used to be, an opportunity to repair the two most troubling aspects of her current existence, the stigma of single motherhood and her poverty. The chance occurrence of his return from the army is an opportunity worth taking a risk for, and by leaving her children outside the pub Zoë wagers their safety against their – and her – opportunity of a better life. Although Dave's discovery, later that evening, that the children are Zoë's shocks him, and the film does not present him as a saviour or hero by confirming that he will take up the social role vacated by Mark, its ending suggests that he is considering this possibility. All these hopes and uncertainties are condensed into Zoë's steady gaze at him behind the wheel of his car, as she takes cognizance of the opportunity that is presenting itself: sexual desire is suggested in two brief close-ups of Dave's mouth, then eye, once the date is arranged, but it is above all the agency and intentionality of her look that marks Zoë out as a female protagonist who is anything but objectified, and whose desire to better her situation constitutes the narrative of *Wasp*. The same can be said of *Fish Tank*'s Mia, who furtively casts curious looks at Connor early in their acquaintance that are more conventionally voyeuristic than Zoë's at Dave. Connor is, however, an agent of *Fish Tank*'s narrative like Mia (albeit a less important one than her), whereas Zoë alone possesses this status in *Wasp*. Having given just a few examples from Arnold's film-making of looks by women that cannot be accommodated by psychoanalytic film theory's division into an active-sadistic subject and passive-masochistic object of the gaze, I would like next to extend the range of possible forms that cinematic looking can take and shall return in order to do this to two films discussed in the previous chapter – Potter's *Orlando* and *The Tango Lesson*.

The embodied and active eye in *Orlando* and *The Tango Lesson*

As established by my commentary in Chapter 3 on the diverse forms of physical activity undertaken by Tilda Swinton in *Orlando*, the affirmative energy of becoming-woman spills out of almost every scene of the film. There is one scene that stages the look in particular as desiring, however, and tellingly, it also suggests looking to be an embodied action rather than only a mental or psychological one. After Orlando encounters Shelmerdine (Billy Zane) and is tending to his injured ankle at her country seat, she confesses to the camera that although she feels she is about to faint, she has never felt better in her life, and the action cuts to their love-making. Stereotypically gendered bodily postures are reversed here, as Shelmerdine (with his flowing hair and sensuous mouth) lies back to be stroked by Orlando and the camera, in several close-ups on his face. So intense is Orlando's/the camera's gaze upon him (Figure 4.1) that at one moment, he registers embarrassment and perhaps a wish that she relax the attention she is directing at him. The camera then cuts to a tracking shot along a human torso, which we expect (for continuity reasons) to be Shelmerdine's, but which is revealed by its curves to be a woman's rather than a man's. The camera gently caresses Swinton's torso from hip to neck and face, and ends on a long close-up on Orlando's eye (Figure 4.2) that connects it to rather than separating it from her unmistakably female body. In addition to privileging the woman's look over the man's during the film's single scene of love-making, the shot reminds us insistently that the look itself is embodied and incarnate. Speculatively distinct modes of feminine and masculine desire are undermined by the blurring of gender identities evident throughout Orlando and Shelmerdine's encounter (they instantly recognize one another as kindred spirits and fellow lovers of travel and freedom), but there is no confusing their female and male bodies, or disputing that her woman's look is privileged over his.

If the encounter with Shelmerdine is the moment in *Orlando* at which looking takes on its greatest diegetic importance, the look is consistently employed by Potter to register the self-consciousness and playfulness of Woolf's fiction, in looks to camera by Swinton that perfectly complement the film's clipped, witty dialogue. The first of these, as Orlando the Elizabethan youth sits alone beneath an oak tree away from court, pairs a look with Orlando's first words, as he breaks into the voiceover's introduction to his character just as it utters the word 'he', correcting it to 'that is, I'. Swinton's look revolves sharply round to camera for just the time it takes to pronounce these three words.

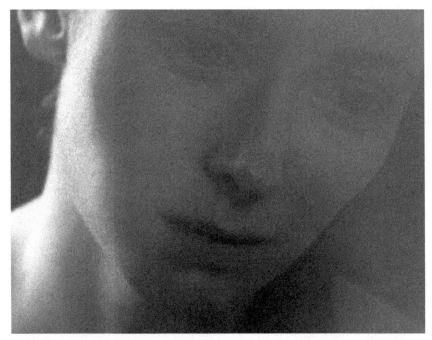

FIGURE 4.1 *Orlando stares at Shelmerdine,* Orlando

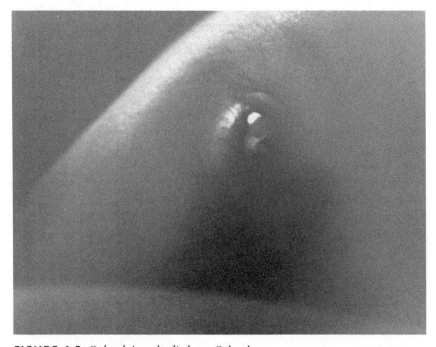

FIGURE 4.2 *Orlando's embodied eye,* Orlando

So much about modernist stream-of-consciousness fiction is condensed into this moment, which by matching a breaking of film's 'fourth wall' with an interruption of one of only two passages of third-person narration in the film creates an exact visual equivalent for the destabilization-through-subjectivity of the fictional universe practised regularly by Woolf and her contemporaries. Remarks Orlando makes to camera throughout the film are often related to literature: catching the closing moments of a performance of Shakespeare's *Othello* on the ice of the river Thames just as it begins to thaw, s/he turns to the viewer to say 'Terrific play!', and after retreating from disappointment in love into a life of reading and delivering an extract aloud from the top of the library's ladder, declaims 'Ah, poetry!'. Appealing to the viewer, Orlando's looks to camera, therefore, usually perform a communicative rather than a disruptive function, such as seeking reassurance for awkward moments – for example, the teasing by poet Alexander Pope during her first society outing as the Lady Orlando. Later, when the modern-day Orlando meets the publisher to whom she has sent the manuscript of her four hundred-year narrative and he inquisitively asks her 'How long did this take you?', she looks to the viewer for corroboration of the improbable truth, unable to make a credible reply. Swinton's meticulously performed looks to camera occur during Orlando's time as a man and as a woman, but in so far as Orlando-as-woman is just as able to register the self-consciousness of Potter's film as when she is living a man's life, no difference along a continuum from active to passive looking is made by his/her gender transformation.

In *The Tango Lesson*, looking is consistently thematized as part of the film's self-conscious treatment of film-making: it is what defines Sally as a film director. Two films in fact compete with one another to produce *The Tango Lesson*, the first a sumptuously costumed drama about the Paris fashion industry Sally struggles to write in the opening scenes, the second a 'more personal' project about the Argentinian tango. The first, which proves to have been a real project of Potter's by becoming *Rage* (2009), although it has been transposed to New York as the Hollywood producers Sally meets in *The Tango Lesson* suggested it should be, is in glorious colour, the second in black and white. In the scenes of the aborted fashion film seen in *The Tango Lesson*, the red, blue and yellow silk dresses of the three correspondingly named models assault the eye with the richness of their colour, offering an instance of to-be-looked-at-ness that points up the lack of glamour in the dance scenes that follow. From a spectatorial point of view, however, the film can be said to reverse the association of masculinity and femininity with looking and to-be-looked-at-ness respectively, since spectacle and glamour are concentrated in the figure of the professional dancer Pablo, with Sally's delight in watching him perform a feature of several scenes(Figure 4.3). When Pablo becomes enraged by Sally's failure to follow his lead during their first public tango performance,

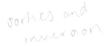
sorties and
inversion

she tells him that he only knows how to be looked *at*, not how to look, and as the project of a film about the tango takes shape, she makes it clear he will have to trust her film-maker's eye in just the same way as she has trusted his skills and talent in dance.

FIGURE 4.3 *Sally sees Pablo dance for the first time,* The Tango Lesson

One early scene in *The Tango Lesson* dramatizes better than any other how looking is every bit as embodied as dancing, a honed, perfected technique: as Sally location-scouts for the abandoned version of *Rage* in the Parc de St Cloud, outside Paris, she runs around pacing out the dollies and levels her camera will need to film the Red Model. As Potter explains in her commentary on the shoot:

This scene was snatched as the sun went down at the end of a shooting day...We had more or less an hour to do about six set-ups, so we ran from location to location as the shadows got longer. My job as a performer was to look – really look – at the locations in the strange (but to me, natural) way that a director looks at a place: seeing it as it is, and, simultaneously, superimposed, seeing it as it could be onscreen. When I saw the rushes I realised, with a shock, that one rarely sees a woman looking out like that on screen. Normally she is dragging the look towards her, as an invitation. (Potter 1997: 4)

The sharp, acquisitive look of a woman prospecting for her film is caught on camera in this scene, and shown to be a thoroughly embodied, physical activity.

If the type of bodily agency proposed by phenomenology's concept of the 'lived body' is dramatized by looking as well as by dancing in *The Tango Lesson*, then the moment at which Sally's agentic looking most challenges Pablo occurs straight after she, he, Gustavo and Fabian, the two Buenos Airean *tangueros* who have trained Sally, have just improvised a virtuoso four-person dance sequence in a disused apartment store they might rent to rehearse and film in. While waiting to see the person who has advertised the space, Sally demonstrates how well she has come to understand Pablo, as she is able to relieve the men's boredom by instructing Pablo to 'set up a rhythm' Gustavo and Fabian can follow, then – appealing to Pablo's narcissism – let him dance solo. The foursome troop down into the store's former basement beauty salon after their exhilarating dance, and Gustavo and Fabian carry Sally to one of the salon's giant chairs, joking in a kindly fashion that their 'queen' should be looked after (thus ascribing sovereign subjectivity to Sally), but Pablo wanders off alone to a chair in front of a mirror and sits gazing at himself, apparently unaware of the reflections of Sally, Gustavo and Fabian in the mirror. Redirecting her gaze from Gustavo and Fabian to Pablo's reflection, Sally walks across to join him in front of the mirror, answering the first direct question he has put to her about *her* look ('Are you looking at me?') with a measured 'yes', then adding that she is seeing Pablo as he will appear on the screen, as the dance star that he is (Figure 4.4). Pablo replies that she cannot in that case 'be here' with him; she has become a camera, with which Sally concurs – she loves Pablo 'With my eyes. With my work'. Disappointed as Pablo may be by Sally's matching of her professional status with his, he can only answer her next question, 'What more do you want?', with one that crosses over into religion and mysticism: 'I want to know ... . why we met'. The action cuts to Pablo and Sally entering a synagogue together.

Guano's reading of the galvanizing power of Sally's look in these two scenes of *The Tango Lesson* brings out how Sally has effectively become her camera, which suggests that her look is 'both disembodied and incarnated, invisible as the mechanical camera stare and visibly expressed through the eyes of a professional woman who declares her desire for her male employee/

FIGURE 4.4 *Sally counters Pablo's visual narcissism,* The Tango Lesson

partner' (Guano 2004: 469). But if we remember Sobchack's qualification of the camera's body as a cyborg body, then there is no contradiction within the embodied status of Sally's look. There is potential friction too between the Lacanian reading Guano makes of Pablo's identity (that his relationship with Sally is what moves him beyond the mirror stage) and the strand of references to the Old Testament and Judaism in *The Tango Lesson*. As Guano points out, the film's midpoint is marked by a baptism scene in which the hierarchical male–female power relationship of tango shifts into one in which Sally is in charge (Guano 2004: 469), and a number of references are made in the film to the Jewish philosopher and theologian Martin Buber, whose best-known book *I and Thou* (1923) outlines an asymmetrical and dialogic form of intersubjectivity very different from Lacan's image-driven one. Sally, Gustavo and Fabian all appear in the mirror into which Pablo gazes in the abandoned department store's beauty salon, but although it is himself he sees as 'real' as against their derealized images, the opposite would be more accurate. (In Merleau-Ponty's essay 'The Child's Relations with Others' (Merleau-Ponty 1964b), empirical psychological research is summarized suggesting that children learn cognitive manipulation of the images of others before they learn to deal with their own image as it appears in the mirror.) By showing a female film director who first physically imitates then becomes her camera, and who effectively takes charge of the looking dynamic between herself and her lover and professional collaborator, *The Tango Lesson* stretches the psychoanalytic feminist understanding of the interrelationship of gender and vision to its limit and beyond, while endorsing and lyrically dramatizing in dance the embodied character of looking.

Male–female intersubjective looking in *Brief Crossing*

Breillat's *Brief Crossing* was one of the ten films commissioned for the Franco-German TV station ARTE's 2003 season Masculin/Féminin, a follow-up to an earlier successful series it had run on a related theme, 'Tous les garçons et filles de leur âge' (1994). The literal crossing of the title is an overnight ferry journey from Le Havre to Portsmouth in which a 30-year-old Englishwoman Alice (Sarah Pratt) meets 16-year-old Thomas (Gilles Guillain), the dialogue of the film moving between French and English throughout. After meeting in the cafeteria, where they share the last free table, Alice and Thomas agree to spend the evening together, talking and drinking, and in due course this turns into a mutually wished-for night in Alice's cabin. During the evening, Alice tells Thomas she has just left her husband, who lives in France, but on arrival in Portsmouth the next morning, she disembarks ahead of Thomas while he is collecting his luggage, and is then seen (first by us, the spectators, and shortly afterwards by Thomas) being met by a man and a child we can only presume to be her actual (not 'ex', and English-sounding) husband. Thomas is left alone and tearful on the quayside. Like Potter's *The Tango Lesson*, *Brief Crossing* is in many ways an allegory of gendered power relations in which looking plays a crucial part. The adolescent Thomas is seen to be of uncertain identity when, running to catch the ferry in the opening sequence, he is almost turned away because his identity card is torn *and* out-of-date, and as he joins the queue for food in the ship's cafeteria, he is presented as younger and less confident than Alice in several ways: she returns a tray Thomas offers her when another one is supplied by one of the cafeteria's staff, and he hungrily accepts the chips she doesn't want served with her set meal of roast beef and chips. The place opposite Alice is the only free one in the cafeteria, but as there is no chair at the table, Thomas goes to find one, and is eyed up by a presumably gay English gentleman with a plummy accent (Nicholas Hawtrey), which identifies Thomas as an object of desire at the same time as being a subject of the narrative. Alice and Thomas's first conversation is filmed in over-the-shoulder shot-reverse shots at varying distances from each of them, with Thomas's eating focused on much more than Alice's. A short distance into the exchange of pleasantries Alice directs, she begins to stare at Thomas, a look that is not entirely continuous, but intense and unusually sustained. It is through the persistence of this stare that she manoeuvres Thomas into addressing her as a potential lover rather than a casual acquaintance, and subsequently into suggesting that they spend the evening and night together: her look is so intent at one point that Thomas is forced to look down into his *crème brûlée*, from which he does not look up again for some moments, by which time he has come to terms with Alice's sexual interest in him. A drama of male–female intersubjectivity begins, and their charged interplay of looks is replicated in their conversation, Alice adopting a slightly bullying 'little boy' attitude in her questions about Thomas's life and schooling, and pooh-poohing the importance of choosing one's career carefully, since, she says, adulthood and money will arrive of their own accord. Just as with the previous exchange of looks, Thomas's measured response to this is that a careful career choice is important; he could for example be a plastic surgeon, practised in taking the money of elderly women desperate to regain their youthful looks.

As Sonia Kruks points out in relation to Sartre's phenomenology of the look, 'in relations of looking there is no reason to assume that human beings are anything but equal' (Kruks 2001: 37) – an assumption entirely at odds with the psychoanalytic division into an active-sadistic subject and passive-masochistic object of the look. For phenomenology, looking is more (or other) than just an expression of (erotic) desire: it is also an exercise of freedom. From a Sartrean perspective on freedom, the cafeteria conversation between Alice and Thomas could be read as an example of oppressive seduction operating through Alice's look, with Thomas (after a pause) exercising his own freedom and transcendence by returning it. In Chapter 8, I shall discuss Sartre's, Beauvoir's and Merleau-Ponty's distinct approaches to freedom in detail, but shall draw here just on Kruks' reading of Beauvoir's thinking on freedom as it relates to looking. According to Kruks, Beauvoir's approach to freedom and intersubjectivity (which are necessarily intertwined) is distinct from Sartre's, which takes the form of a hostile dialectic of consciousnesses. In spite of the epigraph quoting Hegel's version of this dialectic found at the start of her novel *L'Invitée/She Came to Stay*, Beauvoir's approach to intersubjectivity, according to Kruks, developed to allow for a reciprocity of freedoms, and to describe a practical and social rather than invisibly transcendent dynamic. For Beauvoir, it is possible for one person's freedom to be invested in the freedom of the other, something not envisaged by Sartre. As Kruks also importantly specifies, Beauvoir's at-least-partial reciprocity of freedoms 'is not primarily a relationship of the look. Far more than for Sartre, it is expressed and mediated through social institutions and actions' (Kruks 2001: 38).

In *Brief Crossing*, Alice and Thomas's encounter is hardly one of equals: Thomas lies about his age initially but is forced to admit he is only sixteen when the couple go to buy alcohol in the ferry's on-board shop. Alice's look of seduction sets in motion a kind of dialectic of desire to which Thomas responds first with similar actions (a look), and then in mediated, social conversation. At the end of the film, when Alice abandons him to rejoin the husband or partner whose existence the viewer only discovers as she does so, Thomas pursues her long enough to see her get into the family car with the man and little boy who has leapt into her arms as she disembarks from the ferry. Whether she sees Thomas or not is impossible to say, but her look does not waver from her immediate surroundings: she *overlooks* Thomas, looking right past him in a panning shot of which she is in the foreground and Thomas in the background, disconsolately realizing that she has lied to him. Alice has 'managed' matters in such a way that Thomas cannot trace her and make trouble afterwards, and has successfully obtained the extra-marital sexual encounter she seemed to want (how calculatedly it is hard to say, since she also sometimes seems genuinely charmed by Thomas's youth and looks). A Sartrean reading of the film interpreting Alice's and Thomas's brief encounter as a competition of mutually hostile consciousnesses might be made to work, given the way in which looking neatly frames the film's action. But such a reading cannot account for the social and linguistic act of lying through which Alice ultimately comes off better than Thomas: even if an exchange of looks plays a vital initial role, it is not by means of the look that Alice *ultimately* 'wins', and looking, it is suggested, rather than being the expression of a transcendent freedom and consciousness, is just one social action among many when it comes to the negotiation and compromise of freedoms in which human subjects deal all the time. When read according to Beauvoir's theory of partly reciprocal and mutually supporting freedoms, *Brief Crossing* supports a model of intersubjective social relations in which Alice is at least Thomas's equal, and the subject of her own, female desire and look. The existential phenomenology of Beauvoir and Merleau-Ponty allows for the kind of embodied subjectivity Breillat is most concerned to film, and that has now been seen in both *Romance* and *Brief Crossing*. Despite being one of the least known of Breillat's films, barely discussed in the literature on her, *Brief Crossing* offers an intriguingly strong narrative of embodied female desire and looking, and embodied and desiring male–female intersubjectivity.

Transforming surveillance in Arnold's *Red Road*

For her first full-length feature, Arnold directed the first of what was to be a trilogy of dramas produced by Scottish company Sigma Films and based around the same group of Scottish characters,[1] a project named 'Advance Party' by the overseeing Danish producers Zentropa. Casting was undertaken in advance by Zentropa, in one of a number of restrictions imposed in the style of Lars von Trier and Thomas Vinterberg's Dogme 95 manifesto. (The use of handheld camera and natural light were the two other main limits Arnold had to work with.) *Red Road* takes its name from the Glasgow location of some of the film's action – a group of enormous blocks of flats constructed in the 1960s, an attempt at demolishing which in 2015 failed to destroy all the towers – and is a mixture of edgy thriller and intimate personal drama whose central character Jackie (Kate Dickie) works in a Glasgow CCTV centre, monitoring cameras all over the city. From the start of the film Jackie appears somewhat numb, traumatized perhaps, her life consisting of her work, fortnightly meetings with a married man, Avery (Paul Higgins), with whom she has sex, and some family members from whom she has evidently been estranged, without the reason for this being made clear: only towards the end of the film do we learn that her husband and daughter were killed a few years before by a driver high on drugs who crashed into the bus stop at which they were standing. Jackie is a neatly dressed, socially adept woman in her late thirties whose face gives away very little about what she is experiencing emotionally.

Jackie's work at a CCTV centre has tended to lead commentators to assume that because surveillance can be understood as a state-endorsed form of voyeurism, surveillance and voyeurism are what *Red Road* is 'about'. *Red Road* can be classed as a surveillance drama because Jackie takes advantage of what she sees on the CCTV screens – the man convicted of killing her husband and daughter, where he lives and what he now does for a living – for her own purposes, but in my view it departs from the vast majority of films of this genre not only by giving the role of 'voyeur' to a woman, but (as I shall argue) by ethicizing the very act of looking. The line of dialogue that in my view makes this incontrovertible occurs in Jackie's final conversation with 'accidental' killer Clyde Henderson (Tony Curran), when she yells at him as he shambles off to avoid further confrontation 'You didn't even look at me in court!'. Although she has by this point, having insinuated herself into his life,

---

[1] The second film, Morag McKinnon's *Donkeys*, was released in 2010 after considerable delays in production that have also affected the third film of the trilogy, which has still not appeared.

got to know his flatmate Stevie (Martin Compston) and Stevie's girlfriend April (Nathalie Press), attempted revenge by getting him arrested on a fabricated charge of rape, and forced Clyde to talk to her, he still does not seem capable of facing up to his responsibility for the losses Jackie has suffered through the deaths of her husband and daughter. After the early release from jail that explains why Jackie is surprised to see Clyde at liberty when she first spots him on CCTV, he has made a kind of attempt at going straight, in particular by attempting to forge some sort of relationship with the 13-year-old daughter he hardly knows, but his inability to speak to Jackie for more than a minute or two when she attempts to confront him after dropping the rape charge show that he has made little if any progress in coming to terms with his crime – something about which we as viewers can only speculate. 'Shit happens, every day!' is the evasive and defensive response he makes to Jackie's implied accusations of cowardice.

By not even looking at Jackie when brought face-to-face with her in court, Clyde blocked out any acquaintance with the victim of his crime, exactly the kind of knowledge Jackie then seeks out by tracking him down at Red Road, following him to a nearby café where she watches him eat and flirt with the waitress, then attending a party he throws at his flat the following Saturday night. As Patricia Pisters points out in a reading suggesting that *Red Road* is a new kind of thriller driven by affect rather than traditionally constructed suspense, every kind of emotion is mixed up in Jackie's quest to know the man who has so fundamentally altered her life – fear, desire, anger and disgust (Pisters 2014: 89). After accepting Clyde's sexual interest in her and dancing with him intimately at the party, Jackie is unable to sustain this closeness, runs out of the flat and vomits in the lift, only to return to Red Road a few days later by seeking Clyde out in the local pub. The knowledge of Clyde she compulsively desires is provoked and partly delivered by visual means, certainly, but is above all embodied and intimate: as she eventually says to him, she wants to know about her husband and daughter's final moments just before Clyde's car veered into them. For Jackie, then, looking is both epistemological (or epistemic) and ethical: CCTV is the means she avails herself of in order to investigate an aspect of the deaths of her husband and daughter that no one but Clyde knows anything about.

Of course, the ethical and interpersonal nature of the knowledge Jackie acquires by insinuating herself into Clyde's life does nothing to detract from the power of those who monitor the CCTV cameras, which function like Jeremy Bentham's Panopticon in just the way theorized by Foucault in *Discipline and Punish* (Foucault 1977), invading people's privacy in interior as well as exterior public spaces. In *Discipline and Punish*, however, Foucault's emphasis is on the impersonal and even dehumanized, machinic power of the Panopticon, whereas the CCTV centre Jackie works at is presented in *Red Road* as quite a humanized and even a friendly environment, where she can rely on colleagues to cover for her and even to pay attention to an enquiry (Clyde's movements and actions) she admits is of personal rather than professional interest. It is evident from the several scenes where Jackie is seen at her daily task of monitoring activity on Glasgow's streets that she takes the part of the job focused on protecting vulnerable people and animals (a young girl about to spend the night on the street, an elderly man with a sick dog) very seriously. When she spots Clyde get into his van to drive somewhere for the first time, her absorption in what she is discovering leads her to *overlook* a stabbing elsewhere in the city, omitting to zoom in for the close-up shots which, once recorded, will help police identify the attacker. Jackie's guilt at having privileged her personal enquiry over this crime is obvious, but her colleague Frank (Martin O'Neill), not knowing the reason for her lapse of attention, reassures her that anyone is capable of such an oversight. Jackie gains confidence as a result, 'borrowing' VHS tapes from the centre in order to uncover more at home about Clyde's movements. As Jackie is not at this stage spying on Clyde with the intention of prosecuting any criminal activity she spots, her actions can hardly be called 'surveillance', and since Clyde's activity is not sexual apart from the very first time she catches sight of him, it is not thoroughgoing voyeurism either – although there is no doubting Jackie's bodily arousal as she watches Clyde indulge in casual nocturnal sex with a woman who looks as if she is a prostitute. Jessica Lake's term 'sub-veillance', coined in distinction from 'sous-veillance', which has been used to refer to counter-organizational governmental activity (Lake 2010), seems a much more suitable term than surveillance to describe what Jackie is engaged in, though it may be not so much a subversion of the power of those running CCTV operations (Lake's definition of her term) as an *appropriation* of that power for her own, purely personal purposes. If Jackie also subverts the type of looking engaged in by her male colleagues and the majority of CCTV centre workers, it would seem to be in her challenge to the truthfulness of the images the cameras deliver, when she deliberately hits her own face with a piece of stone in order to render the charge of rape she brings against Clyde credible; she does this in the bathroom at Clyde's flat then, as she leaves the building, walks past the security cameras to ensure that her claim is backed up by visible evidence. Fabricated though the charge of rape is, it seems as if the self-injury equates perversely to the embodied knowledge she has gained by getting close enough to Clyde to have sex with him, which is difficult to do (and sexually highly charged) but preferable to the absence of any knowledge at all she has had to live with since the accident. Extreme and unusual though her pursuit of Clyde is, it appears to have the cathartic effect Jackie must at some level have anticipated it would have, since she is now able to visit her husband's parents to talk about where the final resting-place of his and her daughter's ashes should be, a decision they have evidently been wanting her to take for some time. Jackie, it seems, is very aware of the power of images as they circulate in society and less interested in their relationship to truth than in their ability to justify intersubjective claims and counter-claims of the kind that arise from their exchange and manipulation. Or is it that she wants actually to *see*, realized on camera, the pain of not knowing about her husband's and daughter's last moments that has gnawed at her invisibly for so long?

Disclosing the world: Ethical vision in existential phenomenology and women's cinema

In her book of existentialist ethics *The Ethics of Ambiguity*, Beauvoir makes frequent use of the term *dévoilement* and associated verb *dévoiler*, literally meaning 'unveiling' and 'to unveil', but rendered in English by Beauvoir's translators as 'disclosure' and 'to disclose', by analogy with the English terms used to translate *Erschlossenheit*, an important concept in Heidegger's *Being and Time*. (Sartre and Beauvoir had read Heidegger in the limited French translations available and probably also in German before and during the Second World War, and although many of the changes in meaning and connotation brought about by their Frenchification of his vocabulary were challenged by Heidegger, in the instance of *Erschlossenheit*, he seems to object only to aspects of their interpretation and not to the term *dévoilement* itself.) In *Being and Time*, the central term *Dasein* (literally, 'being-there') refers to the type of being that man is, and to the activity of existing, not to subjecthood or subjectivity. 'Disclosure' in Heidegger's work, accordingly, describes the disclosure of the world undertaken by *Dasein*: it is not a conscious or intentional act undertaken by a subject – an emphasis that first appears in French existential phenomenology in Beauvoir's first philosophical essay *Pyrrhus and Cineas* (1944) when she writes 'there is no being except through the presence of a subjectivity that discloses (*dévoile*) it' (Beauvoir 2004b: 136). In claiming this, Beauvoir is adhering closely to the existentialist account of subjectivity Sartre had set out in *Being and Nothingness* the year before, an account that continues to register in *The Ethics of Ambiguity*, which was published in instalments in *Les Temps modernes* before appearing as a single volume in 1947. Disclosure as a mode of unveiling, of making-visible, seems to be at the heart of Beauvoir's thinking of subjectivity in the 1940s, which (as has already been indicated) varies according to which other philosophers she was writing about, while developing during the same period into an understanding of her own much less in thrall to Sartre's than was perceived until the 1980s and 1990s.

Despite never having been given an ethical emphasis by Heidegger, for whom *Erschlossenheit* belonged firmly to ontology, the disclosing of the world described as *dévoilement* by Beauvoir in *The Ethics of Ambiguity* has evidently ethical connotations. As a process of making- or becoming-visible (whether enacted by a subject or not), it fits the actions of several of the female film characters discussed in this chapter – particularly Sally in *The Tango Lesson*, as she prospects for her planned film in Paris's Parc de St-Cloud, and Jackie in *Red Road*, for whom technologically mediated and directly experienced interpersonal vision conveys much of the knowledge she is driven to seek out. The notion of an ethical vision also recalls Catherine Breillat's insistence on the moral or ethical dimension of the film director's look: commenting on Oshima's *Empire of the Senses*, Breillat says that 'ethics in cinema is not to be found in the ethics of the acts filmed, but in the ethical/moral dimension of the look of the director filming' (Breillat 1999b: 18). It seems essentialist, however, to endorse the notion of a wholly or partly ethical look abstracted from the social or fictional context in which it is exercised, so caution should probably be exercised with regard to this statement of Breillat's. Disclosure/*dévoilement* as making-visible or making-apparent is not identical with the act of looking, even if Beauvoir's initial description of it in *Pyrrhus and Cineas* as the act of a subject suggests that it might be.

In an article tracing how Beauvoir's development of *dévoilement* takes it away from Sartre's existentialist framework of 'a being who *makes himself* a lack of being *in order that there might be being*' (Beauvoir 1976: 11), Kristana Arp quotes a vital sentence from early in *The Ethics of Ambiguity*: 'There is an original attachment to being which is not the relationship "wanting to be" but "wanting to disclose being". Now here there is not failure, but rather success' (Beauvoir quoted in Arp 2005: 397). This sentence is crucial because its wording suggests that disclosure is an impulse, desire or 'attachment to being' rather than a subject's act of consciousness, and because it starts to move away from Sartre's presentation of human existence as a 'useless passion'. Speaking of the contemplation of landscape, the sky and 'quiet water', Beauvoir suggests that the joy of disclosure arises from the *temporary* overcoming of man's lack of being (a temporary overcoming is all that is possible):

> I cannot appropriate the snow field where I slide. It remains foreign, forbidden, but I take delight in this very effort towards an impossible possession. I experience it as a triumph, and not as defeat. This means

that man, in his vain attempt to *be* God, makes himself exist *as* man, and if he is satisfied with this existence, he coincides exactly with himself. (Beauvoir 1976: 12)

As Arp points out later in her article, Beauvoir goes on to (re-)associate disclosure with consciousness and to suggest that 'privileged situations' for disclosure exist 'in which disclosure is realized as an "indefinite movement"', with many of the examples of such situations provided by tyranny and other aspects of political life (Arp 2005: 401). In *The Ethics of Ambiguity*, disclosure is inextricable from the independent (non-Sartrean) account of freedom Beauvoir develops throughout the book, a subject I shall return to in Chapter 8, but here I want to emphasize the aesthetically ethical potential of disclosure that arises from Beauvoir's mention of the contemplation of landscape, the sky and water, which seems quite close to the material enworldedness of existence emphasized by Merleau-Ponty. As Arp notes, 'Beauvoir definitely sees both the visual and literary artist to be engaged in the disclosure of the world…The artist does not take the detached contemplative attitude toward the world that the aesthete does. An artist does not just behold the world. His or her art is a project, a way of intervening in the world' (Arp 2005: 403). In Potter's *The Tango Lesson*, the park where Sally location-scouts for the fashion film she will abandon is explicitly presented as *her* world, explored by the character Sally, the director Sally Potter and the audience as views of it alternate with scenes of Sally at her kitchen table trying to write. Similarly, in *Red Road*, images of the world of Glasgow city life shared by consciousness-less CCTV cameras, Jackie and the film's viewers come and go in grainy, low-definition fascination. If some of the zooms-in Jackie effects from her console construct a voyeuristic scrutiny of the person captured – such as Clyde when she first spies him – then others, just as often, contemplate the person in their environment in a way that discloses much about his/her everyday actions, sympathetically, with humour, and without any of the intensity and drama suggested by the notion of the gaze. Panning shots across the full set of CCTV screens suggest the vastness of Glasgow as an urban environment more than the power-laden operations of surveillance culture, and although the rooms of the centre are large, dark and quiet, each resembling a cinema auditorium, staff move between them relaxedly and calmly. Despite the momentary urgency that arises when a violent incident occurs, looking is suggested to be protective and benevolent as much as it is accusatory or criminalizing. And because the trauma caused to Jackie by the deaths of her husband and daughter is eventually laid to rest as a result of information disclosed to her on camera, it can be claimed that vision is an ethical and engaged activity as much (if not more) than it is a detached, objectifying or judgemental one.

Disclosure/*dévoilement*, although developed only limitedly by Beauvoir in *The Ethics of Ambiguity* and taken up by French existential phenomenology in a way Heidegger insists is incompatible with his parallel term, seems like a promising motif to any attempt to forge an account of looking that is both phenomenological and ethical, attuned both to the world on film and the people viewed within it.

In this chapter I have explored looking in relation to sexual difference in five female-authored films, giving particular attention to what I maintain is the superiority of a feminist phenomenological approach over Mulvey's hierarchical division of the gaze into active-sadistic and passive-masochistic forms. (For existential phenomenology, to cite Kruks again, 'in relations of looking there is no reason to assume that human beings are anything but equal' (Kruks 2001: 37), a distinctly better starting point for feminist analysis than a hierarchical binarism.) By illustrating how agentic looking by women is no longer a rarity in film and how female film-makers Potter and Breillat have explicitly tackled the consequences of this shift for male–female intersubjectivity in their dramas, the ground was prepared for an exploration of 'phenomenological' ethical vision carried out by a woman (Jackie of *Red Road*). Looking is one symbolic activity among a number into which existential phenomenology offers multiple insights, and in the next chapter, I turn to the symbolic activity of speaking, the investigation of which by Irigaray's feminist philosophy I shall discuss in three of Breillat's films and in Marleen Gorris's adaptation of Virginia Woolf's *Mrs Dalloway*.

5

Speech

Isolating the language of film from its images and narrative dimension is not often undertaken, so devoting a whole chapter of this book to 'Speech' may require more explanation than the aspects of subjectivity that entitle its other chapters: Body, Look, Performance, Desire and Freedom. 'Speech', here, will refer not only to filmic dialogue uttered by (female) characters, but to their voiceovers and interior monologues, since although these may not constitute speech within the film's diegetic world, they do speak to its viewers and audiences. As a type of language not heard by other characters within the film's story, voiceovers and interior monologues also often feature more knowledgeable or more private and intimate thoughts and feelings than are uttered by characters diegetically. In introduction to this chapter, a few words can perhaps usefully be said too about the contrasting concepts of 'speech' and 'voice'. In metaphysical philosophy, the voice is associated with consciousness, and therefore, in dualist models that separate consciousness from the body (which does not apply to existential phenomenology and the related feminist philosophy I am drawing on), with the mind rather than the body: the voice rises above the alleged mutability and unreliability of the flesh and offers a kind of guarantee of identity and self-certainty, to both the speaker and those listening. In recent years, a plethora of scholarship in addition to feminist phenomenology has challenged this hierarchical privileging of mind over body in which the notion of voice tends to get caught up, and I could, therefore, have elected to focus on the concept of 'voice' instead. I am sticking to 'speech' rather than to 'voice' (or the too all-encompassing 'language') because of the stronger connections speech has to intersubjectivity and communication: it has long been a core concept to the discipline of linguistics, for example. 'Voice' privileges interiority over social relations, and although the films discussed here may turn out to have as much to offer to feminist thinking about interiority as they do to questions of social and political relationships,[1] focusing on 'speech' will allow the intersubjective and ethical dimension of their female characters' speech to be brought out, adding to the investigations of ethical embodiment and ethical vision I began in Chapters 3 and 4. The ethics of speech I shall uncover in the three Breillat films to be discussed in this chapter will also lead me to a consideration of Foucault's employment, in his late work on ethics, of the notion of *parrhesia*, or truth-speaking, and thereby to a confirmation of Foucault's importance to the predominantly feminist-philosophical understanding of ethical female subjectivity posited in my opening chapter.

Language in general has featured continuously in the work of Irigaray since her first book (which preceded even *Speculum*) about the language of the mentally ill, *Le Langage des déments* (Irigaray 1974). In the short lecture-based book translated as the eighth chapter of Irigaray's *Key Writings*, 'Towards a Sharing of Speech' (Irigaray 2004: 77–94), she indicates how vital linguistic communication is to the relational identity she argues to be already characteristic of many women's lives and a desirable development for all post-patriarchal subjectivities:

> The most important mediation for this relational life is language. Language is what allows us to defer instinct, to transform it into desire, to suspend the immediacy of impulse in order to seek means of communication or communion in shared attraction. (Irigaray 2004: 78)

In the introduction to *Part II Linguistics* of *Key Writings*, Irigaray explains that 'the analysis of pathological languages or discourses has been an invaluable help to me in my therapeutic work, but it has also provided me with knowledge and insights concerning sexuate difference' (Irigaray 2004: 35), adding directly afterwards that 'the difference between masculine and feminine discourses' has been a specific focus of her empirically based research, which was conducted without prejudice as to whether any differences observed between masculine and feminine discourses should be cultivated or overcome (Irigaray 2004: 35). Language and subjectivity are inseparable:

> A lack of attention about generation of language, of *logos*, permitted [the authors of Western philosophical texts] to consider as neutral and universal a truth and even a subjectivity in fact related to syntactic and more generally linguistic specific choices. (Irigaray 2004: 35)

---

[1] Eugenie Brinkema's reading of Breillat's *Romance* in 2006, sees the film as an exploration of female interiority.

One of the vital characteristics of subjectivity is that it is articulated *in* speech as much if not more than in writing or bodily movement and gesture: Sarah Cooper has noted that Irigaray associates writing 'directly with the exclusion of the voice and female genealogies in the West' (Cooper 2000: 129), and that 'one only has to look at [Irigaray's] publications to see how important oral communication is to her...much of her written work is a record of oral delivery or exchange' (Cooper 2000: 129). Sexual – in Irigaray's terms, sexuate – difference is, therefore, likely to register in speech in manifold ways: she claims that the linguistic testing of the generation of spoken messages set out in the sixth chapter of *Key Writings*, 'Being Two Outside Tomorrow',[2] reveals the differences 'between masculine and feminine relational behaviours' demonstrated in spoken utterances. These are summarized as follows:

> *women* seek to communicate, especially to hold dialogue, but they address above all to *him* or *them-men*, who do not take interest in subjective exchanges [...]: *men*, for their part, take interest in the concrete object if it is theirs (*my car, my watch, my pipe* etc.) or in the abstract object if it is defined by men and belongs to a community of men to express their psychological states [...]; men avoid staying and talking as two, especially two who are different. (Irigaray 2004: 37–38)

Part of the practical exercises in citizenship Irigaray undertook while working in Italy in the 1990s involved trying to cultivate gender parity in educational programmes in the Emilia Romagna region, where she was employed as a scientific consultant associated with a Commission on parity of opportunities for girls and boys (Irigaray 2004: 39). She worked particularly on language, and describes how she encouraged children of both genders to become aware of differences in their speech and patterns of expression, after which she 'invited them to propose to each other something to make together in respect for their mutual difference(s)' (Irigaray 2004: 39). This speech and language-based work of Irigaray's has been criticized for a lack of rigour evidenced (for example) in the insufficient size of the sample on which she based her conclusions, and such criticisms may be valid, but it is noteworthy that her empirical observations of sexuately differentiated speech correlate closely with the philosophy of relational identity set out in her writings on female subjectivity.

As Margaret Whitford has pointed out (Whitford 1991: 38), Irigaray, despite her association with the movement and theory of *écriture féminine* from

---

[2]This chapter was first published in Irigaray (1996).

the 1970s on, never in fact used this term at all: her research and writings on the sexual differentiation of language employed the term *parler femme*, which first occurs in *This Sex Which Is Not One*. In the 'Questions' section of this book, itself a transcription of a public discussion that took place in 1975, Irigaray is asked about the 'relation or non-relation between speaking (as) woman [*parler-femme*] and speaking-among-women [*parler-entre-femmes*]' (Irigaray 1991b: 137). She replies, rather abruptly, that the latter may be a context in which the former 'may dare to express itself' (Irigaray 1991b: 137). *Parler femme* may be translated as both 'to speak woman' and 'speaking (*as a*) woman', and indicates its link to women-only social contexts and situations through a homonymic pun (*par les femmes*) on women's agency. As Rachel Jones summarizes, '*Parler femme* speaks of a way of articulating the female sex that would allow women to take up the position of speaking subjects themselves, and thereby to relate to one another as women, whose differences and similarities can be registered without mediation through a male voice' (Jones 2011: 16). Irigaray's specification that *parler femme* is distinct from the kinds of speech in which women may engage in patriarchal culture usefully encapsulates its status as a horizon to be attained 'in a different symbolic order' (Whitford 1991: 42). Much of the early literature on *écriture féminine* agonized over whether this form of writing should be located inside or outside the phallocentric Symbolic order defined by Lacanian psychoanalysis that was hegemonic in the feminist criticism and theory of the 1970s and 1980s, but Irigaray's view of this was evidently always that women would only be able to become *speaking* subjects in a transformed, non-phallocentric, Symbolic order. Language and subjectivity are as inseparable for women as they are for men, as Whitford indicates by treating the two issues together in the 'Language and Subjectivity' chapter of *Luce Irigaray: Philosophy in the Feminine*, and *parler femme*, which has gradually given way in Irigaray's writings to a more direct broaching of the question of female subjectivity, 'implies not simply psychosexual positioning, but also social positioning' (Whitford 1991: 49). Because of the way it addresses multiple spectators at once, film may be termed a more 'social' medium than an art form such as the novel, and the co-'presence' of a woman director (virtually), a female protagonist and multiple women viewers (though we do not of course usually know what the proportion of women to men is among the viewers of films directed by women) may create a discursive situation approaching that of a women-only social group, as Caroline Bainbridge explores in the chapter of *A Feminine Cinematics: Luce Irigaray, Women and Film* titled 'Screening *Parler Femme*' (Bainbridge 2007: 99–124). Catherine Breillat is a novelist as well as a film-maker, and her cinema includes some remarkably literary narratives, sometimes based on novels she has published previously.

The language of her films is as vital to their meanings as the images are, ↙
and she has published numerous reflective essays and interviews in addition
to novels and her fourteen feature films. She is, therefore, a very suitable
film-maker on whom to focus in order to explore women's speech, and the
possibility that it constitutes an Irigarayan 'speaking (as) woman'.   + Akerman,
                                                                            Duras . . .

Speaking (as) woman in *Tapage nocturne/ Nocturnal Uproar*, *Romance* and *Brief Crossing*

In her preface to a set of five 25-minute interviews with Breillat conducted
for the French radio station *France Culture* and transcribed into book form,
Claire Vassé remarks that it was only when she came to conduct these
interviews that she understood how 'atypical' Breillat's relationship with
speech is (Breillat 2006: 7). She then explains that this atypicality has nothing
to do with the eloquence that might be expected of a Parisian intellectual,
as what is distinctive about Breillat's speech is not its rhetoric or the way
it conveys well-formed opinions, but an improvisatory quality that allows
Breillat to develop her ideas as she talks, constructing herself and 'finding'
herself as she goes, narrating herself as if she is simultaneously conducting
an enquiry.[3] As I shall go on to argue of the three Breillat films to be discussed
here, a striking diversity of forms of speech including monologue (both
'interior' speech voiced on the film's soundtrack and diegetic conversations
that tend towards the monologic) and letters spoken aloud is found amid the
speech of their female protagonists. (In one film I shall not discuss, *Fat Girl*
(2001), Breillat also includes poetry and music she has composed herself, in
the form of songs communicating the state of mind of teenager Anaïs, who
reflects upon her virginity with a maturity beyond her years.) The extensive
use of an interior monologue on the soundtrack of *Romance* – and in fact
also at eight separate moments in *Nocturnal Uproar* – marks a coincidence
of (interior) voice and speech that is especially suggestive where female
subjectivity is concerned, partly because the feelings and thoughts voiced
are to do with the woman's sex life or sexuality, and partly because the female
characters in both films are on a quest that resembles the improvisation and
self-searching Vassé observes in Breillat's own spoken language.

---

[3]'Catherine Breillat speaks in order to move forward, to construct and to find herself. She does not
speak so much to narrate herself as to create a space in which thought can blossom, transform and
elaborate itself, narrating herself in the manner of an enquiry' (Breillat 2006: 7).

Nocturnal Uproar, Breillat's second film but the first to receive a proper release, was shot in the productive context of French feminism of 1979, the same year that her novel *Tapage nocturne* was published.[4] Anticipating her much later autofictional reflection on the activity of film directing, *Sex Is Comedy* (2002), its chief protagonist is a young female director, Solange (Dominique Laffin) who leads a liberated if disorganized personal life, and although married to Bruel (Daniel Langlet), conducts multiple affairs with men, first a physically appealing actor named Jim (Joe Dallesandro), and then a cerebral fellow-director called Bruno (Bertrand Bonvoisin). The film, which had a limited release in only ten cinemas in France and just in Italy and Portugal internationally,[5] caused a stir for mostly regrettable reasons, with some critics pillorying it both for its literariness (a lack of attention to *mise en scène*) and the noisy narcissism of its heroine, who vocalizes both the transitory pleasures love brings and her prevalent discontentment continuously, to her lovers themselves, to her friend Emmanuelle, played by Breillat's older sister Marie-Hélène, and to her long-suffering husband, who tries to imitate what she tells him her lovers do in bed in an apparent effort to win back her fidelity.[6] Where press reviews of films directed by women in France are concerned (and until well after the late 1970s), criticisms of narcissism or exhibitionism are levelled at dominant female characters or women directors who act in their own films much more often than in other countries, and *Nocturnal Uproar* seems to exemplify this tendency particularly well. A number of critics penned digs at the film's alleged dramatization of a new generation of desperately sincere and (by implication) attention-seeking film writers, directors and performers, although Claire Clouzot denies that it had any contemporary or sociological relevance (Clouzot 2004: 46–47).[7] Interestingly, the low-budget film was supported by France's coveted (if not rare) state funding, the *avance*

---

[4]The novel has not been published in English. As noted of Breillat's films in Chapter 3, the more provocative *A Real Young Girl* (1976) was only released in 2000 after *Romance* brought her acclaim. *Nocturnal Uproar* is the only film from the 1970s discussed in this book, which deliberately focuses on films from the 1990s, 2000s and 2010s, but I am including it for its striking anticipation of aspects of *Romance* and *Brief Crossing* as well as for its intrinsic interest for the issue of speech.
[5]http://www.imdb.com/title/tt0134993/releaseinfo?ref_=tt_dt_dt. It seems also to have had a kind of revival at the 2009 Berlin Film Festival, 30 years after its initial release.
[6]Claire Devarrieux, '*Tapage nocturne*. Des cris, des cris', *France-Soir* 08/10/79, and Michel Marmin, 'Lamentations narcissiques', *Le Figaro* 01/10/79. Marmin describes the film as 'literary in the worst sense of the term, visually hopeless' and says its 'cinematic mediocrity [*pauvreté*]' is aggravated by an evident failure on Breillat's part to direct her actors at all.
[7]See Devarrieux (note 6 above) and Caroline Babert, '*Tapage nocturne*: le malaise d'une jeune marginale', in *Le Matin* 26/09/79.

an antidote
to film theory
dimension of dialogue
etc.

sur recettes, at a time when films directed by Marguerite Duras, Jean-Luc Godard and Alain Robbe-Grillet failed to obtain it.[8] Although Breillat's interviews and television appearances around the film's release brought her a certain amount of national attention for the first time, her film was widely criticized for its clumsiness and uncertainty, and for the mediocrity of its script (Fieschi 1979). Although I don't want to claim merit for *Nocturnal Uproar* that it doesn't possess, what is of particular interest about it, to my mind, are some of the qualities of the film's (rather than just its characters') speech, and the possibility that its rather aggressive address of its spectators' senses (the film's untidiness and Solange's incessant 'lamentations') is an only semi-aware attempt on Breillat's part to appeal particularly to the women in her audiences.

Talking too much is a problem of Solange's, she is aware: in her second brief passage of interior monologue on the film's sound track, she comments 'I can't stop talking. And actually, that's how I find out what I think'. Solange would like everyone to talk about themselves as freely as she does: her opening gambit to Bruno, which he twice refuses with a smile, is 'Tell me your life story, it's all I'm interested in'. Saying 'I love you' to a man, however, is more serious, a declaration it takes Solange some time to build up to, and an act whose effects she tries to calculate before sending Bruno what she calls her 'broken down' or 'distraught' love telegram ['télégramme d'amour décomposé'], which is actually three telegrams bearing the syllables 'je' 't'' and 'aime'. In fact the film seems to suggest that speech is as much under the fragmenting influence of the death drive as Solange's desire is, since shortly after having communicated her love to Bruno things go back exactly to how they were before, except that she starts giving her phone number out to other men as well, specifically a rock musician she then also takes up with. Not long afterwards a pattern of domination and submission begins to set in between Bruno and Solange, leading to her writing him a love letter that is read out on the soundtrack as the sixth and by far the longest passage of her monologue, as she walks to a hotel room through the snow with another new lover met in a café. As with her earlier declaration of love to Bruno, Solange resorts to writing, but what the film resorts to is speech: the letter declares itself to be 'a letter in which I give you the word I for some unknown reason cannot utter' ['une lettre de parole … parce qu'inexplicablement je n'arrive pas à en avoir']

---

[8]Hervé Delila in *Libération*, 26/09/79.

Nocturnal Uproar evidently anticipates Breillat's *Romance* in its depiction of a sexual relationship patterned by submission and domination as well as in its deployment of different forms of language, but *Romance* is a far more controlled piece of film-making, even if Breillat divulged in an interview about the film that she was incapable of detaching herself from the material comprising it – that she had no 'ironic distance' as she directed.[9] The *scénario* of *Romance* published in the year the film was released (Breillat 1999a) is actually a separate work from the film that contains commentary and 'stage directions' making it resemble a play more than any other literary form, or – since the additional *didascalies* often offer interpretations of the characters' words and states of mind – a strange mixture of play and novel. The film's literariness is commented on by Leslie Felperlin, who notes the linguistic root shared by the French *roman* and *Romance*, as well as that Marie's voiceover is heard in 'nearly every scene' (Felperlin 1999: 12). Language is also central to Thierry Jousse's view that for Breillat, sexuality is 'above all an intellectual matter', and that *Romance* is fed by this 'cerebral, linguistic, mechanical fuel', 'inhabited by an obsessive interior voice which is not a spiritual supplement to a mechanical body but the very place from which it emerges, the source where it is generated' (Jousse 1999: 40).

From the first scene showing the refusal of her boyfriend Paul to have sex with Marie or even touch her, her voiceover describes the 'invisible imprisonment' and 'silent Sharia' (Breillat 1999a: 29) of the clinically white atmosphere of Paul's bedroom, and his utter non-responsiveness to her caresses and requests that he not wear underclothes while in bed with her. The two matters on which it comments insistently are how oppressed she is by her 'intimacy' with Paul and her other lovers, and her own, highly philosophical reflections on her own desire and feelings. There is, therefore, a strongly intersubjective dimension to the voiceover, which works to distance her – and perhaps also the film's viewers – from both the men in whose company it is spoken and the visual action taking place on screen: just as Breillat's epigraph to the *scénario* suggests that the words of *Romance* are 'like Marie's soul' (Breillat 1999a: 23), Marie's interior monologue articulates her subjectivity more than any other element of the film.

With the exception of the 'delicious' (Breillat 1999a: 34) initial kisses she exchanges with Paolo outside the all-night bar where they have met after Marie drives there in rebellion against Paul's indifference, described by Marie as a 'miracle' of pure and 'completely childlike' desire (Breillat 1999a: 35), the feelings she voices about her sexual relationships are predominantly gloomy and negative. A man incapable of desiring her physically is 'a well of unhappiness'

---

[9] 'I have no distance from the film … I had no distance. I made it as I was doing it; the film happened as I was shooting it', Breillat (October 1999).

and 'an abyss of suffering' (Breillat 1999a: 32), and she recognizes that her need
to continue seeing Paul despite his callous treatment of her is an undignified
'leech-like' clinging (Breillat 1999a: 39). She does not want to look at the
men who penetrate her, preferring to be a 'hole' which gapes obscenely and
constitutes a paradoxical kind of concave purity: 'It's metaphysical: I disappear
in proportion to the cock claiming to possess me. I hollow myself out' (Breillat
1999a: 43). In her quest for a sexual subjectivity she is only ultimately able
to attain through motherhood and submissive BDSM sex with Robert, she
interrupts her relationship with Paolo after she begins to feel fondness for him,
proclaiming in her voiceover 'It's a question of integrity' (Breillat 1999a: 44). But
during the lengthy explicit scene of intercourse with Paolo that precedes this
decision, it is obvious that Marie needs to talk about sex and desire as much
as she wants to experiment with them, and that Paolo is patiently enduring her
particularly discursive desire rather than relishing it. In the extended passage of
monologue that begins as Marie returns to Paul's flat after her first experience
of bondage sex with Robert, she confides that her ideal sexual experience
is one of 'raw desire' in which all she is for her male partner is 'a pussy he
wants to stuff' (Breillat 1999a: 57), and that she is 'easy prey' for a man like
Paul because fundamentally, she dislikes her body (Breillat 1999a: 55). Marie's
encounter with 'the man on the stairs', who offers to pay to perform oral sex
on her, is the nadir of her self-abnegating tendency and a moment at which
Breillat seems to be engaging with the misogynistic myth that deep down,
all women want to be raped, as here Marie breathily articulates her desire to
have sex with a stranger and be 'a good-for-nothing and an idiot men hang
around with just for the idle pleasure of it' (Breillat 1999a: 57). Women get off,
she says here – a view it seems to me she has overcome by the end of the
film – on dishonour and discredit (Breillat 1999a: 57). Since her consensual act
of sex with the stranger turns into a quasi-rape that leaves Marie sobbing and
contemplating whether she is not actually a self-destructive nymphomaniac
who would relish being a victim of Jack the Ripper (Breillat 1999a: 58), her
declaration to the man that she feels no shame seems to me like the one
moment in *Romance* at which she cannot be entirely sincere. Significantly,
though, she declares this aloud to the man as he makes his escape rather than
in voiceover, reinforcing the notion that Marie's language in the film is divided
into an intimate, self-searching form of interior speech in which she builds
her growing sense of subjectivity and the much less authentic kind of social
discourse she engages in with her lovers and others.

When filming *Romance*, Breillat recorded Caroline Ducey's passages of
monologue as soon as possible after shooting the scenes in which they
would be heard, in order that the emotion of performing them be detectable
(Breillat and Denis 1999: 44). '[The voiceover] had to be spoken under the
influence of what had just happened on set, which transformed Caroline's

voice, putting her in a state of exaltation, rage or despair, at her limit' (Breillat in Breillat and Denis 1999: 44). Breillat's description of the voiceover attributes to it exactly the discontinuous, rather illogical quality Vassé notes in Breillat's own speech; new sentences are often generated by the powerful emotions being experienced rather than in any rational sequence with what has gone before (Breillat and Denis 1999: 44). And in the dialogue with Claire Denis about the film set up by *Cahiers du cinéma* – a context that itself seems to conform to *parler femme* as the social discourse Irigaray defines it as – Breillat suggests too that Marie's subjectivity is constituted by the voiceover as she finds her way through it: 'by pronouncing it Marie pronounces herself. It's when she can formulate it that she advances' (Breillat and Denis 1999: 44). This articulation of subjectivity is particularly noticeable in the closing scenes of *Romance*, in which Marie's monologue takes on an increasingly narrative function; it serves to report, for example, that visiting Robert for bondage sessions (only two of which are dramatized) has become a regular habit of Marie's, and that it is during the unusually brief moment of sexual contact with Paul brought about by her growing sexual confidence that he impregnates her. At this moment Marie addresses the viewer directly for the only time; 'Would you believe it?…that's how he got me pregnant, the filthy egoist…without any real pleasure, even for him' (Breillat 1999a: 64). In the dialogue between Breillat and Denis about the film, Denis observes that Marie's monologue is unusual among filmic voiceovers for the way it reinforces the presentness of the action: 'The *voix-off* often tends to place a film in the past. In your film, it's a specific interior monologue that forms part of the action: it *pronounces* the film' (Denis in Breillat and Denis 1999: 44).

Brief Crossing, perhaps because it was made for television and has never had a cinematic release in France or internationally, despite enjoying considerable success on the festival circuit, makes no use of voiceover at all. In its longest, central scene, however, where Alice and Thomas sit drinking in the ferry's bar and discothèque for some time before Thomas drags Alice onto a dance floor that has by then emptied, dialogue and conversation is subordinated to an insistent, if fragmented, monologue that narrates Alice's views about relationships and the difficulties women face as wives and mothers. Breillat structures this scene in four parts, three of which are a short 'prologue' during which Alice drinks her first large brandy, a section where she entertains Thomas with a commentary on how the ferry's evening magic show – a version of the woman-disappears-and-reappears-in-a-box trick – serves as a parable on patriarchy's treatment of women, and the closing 'dance' section, during which Alice taunts Thomas so mercilessly that he walks off and has to be tracked down on the ferry's dark and windy deck in order to keep on track their mutual understanding that they will sleep together. The couple's lengthy monologue-style 'conversation' is the second part of the scene, filmed by Breillat in slow, fluid panning shots that move around the two characters in turn, suggesting the meaning of Thomas's reactions to Alice's views from his expressions and gestures, since he so seldom speaks.

Bitterness at women's lot is the prevalent subject of Alice's discourse, as she consistently generalizes her own experience into that of all women, claiming that this follows a pattern of seduction followed swiftly by enclosure within a domestic setting that they then maintain and service without recognition or appreciative attention of any kind from their male partners. Without making any mention of motherhood, but stating that she has just (the day before) left her husband of eight years, Alice claims that disillusionment with adulthood on women's part is 'ineluctable', and lays the blame for this squarely with men: 'It's you men who make us like this, men make us grow old' (one of the few statements at which Thomas protests, mildly). In a manner that strikingly recalls Irigaray's observation that women's speech is typically addressed to '*him* or *them-men*' (Irigaray 2004: 37), Alice then launches into a diatribe against men considered as a social group or class, directed at Thomas as its representative:

When you add everything up, men are all the same. [...] It's true, isn't it? That's what men are like? You're all like that. You're right, it's your strength. [...] Men don't want to live with us as part of a couple, they just don't! It's so unfair. [...] They're simple and we're complicated. [...] Only women get mutilated by life, because they are more generous than men.

It is only in Alice's cabin the next morning that Thomas eventually objects to being classed as part of a group all branded with the stamp of patriarchy, by which point Alice agrees he is an exception, 'much more charming'. In the much longer scene in the bar, she mercilessly condemns men as a species, pausing only to get the breath to continue her diatribe. Women have no real alternative to marriage, she argues, because the stigma of remaining single is worse than the suffering marriage brings, and even if she thinks her husband has been faithful to her and so cannot reproach him with adultery, he lost interest in her three months into their marriage, and has treated her like a 'thing' or domestic object ever since. Once she has found fault with every possible aspect of men's treatment of women, Alice begins to pick on men's inferiority in areas such as ageing (Thomas has attractively bushy hair, but should watch out, because he might soon lose it and be left with only a shiny bald pate), and men's overall contribution to society, which amounts to no more than the sterility of bureaucrats incapable of any meaningful (reproduction; it is clear that Alice views all men as suffering from a kind of 'womb envy'. Despite revealing through his facial expressions that he does not really agree with her, and occasionally uttering a few words to this effect, Thomas is incapable of meaningful objection to the torrent of condemnation and criticism Alice pours forth to him, and seemingly only further attracted to her by the passion fuelling her diatribe. The language Alice uses to vent her bitterness and disillusionment is not particularly eloquent or rich, albeit peppered with metaphors, and it is above all its incessant flow and harshness that marks out the way she speaks in this scene as quite distinct from her relatively gentle manner in the rest of the film.

In the three of Breillat's films I have discussed here, women's speech is highlighted as distinct from gender-neutral spoken language in several ways. In *Nocturnal Uproar*, Solange uses talking – as Breillat herself is observed to do by Vassé – as a kind of psychotherapeutic 'free association', an environment in which to discover what she thinks and who she might be, and she experiences the limits of speech as the limits of her sexual and social relationships. The centrality of Marie's interior monologue to *Romance*, and its focus on her most intimate feelings about her own body and desires, suggests that it might be addressed first and foremost to the film's female spectators, while the recurrence of a 'monologic' style of speech in the scene that could be considered the dramatic centre of *Brief Crossing* indicates that there is a consistent connection between Breillat's innovative uses of cinematic speech and the gender of the women in whose mouths she puts it. The searching, inquiring, private and intensely emotional modes speech takes on in these films can, I think, usefully be described as both 'ethical' and 'moral': ethical intersubjectivity is emphasized by most of its occurrences, and in each film, the social position and moral situation of the female protagonist are at stake just as markedly as that of Jackie of *Red Road*, whose ethical vision I explored in Chapter 4. A further reason why Solange's plangent and rather logorrhoeic monologues in *Nocturnal Uproar* (although her words in her letter to Bruno are highly controlled and quite poetic) can be described as 'moral' is that they touch on issues of truth and lying: despite repeatedly describing her love for Bruno, her letter also declares that she is capable of 'lying love letters' [les lettres d'amour mensongères]. In *Romance*, when articulating her view that Paul's refusal of intimacy with her 'dishonours' her, Marie's monologue takes on a particularly moral flavour, insisting, 'Language must be attended to, because it is true [c'est une chose vraie]: Paul dishonours me' (Breillat 1999a: 32). Speaking truth as opposed to lying is raised even more starkly by *Brief Crossing*, where the spectator discovers only in the closing moments of the film that Alice has not just left her husband of eight years in France as she has told Thomas, but is very much still married (or in a stable relationship) and has a child. In an interview accompanying an early DVD release of the film,

Breillat described Alice using the same expression coined by Jean Cocteau to depict his bogus soldier *Thomas l'imposteur*, 'a liar who tells the truth'.[10] So although Alice does lie by not revealing her real social status to Thomas, Breillat attributes a soothsaying role to the views about men and patriarchy expressed in her quasi-monologue in the bar. Alice's act of deception remains one of opportunism that can be criticized on moral grounds: her speech, however, Breillat insists, is 'true'. In some lectures Foucault delivered in 1983, in the context of his late work on ethics and the care of the self, *parrhesia*, or truth-speaking, is one notion he draws upon, and extends into the notion of the 'parrhesiastic contract'.[11] Assuming that there is a relationship between the prevalent shame and candour of Breillat's female protagonists and the truths they speak about themselves and about men as a class of society, and bearing in mind that listening to their speech and participating in the process of formation of their subjectivities is what we do as spectators of Breillat's cinema, can we suggest that the feminist political work done by Breillat's films takes place through a kind of parrhesiastic contract with her spectators enacted *in* her films and supported and furthered by interviews and other paratexts? If so, then might the true speech she ascribes to Solange, Marie, Alice and some of her other female protagonists contribute to allowing her female spectators to become post-patriarchal female speaking subjects?

Feminizing speech in Marleen Gorris's *Mrs Dalloway* (1997)

As my discussion of Sally Potter's *Orlando* in Chapters 3 and 4 indicated, adapting Virginia Woolf's fiction for the screen poses particular challenges (as well as opportunities) to directors willing to take on the communication of Woolf's narratives to the larger audiences commanded by cinema. When Marleen Gorris, director of the award-winning *Antonia's Line* (1995), opted to direct an adaptation of *Mrs Dalloway*, one of Woolf's best-known and most admired novels, she did not know that a new generation of readers would be drawn to Woolf's novel within a year of the release of her film by Michael Cunningham's novel *The Hours*, published in 1998 and itself

---

[10]Breillat repeats the gist of this parallel in an interview with Claire Clouzot in 2000, saying that Alice's diatribe about men and marriage is 'both a lie and the truth. It's a factual lie and true in its essence' (Clouzot 2004: 112).

[11]The transcribed text of these lectures, 'Discourse and Truth: The Problematization of Parrhesia', is available at http://foucault.info/documents/parrhesia.

adapted for cinema by Stephen Daldry in 2002. By inventing a modern-day counterpart to the character of Clarissa Dalloway, the New Yorker Clarissa Vaughan (Meryl Streep), and by making the relationship between Clarissa Dalloway and Woolf herself one of the centres of interest of *The Hours* (like Woolf, Mrs Dalloway is a figure of London society and is of fragile health), both versions of Cunningham's novel may have achieved, by rather cleverer means, some of the work of finding new readers for *Mrs Dalloway* Gorris's film might have done. Assessments of Gorris's *Mrs Dalloway* run the entire gamut of critical opinion, from the view that it is uninspired transcription (Kendrick 1999) to warm praise, with particular appreciation for Vanessa Redgrave's performance in the title role. Leslie K. Hankins' view that the film only half-heartedly attempts most of the ideological critique undertaken by Woolf's novel (patriarchy, imperialism and heterosexism in particular) and remains cinematically conventional (rather than at all avant-garde) by not attempting to enter into the visionary worlds of its characters seems like the fairest all-round assessment (Hankins 1999). Here, though, I am really concerned only with how Gorris and writer Eileen Atkins deal with speech in *Mrs Dalloway*, that is, how the 'disconcertingly polycentric' (Bell 2006: 94) novel is dramatized in a way that makes limited but telling use of interior monologue. I shall also consider how Gorris's film genders the speech of its main characters – Clarissa Dalloway, her husband Richard, her former lover Peter Walsh and Sally Seton, the childhood friend of Clarissa and Peter with whom Clarissa once shared an erotic and intimate kiss.

Gorris's screenwriter Eileen Atkins brought to her film project a good deal of experience of transposing Woolf's prose to stage and screen, having acted the role of Woolf in a one-woman show drawn from Woolf's feminist essay *A Room of One's Own*, itself based on a television film of *A Room of One's Own* she had starred in 1991. She had also taken the part of Woolf's occasional lesbian lover Vita Sackville-West in the play *Vita and Virginia*, in which Vanessa Redgrave had played Vita. With Redgrave cast as Mrs Dalloway for Gorris's production, Michael Kitchen playing the middle-aged Peter Walsh, Rupert Graves the First World War veteran Septimus Warren-Smith and a clutch of well-known British actors such as John Standing, Robert Hardy, Margaret Tyzack and Selina Cadell acting other characters, Gorris's film is in many ways a star-studded piece of heritage cinema focused on faithfully reproducing the streets, parks and interiors of London in 1923, to one summer day of which the action is confined. To this end, Gorris could also call on cinematographer Sue Gibson, who had worked on *A Room of One's Own* and had extensive experience of recreating the mood and atmosphere of different historical periods, which in *Mrs Dalloway* includes the 1890s as well as the 1920s, in flashbacks to a summer spent by Clarissa, Peter and Sally at the rural location of Bourton when all three were aged about twenty. In addition to solving the problems of finding suitable locations to serve as the Dalloways' London house and Bourton, Gibson obviously handled the lighting of the interiors of the film, including its climactic party sequence, with painstaking care (Kaufmann 1998).

The character of Clarissa Dalloway has probably generated more critical articles than any other in Woolf's fiction, with her decision to marry the conventional, reassuring Richard Dalloway rather than the impulsive and passionate Peter Walsh, who is passing through London on the day of Clarissa's party and attends it, forming the main narrative thread of the novel – whose interests seem to be at least as much in the depiction of society and the passing of time as they are in narrative and character. In *Mrs Dalloway*, Woolf's working title for which was *The Hours*, her prose is focalized (as suggested above) through the perspective of an unusually large number of characters, major and minor, with the moral agency of Clarissa not privileged over that of other characters in any way: one typical example of this occurs as she greets her guests at the party, when she is described as 'at her worst – effusive, insincere' (Woolf 2012: 170). There are a number of ways in which film can attempt to convey the constant fluctuations of perspective, feeling and temporality created by Woolf's stream-of-consciousness technique, and Gorris's film employs three in particular, in addition to Sue Gibson's fluid camerawork – the flashbacks to Clarissa, Peter and Sally's youth for narrative purposes, the replaying of moments from the past for *affective* purposes and voiceover/interior monologue to convey the perspective or thoughts of a particular character at a particular moment. I do not really share the views expressed by some critics that the transitions to the past Gorris effects in *Mrs Dalloway* are an unsubtle or clunky way of dealing with the novel's seamless shifts between past and present, since they are inserted at judicious moments, and often linked to the film's present moment of 1923 via dissolves or temporarily superimposed images that ease the viewer gently from one time period to another. The film ends, for example, with a dissolve to a still image of Clarissa, Peter and Sally on the lawn at Bourton, taken from an earlier scene in which Sally and Peter repeatedly teased Clarissa about Richard Dalloway's slightly pompous manner of announcing his name, and therefore maintaining the tension exhibited throughout the narrative between Clarissa's ties to her past and apparently successful, if highly conventional, marriage – although Hankins's view that this ending allows nostalgia and youth to triumph and undermines a certain power of character Clarissa still has in the present (at least over Peter Walsh) also convinces: Gorris's extensive use of flashbacks cannot avoid bringing the film more under the influence of memory than the novel (Hankins 1999: 370). Gorris's employment of voiceover and interior monologue also alters (necessarily, perhaps) the mobile temporalization of the novel's free indirect discourse, and I shall now assess what sort of modification this is.

Eschewing the option of giving a voiceover to several of the novel's important characters – the obvious candidates being Peter Walsh and Sally Seton as Clarissa's intimate friends, and Septimus Smith as the war veteran and sufferer from delayed shell shock whose story unfolds over the day of Clarissa's party – Gorris chooses to have only Clarissa speak in interior monologue about her perceptions of how her day is proceeding. Five passages of monologue punctuate the early scenes of the film as she goes out to buy flowers for the party (meeting the alarmed gaze of Septimus through the flower-shop window as both are startled by the explosion of a car's exhaust nearby), returns to consider which dress to wear that evening and receives the visit of Peter Walsh, who stays only minutes and is interrupted by Lucy the maid just as their conversation has taken an intimate turn, Peter enquiring of Clarissa whether her marriage has brought her happiness (a question she does not have time to answer). The musings of these early passages of Clarissa's monologue concern the ageing process (she is now fifty-two and will have no more children to add to the Dalloways' daughter Elizabeth), her sense that her sex life is over, and Peter Walsh's correct prediction that she would lose the idealism characterizing their trio with Sally, and become the perfect society hostess. (In a flashback to a conversation with Sally about marriage, Sally's opinion is that it is 'a catastrophe for women', to which Clarissa answers 'But it is inevitable, isn't it?') During her brief meeting with Peter, Clarissa's monologue observes fondly how he still plays with his pocket knife in exactly the same way as he did over thirty years before and remarks that the state his presence is able to put her in, so many years after their affair, is 'extraordinary'. Her monologue, then, acts in the early part of the film in the classical manner of personal interior monologue in film, affording viewers privileged access to Clarissa's (female) subjectivity – a more centred and more psychological function than the focalization through a single character Woolf's free indirect discourse slips into and out of throughout her novel.

The momentary meeting of Clarissa's and Septimus's gazes through the window of the flower shop is the filmic equivalent Gorris finds for the paralleling of their stories in Woolf's novel, as Clarissa is constantly buffeted by her memories (she tells both Peter and Sally, when the latter arrives at the party, that she 'has been thinking about Bourton all day') and Septimus struggles with the hallucinations and paranoia that are the symptoms of his delayed shell shock: in particular, he repeatedly imagines the figure of his war comrade Evans, killed as he came 'over the top' of a trench in Italy, advancing towards him. During the day, Septimus and his Italian wife Rezia visit eminent doctor Sir William Bradshaw, who advises that Septimus (since he has threatened suicide) must be cared for at a specialist clinic away from Rezia and London, and arrangements are made, against Rezia's wishes, for Septimus to be picked up and transported there at 5 pm the same afternoon. Until the visit to Sir William, Septimus had been cared for by Dr Holmes, whom both he and Rezia particularly disliked, and it is because Sir William fails to heed their request that it not be Holmes who come to their flat to collect Septimus that Septimus decides to take his life there and then, by throwing himself from an upstairs window onto the spiked railings of the street below. Sir William and Lady Bradshaw figure on the guest list for Clarissa's party, and the way in which both of them mention Septimus's suicide and the related social problem of the treatment of shell-shocked veterans after arriving, slightly delayed, at the party, is experienced by Clarissa, despite her empathy with Septimus, as the highly unwelcome intrusion of death into an occasion she intends as a gift of carefree time to her guests. 'Stop it, stop it! Don't talk of death in the middle of my party! I don't like you, I've never liked you, you're obscurely evil [...] a young man came to you on the edge of insanity and you forced his soul, made his life intolerable, and he killed himself!', intones her monologue before she excuses herself falteringly from the Bradshaws' company and leaves her husband Richard to deal with them. Atkins' adaptation of Woolf's prose into speech heightens the drama of this reaction on Clarissa's part, but more particularly serves as a pretext for the next scene's passage of monologue, by some measure the longest in the film, as Clarissa withdraws from the party into the 'little room' to contemplate the Bradshaws' dampening of her guests' spirits. By making the final passage of Clarissa's monologue consist of thoughts that occur in solitude as she stands by an upstairs window very like the one through which Septimus jumped hours earlier, Gorris both brings the two characters firmly together and privileges interior monologue, rendering it a more significant form of speech than the social communication that dominates her film. This is an entirely conventional use to make of it, and has the effect of psychologizing and personalizing the novel's freer, fickle indirect discourse, as I have suggested, but it may well be a deliberate strategy on Gorris's part to feminize both interiority and the film's speech.

Clarissa's final monologue is a contemplation of the passing of time – how she, Peter and Sally have aged – and of death, especially Septimus's at a young age. Wondering if it is better always to remain young by dying early or to grow old and risk losing touch with 'the thing that mattered' (a phrase that immediately follows a replay of the kiss shared with Sally), Clarissa confesses to 'an awful fear, sometimes, that I couldn't go on, without Richard sitting there, calming reading *The Times* while I crouched like a bird and gradually revived'. This emphasizes Clarissa's strong conventional streak and her timidity, which has also been brought out by the passages of her monologue heard at the start of the party, when Redgrave's performance of Clarissa's fears that the party will be 'a failure' is noticeably more emotional and dramatic than the novel's language suggests. Her final soliloquy is cross-cut with the conversation Sally and Peter are having in the library, which, although based on the novel's dialogue and other indications in its narration, is also rather more explicit about Peter's feelings for Clarissa than the conversation Woolf offers her readers. This leads to an ending that is largely equivalent to but more sentimental than the novel's, in which Sally and Clarissa's youthful attraction to one another is ironed out by Richard insisting that Sally dance with him (to which she agrees), and Peter's acceptance of Clarissa's offer of a dance maintains the triumph of youth and nostalgia identified in the film by Hankins. Clarissa's fears of solitude and death have been diminished by her contemplation of Septimus's suicide: 'that young man killed himself but I don't pity him, I'm somehow glad he could do it, throw it away … it's made me feel … the beauty … somehow feel … very like him, less afraid'. Almost every word of her soliloquy at the window is taken from Woolf's novel, and Clarissa returns to the party in an affirmation of her ties to Sally, Peter, her past and her present. Gorris's deployment of speech and interior monologue in *Mrs Dalloway* may well be cinematically conventional and unadventurous, resulting in a containment of the dancing flights of Woolf's language and a psychologization of the feelings in which the novel deals, but her attribution of monologue to only its eponymous protagonist suggests a deliberate privileging of the importance of female subjectivity and interiority that Vanessa Redgrave performs with sensitivity and conviction.

Gorris's *Mrs Dalloway*, a reading of which has concluded this chapter, is arguably a less feminist work than any of the three Breillat films whose different modes of speech I analysed before it, but despite the fact that Clarissa Dalloway is an improbable feminist protagonist, Gorris's adaptation of Woolf's novel reinforces the notion of the (post-patriarchal) female *speaking* subject in a similar way to Breillat's consistently gynocentric dramas. In this chapter I have drawn on Irigaray's work on gendered speech and *parler femme* rather than on feminist phenomenology *per se* (as well as on Foucault's notion of *parrhesia* or 'true speech') to emphasize the importance of an ethical and embodied speaking female subjectivity in the work of just two women directors: in the next chapter, I turn to the performance of female subjectivity in films directed by Eva Ionesco, Sophie Calle and Laetitia Masson, as well as returning briefly to Potter's *The Tango Lesson*.

6

Performance

The notion of performance was indelibly stamped on the theorization of gender by the appearance of Judith Butler's book *Gender Trouble: Feminism and the Subversion of Identity*, in 1990. Some confusion followed as to the difference between 'performance' in its theatrical sense and the theory of gender performativity Butler set out in the book, meaning that she was obliged to explain in interviews that she was not suggesting that gender can be performed in a voluntarist fashion whereby we choose which gender to be on any given day.[1] As indicated in Chapter 1, the extent to which Butler endorses *any* stability of gender identity amid the continual processes of its performative (re)construction has been picked out by other feminist theorists as a questionable area of her theory. By addressing in this chapter how the notion of performance contributes to the understanding of female subjectivity as conveyed by my corpus of films, I aim not to add to debates about how useful Butler's theory of gender performativity is for female identity, but to show how the notion of performance can complement a feminist phenomenological approach to embodied female subjectivity, with reference to both the subjectivities of characters and those of the directors themselves. The gender performances on which Butler builds her theory of performativity, in *Gender Trouble*, are bodily stylizations such as drag and other types of cross-dressing, and the notions of 'bodily style' and corporeal agency are also fundamental to existential phenomenological theorizing about embodiment and sexual difference, a complementarity that has been little exploited in writings about film.

---

[1] Osborne (1994), 32–39 (33).

Performance, it should also be noted, has not actually been drawn upon by feminist film theorists and critics anything like as extensively as the parallel concept of 'masquerade', first deployed by Mary Ann Doane in 1981 in her seminal essay 'Film and the masquerade: theorizing the female spectator' (Doane 1999). For Doane, writing within a psychoanalytic and semiotic framework, masquerade offered the female spectator a strategy:

> The effectivity of masquerade lies precisely in its potential to manufacture a distance from the image, to generate a problematic within which the image is manipulable, producible, and readable by the woman. (Doane 1999: 70).

Since this book is not aiming to further the focus on spectatorship that was encouraged by apparatus theory (while not ignoring the issue either), I shall not pursue the question of the relationship between female spectator and woman-as-image here. Instead, I shall develop the notion of performance in parallel to Doane's argument about strategic masquerade, focusing on the relationship between the female director and the woman or women in her film rather than on the spectator-character relationship. All four films to be explored in this chapter feature either a documentary-style performance by the director or a fictionalization of an episode or period from the director's life in which her fictional avatar is played either by the director herself or by an actress. In Laetitia Masson's *Pourquoi (pas) le Brésil?/Why (not) Brazil?* (2004) both these techniques are used, that is, Masson appears on screen and is played by an actress, while in Sophie Calle's *No Sex Last Night* (1992), Calle appears as herself, and in Sally Potter's *The Tango Lesson*, already discussed in Chapters 3 and 4, respectively, Potter incarnates a thinly disguised fictional avatar. The first film I shall discuss, Eva Ionesco's *My Little Princess* (2011) is the only one of the four where the director does not play herself at all, partly because the film is a fictionalized autobiography, and partly because it is about her (extraordinary) childhood.

Mothers, monsters and fairy tales in *My Little Princess*

After gaining some attention in the Cannes film festival's International Critics' Week in May 2011, Eva Ionesco's first full-length feature *My Little Princess* was released in France a few weeks later, and over the year to July 2012 in Germany, the Netherlands, Russia and Portugal. Ionesco's was a name already familiar to certain European viewers from her acting role in Roman

Polanski's *Le Locataire/The Tenant* in 1976, when she was barely eleven years old, and possibly also in association with the erotic photography of her Romanian-born though Paris-based mother Irina Ionesco, which gained some renown from the 1970s onwards. *My Little Princess* tells the shocking story of the exploitative relationship between Ionesco and her mother, in which Eva was used as Irina's chief photographic model from a very young age, and, alongside this work and a semi-conventional schooling in Paris that was eventually interrupted by Irina being judged an unfit mother by the city's authorities and Eva being placed in care, taking roles in films such as Pier Giuseppe Murgia's sexually explicit *Maladolescenza* (1977), known in France as *Les Jeux interdits de l'adolescence* [*The Forbidden Games of Adolescence*]. In interviews following the release of *My Little Princess*, Ionesco described how she was still involved in legal action against her mother in an attempt to ban the circulation of her mother's photographs of her, a battle in which she had up to that point had limited success.[2]

The straightforward sense of 'performance' essential to the admiration Ionesco's film won from the great majority of Parisian critics was the acting of its two female leads – Isabelle Huppert as photographer-mother Hannah and newcomer Anamaria Vartolomei as daughter Violetta.[3] For, as already mentioned, *My Little Princess* is carefully crafted fiction rather than simple autobiographical drama, Ionesco having reworked her screenplay several times for different producers. In an earlier version the character of Violetta was played at three stages of childhood and adolescence by three different young actresses, whereas in the final film ten-year-old Vartolomei plays Eva's treatment by Irina from the moment Eva began posing for her mother's photographs up to Violetta's removal to a girls-only facility, where we see her with long blonde hair shorn to a punk style, running away from Hannah who has come to visit her. The film shows Violetta's posing to be a heartfelt wish for maternal affection only forthcoming up to then from her pious grandmother, described by one French critic as a 'short Romanian babouchka',[4] and suggests in its closing scene that Hannah is as unconscious as ever of the abuse she has committed by emotionally blackmailing Violetta into modelling for her explicit, 'slightly pretentious arty photographs'.[5] Isabelle Huppert, who plays the socially pushy, flouncing Hannah with an *insouciance* entirely

[2]See *Le Monde* 29/6/11, *Le Figaro* 29/6/11.
[3]The reviewer for *Le Canard enchaîné* considered the film 'transcended by the dazzling performance of the young Anamaria Vartolomei' (*Le Canard enchaîné* 29/6/11), while *Les Echos* described her performance as 'astounding' (*Les Echos* 29/6/11).
[4]Jacques Mandelbaum in *Le Monde* 18/5/11.
[5]*Les Echos* 29/6/11.

in tune with her many celebrated roles as 'damaged' women, commented about the transmutation of autobiography into fiction undertaken by *My Little Princess* that one way in which she approached the film as fiction despite her awareness of its autobiographical dimension was by not seeking to meet Irina Ionesco, something Eva did not encourage her to do.[6]

A stronger kind of performance at work in *My Little Princess* is seen in the film's *mise en scène*, in the photography of Hannah's outlandishly glamorous style of dress, her lugubrious and macabre artist's studio opposite the Vincennes cemetery, and the very particular atmosphere of bohemian Paris in the 1970s, '[the period] of David Bowie and late Visconti', 'fixed by the photos of Pierre and Gilles that she inspired as an adolescent'[7] which, most critics agreed, Ionesco captures brilliantly. As well as sacrificing any propriety of maternal conduct to her 'art', Hannah gives herself the airs she feels fit her milieu by wearing the satin dresses and sparkling accessories of a 1930s Hollywood starlet, and in a number of scenes Violetta is identically or very similarly costumed, a smaller version of her whimsical mother with matching blonde hair (although with the exception of a temporary dramatically frizzy perm, Violetta's is usually much more natural-looking than Hannah's crimped and peroxided shorter style). The sequence that gives the film its title is probably the best instance of how well Ionesco reproduces the mood of 1970s urban bohemia, of London rather than of Paris on this occasion, when Violetta is taken by Hannah to a photo shoot at a gloomy, Gothic-looking mansion inhabited by a languid, hookah-smoking young man named Updike (played by Jethro Cave, the son of musician Nick Cave). Updike utters the words 'my little princess' as part of the seductive pressure put upon Violetta to adopt compromising poses during this visit, pressure that occasions the most significant rebellion from Violetta so far, although the onset of rebellion has been hinted at in an earlier photographic session in Hannah's studio where Violetta responds to her mother's goading to expose her pubis with a stony-eyed gaze for the first time, despite still complying with the request.

The cinematographer on *My Little Princess* was the experienced Jeanne Lapoirie, who has worked for a number of French women directors including Valeria Bruni Tedeschi and Catherine Corsini as well as for François Ozon on *Gouttes d'eau sur pierres brûlantes/Water Drops on Burning Rocks* (2000), *Sous le sable/Under the Sand* (2000), *8 Femmes/8 Women* (2002) and *Le Temps qui reste/Time to Leave* (2005). In combination with highly effective set and costume design, the film's *mise en scène* and photography create a very particular masquerade of femininity, an excessive, other-worldly glamour that

---

[6] *Les Inrockuptibles* 18/05/11.
[7] *Le Monde* 29/6/11, *Les Inrockuptibles* 14/07/10.

reminded one critic of 'an excentric Bette Davis'[8] and another of 'the visual universe of Pierre Molinier'.[9] Fun is poked at Violetta by her schoolmates for wearing an over-fashionable and perhaps over-revealing halter-necked top in gym classes, implying that the pleasure in fetishistic outfits she is compelled to take by earning her mother considerable sums of money through her modelling (Irina Ionesco's photographs appeared in magazines as widely circulated as *Der Spiegel* and *Playboy*) caused a degree of detachment in Violetta/Eva's awareness of the social norms for 1970s adolescents.[10] Whether Violetta overcomes this alienation once her mother has been judged an unfit parent and she has been taken into care is uncertain, but it is entirely unsurprising that once separated, she rejects the smooth, shiny, glamour-driven aesthetic that is all her mother has given her to imitate, and adopts punk's unkempt, rebellious style. *My Little Princess* is a fascinating film to consider in relation to de Lauretis's call for women film-makers to 'de-aestheticize' the images of their films, because its highly aestheticized *mise en scène* is essential not only in relation to the story it tells, but to the distance from the material Ionesco must have needed in order to make it. The emotional abuse she suffered as a child was committed in images in the first place, and her story is one that could not have been as effectively told in any other medium. The masquerade performed in *My Little Princess* is offset to a degree by its other-worldly, fairy-tale atmosphere and by notes of comedy, but the hardened masks of fetishized femininity embodied and adored by Irina Ionesco are a sombre reminder of the insensitivity and cruelty that can accompany them. In this film, then, performances of femininity construct a fiction that keeps the director's own damaging and unhappy childhood at a distance from her authorial subjectivity, a stage in the development of which is performatively enacted by the filming of her extraordinary story.

Performing the road trip in *No Sex Last Night*

Even a cursory acquaintance with the work of French artist Sophie Calle is enough to ascertain that her artistic projects 'place the energies of performance and process on at least an equal footing with whatever is

---

[8] *Télérama* 29/06/11.

[9] Jean-Marc Lalanne, *Les Inrockuptibles* 29/6/11.

[10] Ionesco explains in interviews about *My Little Princess* that her behaviour once she began to rebel against her mother's coercive exploitation was actually far more violent than is seen in her film, and that she deliberately toned it down in order to preserve the fairy-tale atmosphere she wanted the story to have.

destined to emerge as the end-product' (Gratton and Sheringham 2005: 1–2). Calle's projects date from the late 1970s and are journeys, encounters and performances recorded in photographs, narratives and one feature-length film. Documented versions of some of these projects had been published prior to the 1990s, but the publication by the French publishing house Actes Sud of the box set of seven books *Doubles-jeux/Double Game* in 1998 made Calle's work available to a much broader public than even her numerous solo exhibitions had previously allowed.[11] The phototextuality of the volumes of *Double Game* is the product of her time-based performances, and to read/ view the books is in a sense to view performances which were never 'live', since they stage Calle's life as art. In Calle's sole film *No Sex Last Night*, the English- and French-language project she co-shot with her American lover and sometime-husband Greg Shephard in 1992, the temporality – and, therefore, also the mode of performance – is of course different, nearer to a performative in the sense set out in the speech act theory of American philosopher J. L. Austin, according to which the utterance of certain verbs in specific contexts brings about the action they describe.[12] *No Sex Last Night* is a film composed largely of photographic images rather than an act of speech, but certainly demonstrates the power of film-making to bring about changes in the 'real' lives of its maker-protagonists.

Released in the USA under the more allusive though perhaps more interesting title *Double Blind* and in cinemas and on video in France in January 1996,[13] *No Sex Last Night* charts a journey Calle and Shephard made by car from New York to Los Angeles in January of 1992, arriving in time for Calle to fulfil a teaching contract at a San Francisco Art College for the second semester of the academic year 1991–2. During this trip they were married at a Las Vegas drive-in chapel, and although the movie stops as the ensuing brief period of conjugality begins, a voice-over epilogue added three months after the trip charts the instability and disintegration of the marriage in the months that followed, apparently due to Shephard's involvement with another woman.

---

[11] *Double Game* was published at the same time as an exhibition of the same title was mounted at Paris's Centre national de la photographie, from 9 September to 2 November 1998. Calle gained international recognition and acclaim in the 1990s through numerous projects, a major exhibition in Paris at the Maison Européenne de la Photographie, and a British retrospective that showed at the Site Gallery and Graves Art Gallery in Sheffield and at the Camden Arts Centre in London early in 1999. (Her work had been exhibited in the UK prior to the London show 'Double Games', in a Hayward Gallery–organized national touring exhibition titled 'Imagined Communities' in 1996, and at the Tate Gallery's 'new artists' space in 1998.)
[12] Austin (1962).
[13] FNAC, collection Cinema Portugais, 1995.

Strong connections emerge throughout *No Sex Last Night* to the New Wave of French cinema, in its techniques of handheld cameras (video cameras in this instance) and stop-go editing. The photographic element of the film lies in its frequent use of still photographs for off-the-road sequences, in garages, motels and at city-stops: all the driving sequences of the film are moving pictures. The closing dedication of the film is to acclaimed French documentarist Chris Marker, and its particular homage to Marker seems to lie not only in the still photographs interspersed with the footage shot on Calle and Shephard's video cameras, but in the extensive use of voiceover, preferred by Marker more than other documentarists over the interview technique that tended to be used in ethnographic or sociological work. Marker's film *La Jetée/The Pier* is given special mention in Calle and Shephard's dedication: towards the start of *No Sex Last Night* a short *photo-roman* of Calle throwing flowers into the sea to mark the funeral of her friend, the writer Hervé Guibert, then taking place in France alludes directly to *La Jetée*, both in its images of the pier Calle finds for the purpose and in its measured use of stills which are filmed in colour, but (except for the flowers Calle throws into the water) are so washed-out as to appear black and white. Calle's homage to Marker is also vital to any consideration of the genre of her film (postmodern road movie? video essay? autobiographical film?), since Calle affirmed in an interview that *La Jetée* was the only film in her mind when making *No Sex Last Night*, rather than any road movie precedents. 'The first time I saw [*La Jetée*], years ago, for the only time in my life I was jealous and I wished I had done it. *La Jetée* gave me the right to seek to make my own movie. It was not in my head when we started but I guess it came back when we watched the first few days of recording' (Calle in Cooke 1993: 4).

The genre or mode of *No Sex Last Night* is therefore mixed; early on it features a ceremony of mourning Calle builds into the narration of the film by recording on its soundtrack her phone call to the dead Guibert's answering machine, but its dominant stylistic mode, in semi-adherence to the tradition of *cinéma vérité* inaugurated in the late 1950s and early 1960s by Marker, Jean Rouch and others, is nostalgic homage to the New Wave. Its repetition of New Wave innovations at a moment when they are no longer technically or aesthetically innovative strongly suggests the postmodern recycling of worn-out devices (Ince 2005), but may equally well be read as an attempt on Calle's part to perform her way into a male-dominated history of innovation in which women film-makers hardly figure.[14] In order to tease out how this performance works and what performative force it bears for Calle's subjectivity (if any), I

---

[14]On the domination of the New Wave by male directors, see Sellier (2008).

shall examine the theme of driving in *No Sex Last Night* and how the three-way relationship between Calle, Shephard and his Cadillac (in which they drive as far as Los Angeles) sets up the dynamic of their brief though happy marriage.

When Calle arrives in New York at New Year of 1992 expecting Shephard to have made preparations for their road trip, he does not meet her at the airport as arranged, and nothing is ready: 'the camera was not purchased, he had lost his driving licence, not said goodbye to his friends, not cleaned the trunk; any excuse would do'. Despite sensing that he no longer wants to drive to California with her, Calle organizes everything 'to protect my trip', which as far as she is concerned must go at least far enough to allow her 'to symbolically bury my friend Hervé by the sea', since she has left France as he is dying and is missing his funeral. Calle's decision to make the trip is thus a pure and positive affirmation of life over death that she articulates by saying 'I didn't want to wait in Paris for him to die: leaving was my way of believing that Hervé would live', and 'if we cancel this trip it would be a double failure: that's why we must go'.

Once they are on the road, the couple's fragile 'relationship', which was struck up in January 1991 when Shephard visited Calle in Paris almost exactly a year later than he had promised at their initial meeting in New York in December 1989, is seemingly undermined by phone calls Shephard makes and letters he writes to at least one other woman. Lying is a problem of his Shephard is aware of and that figured in the couple's first meeting, when Shephard lent Calle his New York apartment for two days and she found there the words 'Resolutions for the New Year: no lying, no biting' scribbled on a piece of paper underneath a cigarette packet. Calle is jealous of Shephard's communications with other women, and almost the only affection seen between the couple before their drive-in wedding occurs when she tackles him about how the dishonesty of his behaviour hurts her (she would prefer to know who he is calling), and Shephard agrees to tell her, leading to unguarded contentment on Calle's part that he catches in an intimate close-up (her video camera has dropped onto her lap, whereas in the preceding semi-confrontational conversation, both she and Shephard take refuge behind their respective cameras, which both, unusually, figure prominently in the shot).

No Sex Last Night can in general terms meaningfully be described as a 'bisexual' film, since there is a male as well as a female agent of the narrative, and the editing of footage from the two video cameras used, along with Calle and Shephard's separate voiceovers, allows the viewer to adopt either perspective. In the terms of psychoanalytic feminist film theory, the film offers the spectator the constantly oscillating identificatory position and restlessly bisexual kind of female spectatorship described by

Laura Mulvey in 'Afterthoughts on "Visual Pleasure and Narrative Cinema"'
(Mulvey 1989b). In seeking to theorize the position of the woman spectator
she had been criticized for omitting from her first essay, Mulvey sets out
the possibility of a bisexual form of identification for the female viewer, in
which a psychoanalytically 'correct' identification with the passive aims
of femininity usually set out for the female viewer in the film narrative is
perturbed or interrupted by a masculinization of sexuality and of looking that
women spectators have ample opportunities to acquire, given the 'masculine'
narrative grammar of the majority of film texts. This identification with the
masculine viewing position is enabled by regression to the childhood 'phallic
phase' of femininity, and acts as 'a last-ditch resistance, in which the power
of masculinity can be used as postponement against the power of patriarchy'
(Mulvey 1989b: 37). It can certainly be argued that *No Sex Last Night* offers its
female viewers a normatively feminine identification with a particular passive
aim of femininity – marriage, which is wished for by Calle (she expresses the
desire to be married once [une fois] and not to be an old maid [vieille fille]),
in a strong strand of romantic idealism demonstrated in the film and in some
of her other phototextual projects. A vicarious, mediated form of the gaze is
displayed particularly clearly in one of these, *La Filature/The Shadow*, in which
Calle asks her mother to hire a private detective to follow her through Paris
photographing her, corresponding exactly to the provisional masculinization
of the gaze suggested by Mulvey in 'Afterthoughts on "Visual Pleasure and
Narrative Cinema"'. But even if the Freudian theory of femininity allows
for the active desiring of passive aims – and might, therefore, account for
Calle's rather than Shephard's desire sustaining their road trip, such a reading
is complicated by the provisional three-way relationship between Calle,
Shephard and his Cadillac, which I shall now look at closely.

The rhythm of the central part of *No Sex Last Night* alternates driving
sequences and a number of visits to friends and relatives (artists Bruce
Nauman and Susan Rothenburg, Shephard's sister and her children) with a
series of photographic stills of unmade motel beds over which Calle's voice
melancholically intones the title of her film. As the non-event of the sex Calle
was obviously hoping would happen on the trip becomes routine, the 'no
sex last night' refrain commutes to just the monosyllable 'no', a negativity
matched by the repeated breakdowns of the Cadillac. Over the course of their
three-week trip, Calle counts the hours she and Shephard spend in diners,
restaurants and garages while the Cadillac undergoes a seemingly unending
series of repairs – it runs out of petrol on the first day, the windscreen wipers
need replacing, then the power steering mount, then there is a two-hour
delay due to overheating, then a $600 bill for a new carburetor (a seven-hour
stop), then a new transmission that costs $700 and takes fourteen hours to

fit. Despite these interruptions and the expense of repairs Calle alone appears to be paying for, driving – which the couple share – brings them together: Shephard observes in his voiceover 'I feel safe in the car…. there's something about the road we both seem to need', and after Calle – at the wheel at her request – flirts with a Texan cop she gives a ride to, she comments 'This car has become my home… it's as if I'd let him into my home'. As they approach Las Vegas, the idea of getting married (mooted before the trip by Calle) resurfaces, in Shephard's rather than Calle's voiceover – a subject he broaches since he knows it is one of her aspirations for the trip. As they drive around Las Vegas looking for a hotel suited to a wedding night in case Shephard should find whatever it will take to resolve him to go through with the wedding, they pass the Little White Chapel '24-hour drive-up wedding window', at which he lets out an exclamation of recognition: 'That would be the place we'd do it, then!' It is the next morning rather than the evening of their arrival that Shephard formally proposes to Calle and they return to the Little White Chapel, but the importance of the motorized, all-American *style* of the wedding opted for (one that conforms perfectly to their journey) should not be overlooked. As if to reinforce the importance of the car, driving and motorization to the narrative of *No Sex Last Night*, the couple cannot find a motel room after leaving Las Vegas, and their actual wedding night is spent, chastely, *in* the car, at a beauty-spot called Dante's View in Death Valley National Park. Like the wedding itself, this is a confirmation that their marriage is a three-way one to which the involvement of the American road-based and drive-in movie culture of their film is as indispensable as either of its spouses.

By this point in *No Sex Last Night* it is clearer than at the start of the trip that making the movie has been a kind of lure on Calle's part, and her idea of getting married in Las Vegas, a sort of wily challenge there is pressure on Shephard to accept, because without it their film would lack the narrative climax required by all good journey narratives. The challenge is above all to Shephard's masculinity, since participation in a legislative ceremony and the supplying of closure to their film-text are acts conventionally attributable to male rather than to female authorship. Perhaps surprisingly, though, marriage does indeed appear to have a performative effect upon the couple's relationship, in that it produces in Shephard the physical desire for Calle whose absence she has considered 'a failure' throughout the coast-to-coast journey, and about which Shephard has admitted at one moment to a modicum of shame. Now, like a traditional proprietorial husband he feels possessive towards Calle, while she says only that their sex life becomes 'the opposite' of what it was. Marital happiness lasts only a few months, however, and in the epilogue to the film (which the two film-makers recorded separately) the relevance of the three-way relationship between Calle, Shephard and the Cadillac is revealed by her *esp. autopichonal, self-reflexive*

admission that it is in the car that she finds a black plastic bag full of letters Shephard has written throughout the summer to an unidentified woman, 'H': Calle reads them all, is not convinced by Shephard's explanation and is unable to overcome her jealousy. Despite fulfilling her wish not to remain a permanent 'old maid', the performance of a road trip to which Calle committed with *No Sex Last Night* has revealed, along with the affirmation of life she set out with, considerable fragility and vulnerability in her relationships with men, and difficulty enduring any rivals for her affection.

The subject of *No Sex Last Night*, like that of Calle's phototextual projects, is everyday life, and so the experiences it documents cannot be those of a (masculine) metaphysical subject *of* its experience, because of the stake of her subjectivity in the projects she invents: her subjectivity *is* experimental, unfinished, in process or '*en jeu*'. Much of her 1970s and 1980s work is characterized by a loss of self or stake of un-'experimented'(untested) desire in the approach to the other (as Baudrillard says of *Suite Vénitienne*, 'she who follows is herself relieved of responsibility for her own life as she follows blindly in the footsteps of the other' (Baudrillard 1983: 82)). In *No Sex Last Night*, however, she co-conducts a bolder kind of experiment with this inventive, self-displacing and non-self-identified subjectivity. The experiment both succeeds and fails, in so far as she reaches California as the married woman she wistfully wished to be, only for the marriage to collapse again shortly afterwards. The road trip undertaken by Shephard and Calle in *No Sex Last Night* exposes the performativity of both male and female subjectivities, but with greater emphasis on Calle's, since she is the instigator and funder of the trip and of the project. She may end both film and project as the single woman she started out as, but during it the performativity of life-as-art and of female subjectivity has been explored and revealed in an essentially self-reflexive, unusual and thought-provoking film.

Domestic dances: performed co-authorship in *The Tango Lesson*

By being almost entirely in black and white, *The Tango Lesson* marks a step back from the resplendent colour Sally Potter screened so magnificently for the first time in *Orlando*, but nevertheless offers various alternative visual and aural pleasures – a memorably melancholy-tinged yet restlessly repetitive 'tango' theme, a romantic narrative, and many scenes of expert dancing by Pablo Verón, Potter herself and diverse practitioners from the tango halls of Paris and Buenos Aires. These pleasures were noted even by critics who found

Potter's decision to play the lead female role in the film herself misguided or self-indulgent.[15] *The Tango Lesson* is obviously a personal film, though not strictly speaking an autobiographical one, since the fiction of protagonist Sally's romance with (real-life) tango dancer Pablo Verón reveals no reliable facts about the 'real' relationship between Potter and Verón. (Whereas Potter trained as a dancer, the fictional Sally's reply to Verón's question 'do you know how to dance?', which he asks at her first lesson, is 'not really'.) The aspect of the film I shall explore here is how the creative processes of dancing and film-making are staged in the 'more personal' film Sally opts to make when she decides not to compromise on the demands made by Hollywood producers of her film project about the Paris fashion industry. Feminist critical readings of *The Tango Lesson* including my own have, quite understandably, focused on the tensions between Pablo and Sally stemming from the inherent gender bias of tango as an art form, but in so doing have perhaps overlooked a commentary on co-creation and co-authorship that is visible in the film's *mise en scène* and detectable in its dialogue, and which depends for its existence on the status of dance and film as *performed* arts.

The opening shot of *The Tango Lesson* is an overhead shot of a pure white, circular, table standing on new-looking wooden flooring in what looks like a converted warehouse apartment. The table, it rapidly becomes apparent, is film-maker Sally's writing table: she places on it a pad of white writing paper whose topmost sheet is blank and takes up a pencil to write, as the shot changes to a close-up on the pencil's freshly sharpened lead. The blank writing pad seems metonymically linked to the clutter-free white table: this is a professional yet domestic setting whose importance to Sally's work as a film-maker becomes apparent in a second similar scene after her meeting and first tango lesson with Pablo in Paris, when neurotic moments of composition (Sally screws up whole sheets of barely used paper in order to begin afresh) alternate with equally neurotic inspection of marks on the table and a crack in the flooring, neither of which are visible to the film's viewer. Sally is able to leave for some concentrated tango practice in Buenos Aires because her work (and living) space will be out of action for 'a couple of weeks', but the

---

[15]This is not a view I agree with, as comments in earlier chapters have probably already indicated, but French press critics (for example) mentioned 'a narcissism not always in good taste' (*Les Echos* 10/04/98) and criticized the lack of sensuality and expressivity in Potter's dancing (Jérôme Provençal in *Les Inrockuptibles* 8/04/98). In interview with Catherine Fowler, Potter admits to having been 'taken aback' by the criticisms of narcissism provoked by performing in the film herself, and adds that doing so made her feel vulnerable rather than vain' (Fowler 2009: 125). She also defends the 'sturdy tradition' of integrating the persona of the artist in a work as 'a way of exposing phoney transparency and objectivity' (Fowler 2009: 126), a defence of subjectivity that could be argued to be particularly important for feminists ['An Interview with Sally Potter', 18 August 2004, 109–133].

rootedness of professional artistic identity in personal space is reaffirmed when she returns and has to leave again, this time because of a leaking roof and for Paris. It is affirmed too by the location of several scenes in Pablo's Paris apartment, the parquet flooring of which allows it to double as a dance studio. The humour and charm of one of the most memorable of the film's many dance sequences, Pablo's tap performance in his kitchen and on the mantelpiece of his apartment's *salon*, above a roaring fire, depends on the domesticity of its setting and choreography (Pablo detaches and rinses salad leaves in between moves), even while the restricted space he is dancing in displays his athleticism and the grace and fluidity of his movements to greater advantage.

FIGURE 6.1 *Sally and Pablo dance in the rain in Buenos Aires,* The Tango Lesson

Dances Sally and Pablo engage in along the walkways of the Seine in Paris and in the docklands of Buenos Aires (the film's final sequence) are perhaps the most spectacular sequences in *The Tango Lesson*, and the film does generally make greater use of public spaces than it does of domestic ones. The inclusion of a particularly bodily kind of domestic space, however (Sally pads about her wooden floor in thick woollen socks practising her tango steps while she struggles with her film project), emphasizes both the dependence of Sally's and Pablo's respective professions on material space (for film-making, locations, and for tango, performance spaces) and the precariousness of that dependency. There are perhaps two things in addition to an obvious shared passion for tango that enable the couple to 'begin again' after several arguments that threaten their relationship (depicted only as a romance, not a sexual affair), the all-consuming character of their respective artistic occupations that is signalled by this inclusion of domestic spaces in the film, and the fact that dance and film are both time-based, *performed* art forms. A quasi-contract between tango and film is alluded to in their first conversation in Paris, when Pablo ascertains from Sally that she works in cinema, she asks 'do you give tango lessons?', and he replies in the affirmative. (This quasi-contract is revisited in the conversation in front of the mirror in the disused hairdressing salon in Buenos Aires I commented on in Chapter 4.) The implication that Sally is more aware than Pablo that for artists such as the two of them, work is the greater part of their personal identity is not pursued, but it hangs over the following, final scenes of the film, when a less narcissistic and more humble Pablo allows Sally to answer further questions he puts to her about identity, exile and belonging. The moment at the end of *The Tango Lesson* when it becomes clear that the film Sally has been preparing about the tango and Pablo is the film we have been watching marks the fusion of the arts of tango and film, and the conclusion of a period of collaboration or co-creation that also merits a description as co-authorship, a co-authorship dependent upon their respective skills as performers. Film directing and tango dancing are discrete forms of art practice, but are both carried out by an essentially open-ended, performative mode of subjectivity inseparable from the body of its practitioner. Rather like my discussions of male–female intersubjective looking in Breillat's *Brief Crossing* and *The Tango Lesson* in Chapter 4, this short return to *The Tango Lesson* has brought out co-authorship between a woman and a man at the level of filmic performance, an element of the film it is easy to miss because of the de- and reconstruction of the male–female gender hierarchy that dominates its action.

Why life, why art? Self-reflexive creation in *Why (not) Brazil?*

By some degree the most complex of the films considered in this chapter, *Why (not) Brazil?* is the fifth feature film directed by Laetitia Masson, who established herself during the 1990s wave of new, young talent referred to by critics of French film as *le jeune cinéma français*. Masson's previous film

La Repentie/The Repentant (2002) had failed both commercially and critically, and in the second scene of *Why (not) Brazil?*, which was released in France in September 2004, the director, sitting at her kitchen table, introduces herself to camera and declares that she has not worked for two years and has just been told she is 10,000€ overdrawn. Such direct self-exposure both draws attention to 'the links between emotions, work and money', Masson has described as the main concern of her film-making (Masson 2007), and introduces the issue *Why (not) Brazil?* will grapple with, the difficulty – and perhaps impossibility – of adapting a first-person text to film.[16] Masson's source text for this film-making experiment is the 2002 novel *Why Brazil?/Pourquoi le Brésil?* by Christine Angot, in which the relative youth and open future of Brazil as a nation acts as a metaphor for the hope and euphoria experienced in a new love affair – Angot's relationship with the cultural commentator and publisher Pierre-Louis Rozynes. Angot had been catapulted to the centre of French literary culture in 1999 by the success of her novel *L'Inceste*, after which she published several novels in rapid succession and collaborated with Masson on an adaptation of one of her short stories.[17] As the title *L'Inceste* indicates, parental abuse – in Angot's case by the father who had left the family home before she was born and only recognized her as his daughter when she was fourteen – became one of the shaping influences on Angot's writing, leading her to what she describes in one of her appearances in *Why (not) Brazil?* as an uncensored 'hatred of secrecy' [*haine du secret*], a type of self-exposure that involves intense and violent 'moments of creation' and, therefore, puts subjectivity at risk. In interviews about the film, Masson emphasized that although her own personal life is more settled and stable than Angot's (she is married to the publisher Jean-Marc Roberts and has two children), she had to go beyond her usual limits in order to engage at all convincingly with the kind of material in which Angot's novel deals. ('To be faithful to Christine's work, I had to surpass my limits and get outside myself as she does. To the point of endangering my marriage. This is the risk that drives me to direct'.[18])

The complex *mise en scène* of *Why (not) Brazil?* begins directly after Masson's revelation to camera of her parlous financial state, when the same declaration is made by a fictional double of Masson played by Elsa Zylberstein, cut short this time by a phone call offering her work from Maurice Rey (Bernard Le Coq), a thinly-disguised pseudonym of one the film's actual producers

---

[16]Jonathan Romney quipped that the film could be described as 'self-referential fiction … about the difficulty of making films when you're Laetitia Masson' (Romney 2008: 44).

[17]*Emmenez-la* was one of the six short films directed mainly by writers and broadcast on the French TV channel Canal+ on 30 April 2001.

[18]Barbara Théate, *Journal du dimanche* 19/09/04.

Jean-Michel Rey. The difficulty of adapting Angot's first-person narration of her relationship with the Jewish Rozynes to the screen is confirmed at their meeting the next day when the fictional Masson declares it 'inadaptable', although the pressure of having reached her overdraft limit quickly changes her mind. Masson, therefore, opens her film by framing her director's identity as one working for solely commercial reasons and the interest of bringing the story of a personal friend of hers to a wider audience, with the considerable restrictions on creative freedom these limits entail. A lengthy prologue ensues that is the first of ten chapters of wildly different lengths in *Why (not) Brazil?*: titled 'Alone', it shows both Masson and her fictional double preparing her adaptation by drafting a script and attempting to cast it, but above all trying to identify with the solitude and readiness for a love affair described by Angot at the start of her novel. The fictional Masson explains to her on-screen husband (Marc Barbé) and her producer that she needs to relive new love in order to film it, attends a fruitless evening of speed-dating at which she lies about being married, and finds herself attracted to her son's paediatrician (Pierre Arditi), who like Angot's lover is Jewish. Upon discovering that the paediatrician has recently left his wife but met another (married) woman he is drawn to, the fictional Masson asks if she can use the story of his new love in her film project, then writes him into her script despite the paediatrician's decision not to pursue the affair. When her husband slams a copy of the script down on their kitchen table and demands to know what is going on between his wife and the paediatrician, the fictional Masson replies simply that her interest in him is the only connection she has so far found with the excitement and hope Angot writes about in *Why Brazil?* The estrangement this creates in her marriage is doubled shortly afterwards in an apparent abandonment of the film by its producer, who refuses to put up any more money until Masson makes more and faster progress with the project. Now, the real Masson reflects in her voiceover, she has no producer, no money, no actors and not much of a marriage, making her much more genuinely alone than three months previously – a situation much closer to the struggle to write and find love narrated by Angot.

As an autofiction about the process of directing, *Why (not) Brazil?* resembles a film I shall discuss in the next chapter, Catherine Breillat's *Sex Is Comedy* (2002),[19] although that focuses on the difficulties of coaxing convincing performances out of actors rather than, as *Why (not) Brazil?* does, on a director's struggle with her material and a limited budget (it was

---

[19]François Truffaut's *Day for Night* (1973) is the classic reference in French cinema of an autofiction about the process of film directing and is mentioned in a conversation between the fictional Masson and her producer.

produced for only €1 million and shot in just five weeks (Audé et al. 2004)).
What is performed in the film, in addition to the professional and domestic
life of a female film-maker, is Masson's difficulty in adapting for the screen
material she cannot identify with except through her 'recurring fascination
with the dynamics of origins, fate and intervention' (Dobson 2012: 149),
which surfaces in the Jewishness of Angot, Rozynes and the paediatrician.
A second successful identification of Masson with Angot occurs in the
performance of Elsa Zylberstein who, from the start of the second chapter
of the film onwards, appears as Angot (as well as Masson) alongside Marc
Barbé as Rozynes (as well as Masson's husband).[20] In other words, Masson's
identification with Angot is much more easily accomplished visually than it is
for Masson as a social and psychological human being. Once the spectator
has been introduced to the fictional Angot, the scenes of her initial meetings
and first sexual encounter with Rozynes follow the novel closely, although
two possible versions of the first sex scene are intercut with one another as
if to indicate both the importance of the passion at the core of Angot's story
and Masson's ambivalence about how to film it. (Later in *Why (not) Brazil?*
Masson will consult Angot about the issue of her Jewishness and about the
difficulty she is having protecting her family from the exposure to which the
film is subjecting her – a protection Angot declares to be 'impossible' – but
how to screen the novel's descriptions of sexual love is, perhaps tellingly, a
thought process Masson keeps to herself.)

The two aspects of the directing process that *Why (not) Brazil?* particularly
emphasizes are the examination of the relationship between Masson's life
and her work precipitated by having to adapt a friend's uninhibitedly personal
narrative and, ultimately, the limits of her ability to identify with Angot's
rejection of all secrecy and shame. The first of these is dramatized by frequent
passages of analytical commentary in voiceover and by lingering shots of the
real Masson filming herself before her full-length bedroom mirror. Angot's
writing bares everything, but 'I do not film everything', Masson declares, even
going so far as to suggest that she may be the worst possible person to adapt
Angot's novel because it repeatedly sends her back to herself when her life,
she is now convinced, is not suitable film material. Whereas Angot's creative
process takes constant risks by revealing everything she experiences in her
close relationships and thereby denying her lovers, family and friends, and the
privacy she does not seek for herself, Masson has exposed only herself to the

---

[20]Journalist Emmanuel Frois commented that Zylberstein pulled off the challenge of playing the
film's two key roles 'perfectly', while Zylberstein herself said in an interview that she found the
challenge a gift, and that she shared Masson's desire for an intimate understanding of Angot while
not identifying with Angot's hatred of secrecy (*Le Figaroscope* 15/9/04; *France-soir* 15/9/04).

camera, and employed an actor to play the part of the one new acquaintance she feels has actually altered her emotional status quo since she began work on the film – the paediatrician. In order to rescue any vestige of authorship – of 'the so-called truth' of Angot's book or of the adaptation – she must go and film him, 'at the risk of my husband seeing me as I really am, moved by another man, and at the risk of involving the paediatrician in something unprofessional, intimate and public'. A scene follows with Haïm Cohen in which Masson is visibly if shyly attracted, but pursues the questions about Jewishness she is convinced underlie Angot's attraction to Rozynes and her own sense that Haïm Cohen is 'the film's only true encounter'. Having taken the only risk within her power that can make her film comparable to Angot's novel, there is nothing else to film that interests her, and no further way to add to the project, which has reached its limit: 'I don't adapt, and I don't adapt myself'.

Once its self-reflexive meditation on adaptation has been stretched to a point at which it appears to fail – Masson gets a friend to tell Maurice Rey that she is abandoning the project and temporarily disappears – Why (not) Brazil? ends with Masson's reappearance on a station platform from which she is evidently returning home. This sequence is intercut with images of Angot walking alone along one of the Normandy beaches we have seen the fictional Angot visit with Rozynes. Before the cut to footage of Benjamin Biolay performing the song that is playing on the film's soundtrack (the string instrumentation and lyrics of his romantic ballads have been used in a pointedly self-conscious fashion throughout the film to announce that a romantic or sexual scene is beginning and the viewer's emotions should be engaged), we also see fleeting images of Elsa Zylberstein and Marc Barbé individually, a reminder of how the double roles taken by these two actors have mediated between reality and fiction and between novel and film. Angot's and Masson's status as the respective creators of Why Brazil? and Why (not) Brazil? make them the film's third couple alongside Masson and her husband and Angot and Rozynes; theirs is a friendship that, like Masson's marriage, has survived the project and become more self-aware in the process.

In addition to being an absorbing autofiction about the process of directing, then, Why (not) Brazil? reveals a woman director salvaging authorship from a professional and financial crisis. Unable to attract any stars because of the complexity of her subject (Emmanuelle Béart, Charlotte Gainsbourg, Jane Birkin and Romane Bohringer all find reasons to refuse the role of Angot), Masson nonetheless manages to 'cast' well-known actors Daniel Auteuil and Francis Huster by filming her conversations with them about playing Rozynes. Auteuil is made visibly uneasy once he realizes that his conversation with Masson will form a scene of her film, while Huster roundly condemns both Angot's novel and Masson's adaptation of it: *Why Brazil?* was not the 'truth' Angot's previous work led him to expect, and any adaptation is a waste of time and worthless, since repeating the novel will compound its faults. The appearances of Auteuil and Huster in *Why (not) Brazil?* are revealing where Masson's views about her status as a woman director are concerned, because in the director's interview included on the DVD, she rejects the suggestion that adapting a woman writer's novel continues her oeuvre's tendency to focus on 'strong' female characters and emphasizes that the participation of Auteuil and Huster in the film pleased her as much as the agreement of any high-ranking star to play Angot would have done. Masson ultimately seems as interested in her male actors and characters as in female subjectivity, and *Why (not) Brazil?* does not fit at all easily into the category of 'women's cinema' (a category Masson is not interested in). The film may have been a project she was compelled to accept against her better judgement, out of professional and financial necessity, but the complex *mise en scène* and absorbing treatment of self-reflexivity Masson salvages from this situation offers unusually honest insights into the everyday life and professional challenges of an already-successful woman film-maker, a rarity among recent films directed by women.

In this chapter I have discussed four films in which the subjectivity of the female director herself is dramatized in her film, through either a documentary-style performance (*No Sex Last Night*), a fictionalized performance (*My Little Princess* and *The Tango Lesson*) or both together (*Why (not) Brazil?*). These analyses have shown how the notion of performance can complement a feminist phenomenological approach to embodied female subjectivity, by allowing a female director's self-reflexive approach to her own subjectivity to be explored as it is performed. Ionesco, Calle, Potter and Masson adopt different performance strategies for filming their own lives and approaches to those lives, and the concepts of performance and performativity afford us insights into those approaches that parallel those about female spectatorship afforded by the many 'applications' of Mary Ann Doane's concept of masquerade that were undertaken in an earlier phase of feminist film studies.

7

[handwritten: an effort to introduce a political angle to film-philosophy m emphasis on the social]

Desire

One of the oldest of philosophical concepts, 'desire' is perhaps also the most geographically widespread, since it features in Eastern religions such as Buddhism as well as across Western philosophy and theory. Associated particularly, after Aristotle and Plato, with German philosophers Schopenhauer and Hegel, it came to the forefront of enquiry in Freudian and Lacanian psychoanalysis, Freud using several terms to theorize it (the drive (*Trieb*) and *Wunsch* as well as 'libido') and it has continued to play a role in film theory and philosophy, particularly in relation to the desire(s) of the voyeuristic spectator. The question of desire, frequently approached in anti-Oedipal mode since the publication of Gilles Deleuze and Félix Guattari's *Anti-Oedipus* in 1972, is often considered inseparable from the question of subjectivity, and may be as important to ethics and the ethical as how questions of subjectivity are approached,[1] but formulating a concept of 'female desire' is not a route feminist film studies have tended to favour, because of the risks – even more pronounced than when broaching female subjectivity – of producing ahistorical and essentialist readings. Desire is what links the four films I shall discuss in this chapter, Andrea Arnold's *Fish Tank* (already treated in Chapter 3), Lynne Ramsay's *Morvern Callar* (2002), Claire Denis's *White Material* (2010) and Catherine Breillat's *Sex Is Comedy* (2002), and although it is mainly the desire of the female protagonist of each film that I shall discuss, it is not my aim to suggest that there is anything essentially 'female' at work: the desires of these women are fully social, arising from and responding to the situations in which they find themselves – restrictive, embattled circumstances in each instance. I shall approach the potential traps

---

[1]See, for example, John Rajchman, *Truth and Eros: Foucault, Lacan and the Question of Ethics* (Rajchman, 2009).

set just by employing the notion of desire, rather, via the concept of *economies of sexual subjectivity*, suggested by a number of expositions of Irigaray's work to be a way in which desire manifests itself in social formations.

In *Irigaray and Deleuze: Experiments in Visceral Philosophy*, as Tamsin Lorraine expounds 'the project of describing and giving voice to the feminine other [Irigaray] believes to have been silenced by a masculinist economy of subjectivity' (Lorraine 1999: 21), she almost incidentally suggests a framework for Irigaray's theorization of women's desire. The patriarchal repression of women's means of symbolizing their relationship to their origins (the maternal body) might, Irigaray suggests, be remedied in a range of ways, and these entail not just a change of representations, but a different mode of desire. Whereas men (in Freud's account, critiqued by Irigaray in *Speculum*) relate to mother-substitutes as objects of desire, repeating the hierarchical, dominating subject-object divide familiar from philosophical accounts of subject-object relations, women, in Irigaray's words, 'do not try to master the other but to give birth to themselves' (Lorraine 1999: 32). Women's desire is not possessive: '[u]nlike masculine desire, her desire does not necessarily take the form of a desire to possess a discrete entity' (Lorraine 1999: 31). Instead, it reaches out to and touches the other (woman), operating in a non-hierarchical, horizontal manner. 'It is in communion with the world through a touching that touches back that a feminine subject continues to identify with the mother who provided her first nourishing contact with the world' (Lorraine 1999: 32). Rachel Jones confirms Lorraine's account of the reading of Freud Irigaray makes in *Speculum* when she states that, for the 'little girl' of Freud's essays on sexual difference who has no way of relating to the mother as a *woman*, 'the possibility of taking pleasure in her own sex is foreclosed. Hence the need to find ways of articulating woman's relation to her beginnings in birth which are not mediated through the male subject, as well as a different, non-phallic model with which to represent female desire in its own terms' (Jones 2011: 139).

A further dimension of Irigaray's theorization of a non-phallogocentric desire arises in a different section of her reading of Freud in *Speculum*, 'Female Hom(m)osexuality'. Here, she discusses how desire circulates among women – or rather, how it is prevented from so doing in a Symbolic order constructed around the masculine subject, and how an alternative libidinal economy would support the formation of female subjectivity (described by Lorraine as the 'feminine on her own') via a differently differentiated economy of subjectivity. Irigaray refers to 'the lack of an auto-erotic, homo-sexual economy' (Irigaray 1974: 102) for women indicated by symptomatic behaviours that occur in a phallocentric Symbolic order, such as hypernarcissism, difficult relations with the mother 'and indeed with all women', 'lack of "social interest" and, more generally, of all sustained interest'. It may be that what is most 'essential' about women's desire in patriarchal social formations is the way it is expressed and circulates, or gets blocked and cannot do either of these things, in general but particularly among women. Irigaray's suggestion for countering such blockages is the construction of a 'homo-sexual' (same sex) economy among women, out of female genealogies and symbolized representations of mother–daughter relationships. In a discussion of this passage in the chapter of *Luce Irigaray: Philosophy in the Feminine* titled 'Maternal genealogy and the symbolic', Whitford emphasizes the importance of an economy of the death drives in bringing about this change in current sexual economies for the benefit of women's sexuality and desire. According to Irigaray, in a sexual economy organized around masculine subjectivity, where the feminine is only a specular other or 'co-opted by the masculine', the '"active" mobilization of the death drives is prohibited for/in female sexuality' (Irigaray in Whitford 1991: 96). Under the particular symbolic organization of the patriarchal social order, women's desires and alternative libidinal economy are 'used' for the representation and sublimation of men's death drives, but are unable to sublimate or represent themselves. A phallocentric symbolic economy allows the representation and sublimation of men's death drives, but not the 'rechannelling, metaphorization or sublimation' (Whitford 1991: 96) of women's.[2] A redistribution of the death drives of men and women would not necessarily reduce the prevalence or intensity of the negative affects with which the concept of the death drive is associated (compulsive repetition, a reduction of tension to the point of inertia, masochism and self-destructive sentiments generally), but it would redistribute them differently among men and women, and thereby modify the character of the desiring economies we currently associate with both feminine and masculine same-sex collectivities. The collective formations of the 'men-among-themselves' (the *entre-hommes*, a term Irigaray employs only in the earliest phase of her work critiquing the patriarchal subject and sociality) and 'women-among-themselves' (*entre-femmes*) would each be more loosely bound and would be more open to exchange with one another, enabling potentially important changes in the symbolic and the social organization of sexual difference and desire.

---

[2] As Whitford notes, the concept of the death drive belongs to psychoanalysis, but Irigaray is using it here to make an argument about sociosymbolic organization, not about the psyche. According to Whitford, Irigaray's critics read her as if she were offering an alternative psychoanalytic theory, when in fact she is 'interrogating psychoanalytic conceptualization itself' (Whitford 1991: 84). 'Lacanians take Irigaray to be talking about feminine specificity at the level of the drives, whereas I take her to be talking about feminine specificity at the level of the symbolic, or representation' (Whitford 1991: 85).

My main reason for drawing on remarks by Irigaray that suggest an approach to desire involving a redistribution of the death drives is that a considerable amount of aggression and violence attaches to the actions and behaviour of the female protagonists of *Fish Tank*, *Morvern Callar*, *White Material* and *Sex Is Comedy*. For Mia of *Fish Tank*, it is uncontrollable behaviour at school and at home that leads her to reject her family and the estate on which she has grown up; the eponymous heroine Morvern Callar cuts up and disposes of her boyfriend's body after his suicide and steals his identity as a promising novelist; Maria Vial, the protagonist of *White Material*, is driven to the violent murder of her father-in-law, while Jeanne, the film-director character of *Sex Is Comedy*, conducts herself in a totally authoritarian fashion in order to complete the shooting of the film we watch her, her crew and her actors work on. All four of these women live or work in difficult – materially impoverished, war-torn or conflict-ridden – circumstances, and for all four, the effort of dealing with and attempting to overcome these circumstances sees them behave with a socially unacceptable degree of aggression or violence. They are not social outcasts, however, and it is precisely this 'inbetween' status as 'bad girl' (Mia), unapprehended criminal (Morvern and Maria) and self-elected autocrat (Jeanne) that makes their challenging or conventionally unacceptable actions worthy of closer analysis. By behaving 'badly' at least in part because they are driven to by circumstances, these women might be said to inhabit a zone in which the symbolic and social reorganization of sexuate desire is taking place, and a modification of the economy of masculine subjectivity going on. The fact that a patriarchal economy of subjectivity is also the upholder and guarantor of masculinist *moral* values is more a Beauvoirean than an Irigarayan emphasis, but the female protagonists of these four films invite comparison with one another in the challenge they present to conventional civilized morality as well as in the extreme and violent behaviour they exhibit.

Mia walks: Movement and struggle in *Fish Tank*

In the eleventh minute of *Fish Tank*, Mia arrives for the second time at the compound where the white horse she has befriended is kept chained up. In this short interval of filmic time that is probably most of an afternoon in diegetic reality (she has spent time in her room after an argument with her mother involving pushing and slapping), Mia has walked twice from the empty flat where she does her dance practice via the block where she, her mother and her sister live, swiftly, vigorously and with a sense of purpose. Her movements seem dictated by the next action she wants to carry out (collect a hammer with which to break open the padlock on the horse's chains, free the horse and so on) rather than calculated in any premeditated way, and in fact she is moving in circles as if under the sway of some kind of repetition compulsion, counteracting the negativity of these circles with the positivity of her intention to give the horse its freedom – an action in which she does not succeed. *Fish Tank* is punctuated with episodes in which the filmic action consists solely of Mia walking, always wearing her jogging bottoms, always fiercely intent upon what she is going to do next, even if it is to slam her bedroom door or flop down on her bed in anger. When her movement is impeded – as it is when she is caught trying to free the horse – she resists, strikes out, kicks and fights, before breaking free and tearing away to escape those who would thwart her. A certain physical courage sets her apart from her mother and Tyler: when Connor takes the three of them out on a drive and wades out into the river to fish with his bare hands, only Mia wades out to help him, as her mother and Tyler stay cowering on the river bank, their arms round each other's waist. 'Trust bloody Mia!' is her mother's comment on Mia's adventurousness.

Whereas Mia's hip hop dancing is a planned, rehearsed form of expression into which she channels her unused energies and desire to escape from her mother and the estate, most of her movements are spontaneous and raw, as if entirely unreflected upon. The morning after she and Connor have had sex and he has consequently walked out on his relationship with her mother, she chases out into the car park after him at a run only to see his black saloon car racing away. Pausing only to change from pyjamas to her usual sweatshirt top and bottoms and to transfer Connor's work phone number from her mother's mobile to her own, she sets out on foot to Tilbury, a distance of at least six or seven miles. Arnold films her at four or five different moments in this walk, despite the drab similarity of the surroundings at each of them, emphasizing the distance involved, which is confirmed when Connor – after the briefest of conversations that is as evasive as it is reassuring – redeposits her at Tilbury station to get the train home. Mia does not get on the train, and the camera cuts from the station platform back to the front drive of Connor's house and Mia once again approaching the front door. Once she is inside the house (accomplished by climbing athletically over a gate and through a rear window) and sees from recorded images on Connor's DV camera that he is married with a little girl, she expresses her horror and disgust in the most spontaneously physical way imaginable, by urinating on the sitting room carpet.

Perhaps the most striking sequence of raw, desiring movement in *Fish Tank*, however, is the revenge Mia wreaks following her discovery that Connor is a father and husband, by abducting his young daughter Keira. This is a sequence redolent with significance about family structure and Mia's place in it: Connor had treated Mia with ambivalent paternal tenderness before they had sex, by carrying her up to bed when she fell asleep on her mother's bed, giving her a piggyback ride, and cleaning and bandaging her injured ankle. Mia had all too briefly had the father absent from her upbringing, and the discovery that this father-figure has a rival (and actual) daughter creates a potentially competitive and violent dynamic between the teenager and the little girl, loading what happens next with menace. As Mia tempts Keira away from the safe enclosure of her home and estate with the promise of ice cream, the only meaning of the sequence attaches to the characters' movements out into undetermined space, across waste ground and to the shores of a threatening-looking man-made lake. As Mia pushes Keira relentlessly forward without knowing where her spontaneous act of abduction is leading, repeatedly ordering the little girl to 'Walk!', the weather is more bright than dull, and windy, so that the minimal verbal exchanges between the characters are blown away and take second place to their effortful progress across open country scattered with brambles and barbed wire fences. After Keira's sparkly pink and silver dress snags and tears on one of these and Mia takes a minute or two to climb over it, a distance opens up between them as if to represent the distance between her and Keira's better social fortunes of an employed father and comfortable house with a garden. For such a sweet-looking little girl, Keira shows an unexpected feistiness not far short of Mia's own, gaining ground over Mia in the chase and thumping and kicking Mia when the older girl tries to restrain her physically. It is only because the lake's edge is reached and cold, choppy water threatens that the conflict is eventually resolved: after Keira half-falls and is half-pushed in, Mia's humanitarian impulses overtake her vengeful ones, and she offers Keira a dead tree branch she finds lying nearby in order to help her out of the water. Shivering, the two girls embrace hastily, both knowing that the abduction is at an end. Keira has no way of knowing Mia's motivation for what has occurred, but Mia – importantly for the film's presentation of her as a damaged, aggressive adolescent – has given vent to her anger at Connor's failure to reveal his social status as husband and father.

In *Fish Tank*, then, a young woman's desire is filmed in all its raw spontaneity, in the fierce, determined walking and actions with which Mia counters anyone who acts upon her (any other subject who would objectify her). Her rebelliousness, which is screened almost entirely through the movement and *mise en scène* of actions without identified objectives, conforms to the '"active" mobilization of the death drives … prohibited for/ in female sexuality' described by Irigaray (Irigaray in Whitford 1991: 96). The manner of Mia's movements stages an aggressively resistant ethical desire for survival that I shall now also identify and discuss in *Morvern Callar*, *White Material* and *Sex Is Comedy*.

On the road to nowhere: Lynne Ramsay's *Morvern Callar*

Morvern Callar, Ramsay's follow-up feature to her acclaimed 1999 film *Ratcatcher*, is based on Alan Warner's 1995 cult novel of the same name. Beginning in the immediate aftermath of the suicide of Morvern (Samantha Morton)'s boyfriend in their shared flat in a lifeless town on the west coast of Scotland, the film follows Morvern through the days and weeks that follow, as she fails to report the death, lies to her close friend Lanna (Kathleen McDermott) and other acquaintances about James's whereabouts, cuts up and disposes of the body on nearby moorland, then uses the money left for his funeral to buy a holiday for herself and Lanna in a Spanish resort. While in Spain, Morvern is in contact with a publisher to whom she has sent the manuscript of the novel found on James's computer after his suicide, the authorship of which she has assumed by erasing his name from the title page and inserting her own in its place. After spending several hours and having sex with a young man in a neighbouring room to hers and Lanna's at the resort, Morvern immediately drags Lanna into a taxi that takes them into the mountains away from the coast, where they encounter a typically Spanish religious fiesta: Lanna participates in this with the same automatic pleasure as she did the swimming-pool games at the resort, but Morvern is enchanted by it, as she is by the wild and sparsely populated landscape. Leaving Lanna asleep by the roadside, Morvern continues her journey alone, hitches a lift and finds a place to stay, then renews contact with the London publisher, who flies out to Spain with his assistant and offers her a contract and an advance of £100,000 she can scarcely believe. Returning to Scotland only to collect a few belongings and tell Lanna what she is doing, Morvern heads back to Spain, which is represented in the closing scene of the film by a dreamy out-of-time sequence in one of the nightclubs she frequents there, to the accompaniment of the Mamas and the Papas' 'Dedicated to the One I Love'.

According to Ewa Mazierska and Laura Rascaroli in *Crossing New Europe: Postmodern Travel and the European Road Movie*, Ramsay's 'often hypnotic, stylistically austere' film resembles other road movies by being 'as much about home as it is about being away from it' (Mazierska and Rascaroli 2006: 191, 192). The question of where Morvern is at home is inseparable from the larger issues of identity raised by both Warner's novel and the film, but it is clearly not Scotland, as unlike Lanna, whose view of her home town is that 'There's nothing wrong with here; it's just the same crap as everywhere else', Morvern is set on fleeing as soon as the financial opportunity presents itself. Like *Fish Tank*'s Mia, Morvern's movements

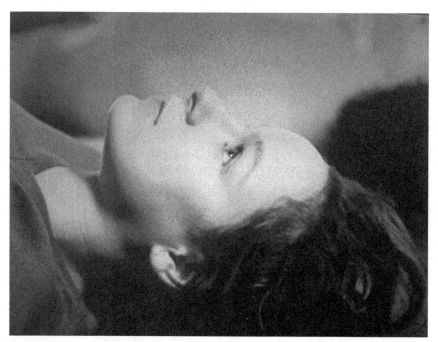

FIGURE 7.1 *Morvern at home at Christmas*, Morvern Callar. *Courtesy of BBC Films*

exhibit a driven character distinguishing her from her home-loving best friend, whose more predictable modes of pleasure are fully satisfied by the leisure activities available in the Spanish resort. Both girls take drugs, drink to excess and party wildly in Scotland, and Morvern is just as drawn to the resort's clubs as Lanna is, but while Lanna flirts with and has casual sex with other British boys on holiday, Morvern remains aloof, only finding emotional and sexual release in the company of another loner – the boy in the neighbouring room who has just heard that his mother has died. It is suggestive that it is directly after the hours spent with this boy that Morvern suddenly forces Lanna to accompany her inland, as if his final words to her, 'I have to go back', present her with a prospect she cannot bear, and drive her onward into the unknown.

How Morvern's identity shifts as she travels is of course central to any interpretation of the film, and commentators have tended to agree that the readiness with which she quits her Scottish supermarket job after taking more leave than she is entitled to (she summarizes the job's value to Lanna in the words 'fuck work') adds up to a *flight* from identity – at least of the socially recognized kind. Mazierska and Rascaroli, reading Morvern as a postmodern traveller who 'does not change identity but plays with it – more precisely, she plays with tourism and tourist identities' (Mazierska and Rascaroli 2006: 194) – conclude that she develops an identity equivalent to 'that of the non-tourist, almost of a resident or of a guest of the community', but that even this is 'only one more form of playing' in so far as it 'does not seem to be final and stably adopted by her' (Mazierska and Rascaroli 2006: 197). Lucy Bolton's Irigarayan reading of the film, taking off from the similarity of the words READ ME on James's computer screen to the instructions to Lewis Carroll's Alice in *Alice in Wonderland*, on a cake and a bottle of magic potion, respectively, to EAT ME and DRINK ME, interprets Morvern as an Irigarayan Alice' who 'steps through the looking glass of convention and social identity into a realm of speechless sensory immersion' (Bolton 2011: 150). This is utterly convincing, but while I entirely agree with Bolton about Morvern's 'lack of attachment to her identity and her life' (Bolton 2011: 152), and the emotional distance conveyed in the blank expressions with which she meets questions and sometimes stares at the camera, the aspect of Morvern that seems to me to account best for her inscrutable remoteness is the negativity of the desire propelling her forward, at first in space and time and then, once she has seen the barren yet beautiful Spanish interior that meets her desire for a simple pleasure-driven existence, just in time. Revealingly, her explanation to Lanna of why she is leaving Scotland for good is 'I'm going again': she does not say 'I'm going back', which would construct the Spanish province of Almeria as an undiscovered paradise or Shangri-La, but draws attention, with the word 'again', to the compulsive force of her wish to escape familiar surroundings and a socially recognized identity. As Bolton says of the stage of Morvern's journey that follows her separation from Lanna, Morvern is quite content to communicate non-verbally with the Spanish speakers she meets: 'There is no pressure of recognition, no demands upon her – she need not speak, as she will not be understood.... The emphasis here is on the immediacy and simplicity of these experiences, the lack of words, the lack of responses required' (Bolton 2011: 163–164) – a symbolically ungrounded life of 'speechless sensory immersion' (Bolton 2011: 150).

There has also tended to be consensus among critics commenting on how *Morvern Callar* translates Warner's first-person novel into visual form, around the view that the film is transformed by Ramsay's sensibility to a degree that makes it 'the sort of adaptation [...] that drives lit-minded (and literal-minded) critics against the wall' (Pride 2002: 5). Ramsay's own view, chiming exactly with Pride's, is that 'The film is quite different from the book, but I think it's truer to Morvern's character than if we stuck on a voiceover to explain everything. I wanted to keep that rawness, the edginess of the book while making this emotional journey. I really tried to distill what I thought was good about it, because here is a man who writes a woman really well' (Pride 2002: 6). Like Mazierska and Rascaroli, who emphasize Morvern's multi-sensory experience of places and landscapes captured by Ramsay's *mise en scène* and cinematography (Mazierska and Rascaroli 2006: 196–197) – Morvern touches the sandy Spanish earth, the twigs and buds of a tree on the Scottish moorland, and a maggot nestling in a rotting carrot in the supermarket – Pride alights on emotional subjectivity as the dominant technique employed to convey Morvern's character.[3] Bolton's reading of the film extrapolates both this multi-sensoriness and Morvern's subjectivity by drawing on Irigaray's essay on the caress in *An Ethics of Sexual Difference* and Laura U. Marks' *The Skin of the Film: Intercultural Cinema, Embodiment and the Senses*, maintaining that 'an alternative philosophical and phenomenological environment' is established by this Irigarayan Alice in her wonderland beyond the logocentric specular economy (Bolton 2011: 151). From her 'visceral and non-verbal' reactions to James' suicide (Bolton 2011: 154) to the series of gestures of communion with the natural environment that follow her burying of the pieces of his body, and the enchanted ease with which she moves through the Spanish landscape, Morvern's sensory and sensual contact with the world, both tactile and auditory, is repeatedly returned to, and – unlike Warner's novel, which closes with Morvern returning to Scotland penniless and pregnant after having spent all James's money – is the note on which Ramsay chooses to end her film. As Bolton says of this out-of-time club scene where Morvern is listening to 'Dedicated to the One I Love' on her Walkman headphones, 'She has removed all the trappings of everyday life that conventionally constitute a social identity – name, job, home, friends, conversation, routine – and immersed herself into a physical environment which occupies her on a sensory level' (Bolton 2011: 165). Ramsay's decision to end her film with this scene both confirms how Morvern's subjective sensory experience has dominated it, and gives the narrative a distinct feminist twist missing from Warner's novel and noted by Mazierska and Rascaroli when they remark that the change 'reflects her unwillingness to constrain her heroine by domesticity or any other factor' (Mazierska and Rascaroli 2006: 198).

Despite admiration for the Irigarayan and Marksian framework with which Bolton demonstrates so convincingly that *Morvern Callar* is a film *about* sensory

---

[3]'Ramsay and recurrent cinematographer Alwin Kuchler construct a remarkable emotional subjectivity, a shimmering use of focus and focal length that disorient our perception at just the right moment. You get the sensation of presence and absence, admiring how she can capture just how it feels to *be* in a room' (Pride 2002: 6).

experience, an aspect of her reading I find unconvincing is its emphasis on the preservation of memory. She takes this from questions Irigaray poses in the essay 'Fecundity of the Caress' in *An Ethics of Sexual Difference*, 'how … can we remember flesh? How can we preserve the memory of touching?' (Bolton 2011: 148), declaring that the latter is 'the problem that *Morvern Callar* attempts to answer' (Bolton 2011: 148). In large part because of Morvern's inscrutable muteness and facial inexpressivity, there is little in the film after her caressing of James's dead body to suggest that she is mourning him at all, let alone that her journey 'is about establishing a communion with her dead lover' (Bolton 2011: 148). Rare flashes of emotion cross Morvern's face in the scene in the Spanish hotel where she has sex with the young grieving man, indicating that the act may mark the end of a period of grieving of her own, but even this is arguable. Attempted communion with her dead lover is an interpretation Bolton suggests of Morvern's muteness (Bolton 2011: 156), but Morvern's move into a largely silent non-logocentric wonderland is necessarily polysemous, and there is no way to be sure that the 'peaceful and undisturbed state of being' (Bolton 2011: 166) offered by Spain and its sensory sunlit or drug-induced realm of touching and hearing is motivated by memories of her lover's flesh. Sue Thornham similarly interprets Morvern as 'a figure of melancholy' (Thornham 2012: 112), but it seems to me that Morvern's rejection of her life in Scotland and its trappings of social identity links more directly to the driven element of her own subjectivity than to emotions or psychology, having more to do with survival than with memory. A view of Morvern offered by Ramsay is that there is something childlike and 'autistic' about her, and that she is above all pragmatic: 'She just takes the survival route. She's very pragmatic. She doesn't even know why she does it, it's almost existentialist. There was an influence of Camus there, *The Stranger*, in that you're not thinking or analysing these acts – you're just doing them' (Pride 2002: 26). This view of Morvern suggests that it is a mistake to read her failure to declare James's death and theft of his authorial identity as part of a philosophically elaborated framework of identity, as grim pragmatism may be more the order of the day. Morvern senses that money and freedom are (quite literally) the way to go, and to interpret her actions as an attempt to preserve the memory of touching her dead lover lessens the separateness of her subjectivity and her aggressive 'survivalist' desire. Morvern's desire, in other words, seems to stem more from her drives than from her emotions, and conforms to the type of death-driven desire that in Irigaray's thinking can contribute to a reorganization of the sexual economies of subjectivity. This reading of her desire is reinforced by the moral puzzles posed by Morvern's flight from social identity (or at least from a sociosymbolically familiar identity), as despite having committed what are strictly speaking criminal offences, the film sees her move into an amoral zone where she remains untouched by the legal consequences of her actions. In view of her femaleness, this zone may correspond to new moral 'territory' acquired for female subjectivity by the reorganization of economies of sexual subjectivity envisaged by Irigaray.

Confronting the patriarch:
Claire Denis's *White Material*

Conflicting desires of manifold kinds structure the diegesis and atmosphere of Denis's *White Material*, shot in 2007 although only released generally in France in March 2010, after over six months on the international festival circuit. Isabelle Huppert plays the film's central character Maria Vial, who is hanging on grimly to the coffee plantation she manages in an unnamed African country, despite its rapid descent into civil war. Also involved in the family business are her ex-husband André (Christophe Lambert) and his father Henri (Michel Subor), seemingly the owner of the plantation: André has a young son, José (Daniel Tchangang) with his second, black wife Lucie (Adèle Ado) as well as Manuel (Nicolas Duchauvelle), the teenage son from his marriage to Maria. The film has a fairly complex temporal structure comprising multiple flashbacks in which it is above all Maria's clothing that identifies the particular moment of the action, so that when we see her take a particular pale pink dress out of her wardrobe and hang it up to be worn the following day, we know the principal, framing flashback will shortly give way to the urgent scenes of violence and destruction with which the film opened, in which Maria tries against all advice to hitch a lift back to the plantation.

Shot in Africa like her first feature *Chocolat* (1988), and her acclaimed drama about the French Foreign Legion *Beau Travail/Good Work* (1998), *White Material* marks Denis's second professional 'return' to the continent at an interval of almost exactly a decade, a regularity she admits she is at a loss to explain.[4] If the politics of French colonialism in Africa were integral to both the first two films, however, then that is not the case with *White Material*, since the historical moment as well as the location of the action is uncertain, and although the warning shouted down to Maria from a French army helicopter to quit her plantation indicates that French forces have been involved in the domestic conflict that is underway, they play no further part in the film. *White Material* grew out of a suggestion made by Huppert to Denis that she adapt Doris Lessing's novel *The Grass Is Singing*, but this would have meant a return

---

[4] *Les Inrockuptibles* 24/03/10.

to the apartheid era Denis was opposed to, and working in an Anglophone African country rather than the Francophone ones familiar to her from the parts of her upbringing in Burkina Faso, Djibouti and Cameroon, since Lessing's novel is about the 1940s in the then-British colony of Southern Rhodesia.[5] One detail pertaining more to Anglophone than to Francophone Africa Denis keeps in the film is the pidgin English from which its title is taken – the phrase 'white material' occurs twice amid French dialogue, referring once (when used by a DJ broadcasting for the anti-government rebels) to the white population itself, and once to a gold-plated cigarette lighter stolen from André Vial by child soldiers, and by extension seemingly to all goods and trinkets belonging to the white population.

Although not 'about' (post)colonialism and, therefore, not thematizing power struggles directly – the critic of the French magazine *Télérama* comments that the film is without heroes, since its characters 'elicit neither admiration nor empathy'[6] – *White Material* is steeped in an atmosphere of tension and violence from its opening darkened frames, an atmosphere owing much to the music of Denis's regular collaborating group *Tindersticks*. Even the many vistas of open, sunlit African landscapes take on a menacing air, as with the exception of the Vials themselves and the two sets of workers who leave the Vial plantation in mid-harvest, most movement is associated with violent intent – such as the two young boys André sees loitering in the bushes near the plantation's makeshift swimming pool, apparently about to attack Manuel. (When Manuel sets off barefoot into open country shortly afterwards in what seems like an ill-advised act of bravado, the two boys track his movements before assaulting and stripping him, a hostility with which the reddish-orange earth and scrub vegetation seems impregnated.) Although little violent action is seen – for example, Denis elides the central moments of the assault on Manuel, who is filmed only before then after it, naked and on his knees – the effects and results of violence pervade the film, palpable in fear, injury and increasingly urgent movement.

Denis's main co-writer on *White Material* was the half-Senegalese but French-born novelist and playwright Marie NDiaye, whose work she says appeals to her because of its lack of compassion and sense of community, 'its gentle and comical sense of brutality'.[7] In interviews describing how Denis and NDiaye collaborated on the film's screenplay, it is evident that no notion

---

[5]Asked directly by a Parisian interviewer whether *White Material* is 'a film about the postcolonial situation', Denis replies simply 'I don't think so' [Je ne crois pas], *Les Inrockuptibles* 24/03/10.
[6]*Télérama* 24/03/10.
[7]To Denis, NDiaye's language is beautiful because of its lack of the 'compassionel' or 'sociétal', 'La Brutalité douce de Marie NDiaye', interview with Denis by Jean-Marc Lalanne, *Les Inrockuptibles* 18/08/09.

of narrative closure – an event that would resolve the multiple overlapping tensions set up by the factionalism of the political situation depicted – governed how they worked; in other words, that the film's meaning lies more in its crescendo of tension and violence than in the outcome of any of the crescendo's narrative threads. The style in which these threads are woven together might be termed 'circular', as the film repeatedly returns to significant characters and locations at different, largely though not exclusively chronologically ordered moments: the best example of this is probably the narrative thread concerning the Boxer (Isaach de Bankolé), a leader of rebel forces whose dead body is picked out by a searchlight in the opening shots of the film and who is subsequently shown wounded (he has been shot in the stomach) and increasingly unable to move around. Every time Denis's camera alights on the Boxer except the first in the film's principal flashback, when he is still able to mount a horse to ride away from a church littered with stinking corpses, he is supine: although a powerful, muscled man whose body recalls those of the legionnaires in *Beau Travail* (and de Bankolé has of course acted for Denis previously, as the house servant Protée in *Chocolat* as well as in *S'en fout la mort/No Fear No Die* (1990)), he is immobilized by his injury and the pain it is causing, his physical power on display and yet stymied, lacking any outlet.

The collaboration of two women on the writing of *White Material*, combined with its repetitive, downwardly-spiralling narrative structure and prevalence of supine or passive male bodies (Henri's as well as the Boxer's, as I shall detail shortly), leads me to contend that death-driven female desire of the kind theorized by Irigaray is at work in the film's composition and 'textuality'. A meaningful reading of *White Material* concerning desire and agency can be built upon the way Denis deploys bodies in her film, in which sexual difference figures strikingly, in the difference of actively desiring female bodies (particularly Maria/Huppert's) from the majority of passive male bodies populating the film. It is, I suggest, this dynamic of sexually differentiated desire that intensifies to produce the act of extreme violence Maria commits as her plantation is destroyed around her. Commentators on *White Material* to date have either glossed over her brutal murder of Henri Vial or, seemingly troubled by the difficulty of accounting for it, have interpreted it as committed in a moment of madness or psychosis. Such interpretations not only overlook a perfectly coherent reading of how conflicting desires and different modes of agency can overlap to produce acts of extreme violence that precisely do *not* resolve the tense and violent situations in which they arose (there is nothing cathartic about the closing scenes of *White Material*, in which the charred body of Maria's son Manuel is glimpsed just before she clubs Henri's neck from behind with a machete), but they undermine any enabling, constructive interpretation of female desire and subjectivity in Denis's film. Maria may strike Henri a fatal blow with a machete, but as a channel for the intense yet threatened desire to stay in Africa and farm the plantation she has tenaciously exhibited throughout the film, this is a perfectly explicable rather than an incoherent, 'mad' or psychotic act.

The casting of Isabelle Huppert as Maria Vial was a core element of the screenplay Denis and NDiaye crafted for *White Material*, because, as noted above, Huppert was a collaborator on the project from the start. Huppert's slight and even scrawny physiognomy was, therefore, essential to the obstinate, tireless, defiant – perhaps also blind and deluded – character Maria Vial became. Although she displays a frailty that some commentators have viewed as pitiful feebleness,[8] it is clear that Denis saw great strength and resilience in the incessant activity with which she is associated in the film, since she describes 'women like Maria' in the following terms:

> Despite only having the build of a wisp of straw, they are very strong, they make sound decisions … It's impossible to shift them an inch. And this tenacity was in a way the subject of the film.[9]

Maria is filmed running through long grass, and riding a moped through the bush with her hands free of the handlebars and her arms high above her head. She drives jeeps at speed along dirt tracks and tractors on more uneven ground (Figure 7.2): she is by far the most mobile body in the film, in direct contrast to Manuel's habitual idleness and the unspecified sickness of Henri that appears to keep him housebound. Her slightness, emphasized by the girlish dresses and gingham shirts she wears, also contrasts strikingly with the physiognomy of most of the male characters in the film – Subor/Henri, whose corpulent frame has featured in *L'Intrus/The Intruder* and more recently *Les Salauds/Bastards* as well as *Beau Travail*, de Bankolé as the Boxer of whom actor Alex Descas says 'He carries the suffering of an entire continent on his own',[10] and the lazier mode of muscularity possessed by Christophe Lambert and Nicolas Duchauvelle.[11] The cumulative effect of these distinctive modes of desire and embodiment enacted just by Huppert is to associate female subjectivity with

---

[8]For example, Asibong (Spring 2011), 154–167 (160–161).

[9]'La Brutalité douce de Marie NDiaye', interview with Denis by Jean-Marc Lalanne, *Les Inrockuptibles* 18/08/09.

[10]'A lui seul, la douleur d'un continent', Descas in Danièle Heymann, 'Politiquement incorrect. L'Afrique comme on ne l'a jamais vu', *Marianne* 20/03/10.

[11]Adrien Gombeaud observes that Subor and Lambert share the same 'wild, tired beauty' [beauté fauve et fatigue] and that Duchauvelle has a 'worrying brutality' [sauvagerie inquiétante], 'Naufrage en pleine brousse', *Les Echos* 24/03/10.

agency, work and production, and male subjectivity with idleness, selfish self-protection, and even defeatism. The solitariness of Maria's defiant stand against a patriarchal economy of subjectivity is summarized in the shot of her alone on the orange dirt road that leads to the Vial plantation towards the end of the film, her diminutiveness emphasized by her pale pink dress and the light skip with which she starts to walk towards the village.

FIGURE 7.2 *Maria driving a tractor on the plantation,* White Material

The contrast of Maria's driven desire and tenaciously active female subjectivity with male bodies all connoting modes of passivity is not enough on its own to make sense of Maria's violent murder of her ex-husband's father, however, and in my view, a second thread of meaning relating to property ownership and the land is also important. Maria is never clearly identified as the paid manager of the Vial plantation, despite fulfilling every aspect of this role, while André, who unlike Henri, Maria and Manuel does not live in the unfinished luxury dwelling the family has obviously aspired to build at a better moment in their economic fortunes, offers advice without it being clear in what capacity he is doing so. Because André favours abandoning the plantation to the civil war and returning to live in France, he attempts to sell it to the village mayor, Chérif, who tries to persuade him the violence has rendered it worthless. Henri, however, refuses to supply the signature required by the document of sale, suggesting that he still has part if not sole ownership of the plantation and all its buildings. The relationships of André, Maria and Manuel to the plantation, as place and as property, could not be more different, as it is only Maria, who says 'I have nowhere else to go', for whom it is a unique and irreplaceable home. Her link to the land also appears quite different from André's, as her desire to get the coffee crop harvested seems to owe as much to respect for the earth and its produce as to economic need or calculation (Maria is the only family member we see working with her temporary labourers to achieve this). Looked at in this light as well as from the angle of her differently desiring attitude to the situation in which she finds herself, there is a logic in Maria's brutal murder of Henri. By killing him she may become sole owner of the plantation that is the only place she feels she belongs, and her possessive yet also grimly pragmatic attachment to 'home' has no other outlet. Maria is, of course, in an extremely emotional state in the closing scenes of *White Material*, when she is seen sobbing on the shoulder of a native woman out of desperation to return to the plantation (it is the mayor Chérif who takes pity on her and transports her there), but this reinforces my interpretation of her act of violence rather than undermining it. In insisting that Maria's murder of her ex-husband's father is an explicable consequence of her sexually differentiated desire rather than a mad or psychotic act, I am of course in no way condoning her violence; the purpose of making a reading of *White Material* that stays close to narrative in so far as it supplies an account of the film's structure and the embodied actions of its characters, has been to offer an account of the unusual subjectivity of its principal character, Maria Vial, whose tenacity and violence correspond to the driven, brutally pragmatic kind of female desire Irigaray suggests may reorganize economies of sexual subjectivity in favour of women.

Authority and the masquerade in Catherine Breillat's *Sex Is Comedy*

Sex Is Comedy, Breillat's ninth film, is above all a self-reflexive meditation on her working methods as a director, and particularly as a director of explicit sex scenes: the film being shot, *Scènes Intimes*, resembles Breillat's previous film *Fat Girl* (2001). In its self-reflexivity *Sex Is Comedy* bears a resemblance to Truffaut's *La Nuit américaine/Day for Night* (1973) and a stronger one to Abbas Kiarostami's *Through the Olive Trees* (1994), itself a meditation on his

And Life Goes On… (1992). In a sense the film is an autofiction like Masson's *Why (not) Brazil?*, in which the central character is Breillat's fictional incarnation Jeanne, impressively played by Anne Parillaud in what the actress herself says was her best experience of *being* directed since Luc Besson's 1990 film *Nikita* (Frappat and Lalanne 2002: 36). Breillat's interviewers in *Cahiers du cinéma* call it self-portraiture (Frappat and Lalanne 2002: 34), and Breillat herself says 'To begin with, I thought I would be making a film like *La Nuit américaine*. I didn't imagine the dimension of self-portraiture' (Frappat and Lalanne 2002: 37). However, *Sex Is Comedy* is far from being a conventional autofiction, as the film does not concentrate on the character resembling Breillat, as a conventional autofiction would do, and its narrative is limited to one episode, the shooting of the film *Scènes Intimes*. The aspects of Breillat it draws out and lingers on are her desire to direct and the agency with which she does so – the intensity of her wish to convey explicit sex to audiences intelligently, and the investment she has as a creative artist in cinema. This is confirmed particularly at the end of the film, when the central, most taxing scene of *Scènes Intimes* is 'in the can', and Jeanne is relieved and happy, even reservedly jubilant, and is pictured warmly embracing the Actress (Roxane Mesquida), also her leading actress in *A ma soeur!*, and then energetically eating a banana amid her assembled crew.

My contention here is that Breillat's representation of the directing of desire in *Sex Is Comedy* offers a *mise en scène* of the enacting of desire (the drives) in a context where the activity *is* representation, and, vitally, artistic representation of which a woman is in charge. The clashes between Jeanne and her male lead (Grégoire Colin) are an important dramatic focus of the film and illustrate the politics of desire represented in Breillat's *mise en scène* of female directing: the relationship between Jeanne and the Actor stands in for Breillat's tussle with male authority in the film industry, and examining closely how it is represented can add to this chapter's readings of aggressively desiring screen women. In *Sex Is Comedy*, a gender ontology appears to govern feminine and masculine identities, with the roles of the Actress and Jeanne starkly opposed to those of the Actor and Jeanne's assistant director Leo (Ashley Wanninger). But these fixed identities – or at least, the masculinity of the Actor and the authority attaching to it – is shown to be a masquerade by the fact that for the central scene being filmed, in which the Actor takes the virginity of the Actress (a repetition of the first *scène intime* between Fernando and Elena in *Fat Girl*), he has to wear a prosthetic penis, a prop that is both taken seriously and mocked by Jeanne's cast and crew. In the section of *Gender Trouble* titled 'Lacan, Rivière and the Strategies of Masquerade', Judith Butler suggests two very different interpretations of Lacan's analysis of Joan Rivière's essay 'Femininity as Masquerade', which she glosses as follows: 'On the one hand, masquerade may be understood as the performative production of a sexual ontology, an appearing that makes itself convincing as a "being"; on the other hand, masquerade can be read as a denial of a feminine desire that presupposes some prior ontological femininity regularly unrepresented by the phallic economy' (Butler 1990: 47). Butler suggests that the first interpretation would 'engage a critical reflection on gender ontology as parodic (de)construction and, perhaps, pursue the mobile possibilities of the slippery distinction between "appearing" and "being"' (Butler 1990). It is just such a critical reflection that my reading of *Sex Is Comedy* will affirm – that the phallic mastery that takes the Actress's virginity is a masquerade, an 'appearing that makes itself convincing as a "being"' (Butler 1990: 47).

From the start of filming in *Sex Is Comedy*, Jeanne is limping around the set due to a foot injury that has put her foot in plaster. The injury is shrouded in mystery and apparently symbolic of Oedipally disadvantaged femininity, since when asked, Jeanne says it is not she that has broken her ankle, but her ankle 'that broke itself. It's the metaphor of the film'. As already stated, the focus of drama in *Sex Is Comedy* is the filming of scenes of intimacy between the Actress and the Actor, and interspersed with Jeanne's instruction of her actors in the movements and gestures that will produce the emotion she wants are a series of *tête-à-tête* conversations with the Actor in which she coaxes, cajoles and bullies him into a convincing performance. In these dialogues she is outspoken to the point of being insulting, and tyrannically insistent on sex being acted as *she* sees it. She bans 'male larking about' [*plaisanteries d'homme*] from the sacred place that is her set, refuses the Actor's own interpretation of himself as 'timid', and lambasts the 'moral ugliness' of an actor who performs with his body but not with his soul. The Actor is subjected to a demeaning comparison with the Actress, to which he retorts that she is no good, and that he is only interested in himself as a unique individual. This – not incidentally an endorsement of the conventional Enlightenment model of autonomous male subjectivity – is precisely the sort of male behaviour Jeanne will not indulge, and although she continues to respond to the Actor's pleas for attention (she frequently puts her arm around his waist or shoulders and walks off into the wings with him to talk things through), she will not engage in any flattery of his narcissism. She complains to Leo that the Actor is 'arrogant… terribly arrogant', and, when the Actor apparently tries to sabotage the smooth running of the 'deflowering' scene by turning Jeanne and her leading lady against one another, claiming that the Actress will not perform nude since it is not in her contract (although in the event she complies uncomplainingly), Jeanne tells him he is egoistic, vain, irresponsible and lacking in professional conscience. The Actor has said several times that he only puts up with Jeanne's authoritarianism because he is getting well paid, and now she throws his words back at him: 'Actors are very well paid for what they do because it's very hard. There, that's it'.

The passionate and often selfish involvement in her film displayed by Jeanne in *Sex Is Comedy* – to prepare for the shooting of the deflowering scene, she expels the entire crew except Leo from the bedroom set for an hour-and-a-half, to allow her the solitary concentration she says artists and writers like her need – reveals aggressive and unyielding desire, a desire to prevail over masculine authority. The Actor character played by Grégoire Colin is in many ways an Everyman figure with the added sensitivity one would expect of a beautiful man – one who on this occasion must act out a woman's vision. The dialogues and relationship between Jeanne and the Actor have an unmistakably symbolic dimension: far more than just a reenactment of a 'war of the sexes', they show uninhibited female aggression towards a male 'artist', an altered sexual economy in which the desire of a woman director is successfully sublimated, and finds its expression in the realization of *her* film. As will be clear by now, I am suggesting that *Sex Is Comedy* dramatizes the altered economy of the death drives called for by Irigaray. Feminine sexualities under the sway of the death drive, along with their association with (self-) destructive impulses, with the drive to repeat and to return to immobility, and with sadism and masochism, often figure in Breillat's cinema, perhaps particularly in the person of *Romance*'s Marie, but also in *A Real Young Girl* and *Nocturnal Uproar*. In *Sex Is Comedy* Breillat achieves a rare degree of reflexivity about the relationship of female sexuality to artistic creation (in this case, film directing). The relationship between female director and male actor that occurs in this context may well draw on Breillat's own experience of directing, but whether it does or not, it is fascinatingly suggestive about uncharted routes of women's desire. Through an 'autofictional' *mise en scène* of her own direction of desire that viewers can recognize from her previous film, Breillat shows women's film directing to be a tussle and a struggle involving an altered sexual economy, a redistribution of men's and women's death drives that allows a female director's desire to be successfully sublimated in the creation of her film.

In this chapter I have discussed four films of the early and late 2000s that feature a particular type of female protagonist, a woman who behaves with an unusual degree of aggression in the pursuit either simply of survival or of the goals of escape and independence. Maria of *White Material* and Jeanne of *Sex Is Comedy* also violently desire proprietorial control (of a coffee plantation and a film, respectively). It is at least in part these women's circumstances that drive them to behave as they do, produce their incessant bodily activity and put them in questionable moral territory, but my point is precisely that they inhabit a zone in which, according to Irigaray, the symbolic and social reorganization of sexuate desire is taking place, and a modification of the economy of masculine subjectivity going on. As I wrote at the start of the chapter, the fact that a patriarchal economy of subjectivity is also the upholder and guarantor of masculinist *moral* values is more a Beauvoirean than an Irigarayan emphasis, but the explicability by feminist theory of these women's extreme and violent behaviour suggests that their challenge to conventional 'civilized' (patriarchal) morality might just represent the beginnings of a new and *sexuate* ethical and moral order.

8

Freedom

Freedom is a concept central to existentialist thought, and the struggles Sartre underwent, from the 1940s onwards, in order to formulate a satisfactory account of human freedom – a trajectory that leads from *Being and Nothingness* (1943) to at least the *Critique of Dialectical Reason* (1960) – are familiar to scholars in the field. The 'new wave' of scholarship on Simone de Beauvoir that began in the early 1980s, in which the supporting role to Sartre's philosophical work that Beauvoir had insistently adopted throughout her life began to be questioned and unpicked, and she was re-interpreted as a philosopher in her own right by a number of commentators, gathered pace after her death in 1986.[1] As suggested in earlier chapters, Beauvoir's identity as a phenomenologist is to the fore in most of these writings, and her relationships with the other chief proponents of existential phenomenology – its founder Edmund Husserl, and Merleau-Ponty, who had studied Husserl's unpublished papers in Louvain in the late 1930s, and whose *Phenomenology of Perception* was published in 1945 just as Sartre and Beauvoir set up *Les Temps modernes* – are under scrutiny.

Freedom is one of the concepts focused on in this post-1980 wave of Beauvoir scholarship, because what emerged from close attention to Beauvoir's 1940s writings was an understanding of freedom not at all in thrall to Sartre's, a much more material and embodied notion of freedom closer to the work of Merleau-Ponty than to that of Beauvoir's elected life companion. Leading contributors

---

[1] Sonia Kruks in *Situation and Human Existence: Freedom, Subjectivity and Society* (Kruks 1990), Kateand Edward Fulbrook in *Simone de Beauvoir and Jean-Paul Sartre: The Remaking of a Twentieth-Century Legend* (Fulbrook and Fulbrook 1994), Karen Vitges in *Philosophy as Passion: The Thinking of Simone de Beauvoir* (Vitges 1996), Debra Bergoffen in *The Philosophy of Simone de Beauvoir: Gendered Phenomenologies, Erotic Generosities* (Bergoffen 1997) and Margaret Simons in various essays collected in *Beauvoir and the Second Sex: Feminism, Race and the Origins of Existentialism* (Simons 1999).

to this new strand of Beauvoirean political philosophy were, as mentioned in Chapter 1, Sonia Kruks, in a later book than *Situation and Human Existence* titled *Retrieving Experience: Subjectivity and Recognition in Feminist Politics* (Kruks 2001), and Toril Moi in her 1999 book of essays *What Is a Woman?*. Moi entitles Part I of *What Is a Woman?* 'A Feminism of Freedom' not just, she says, because freedom is 'the fundamental concept in Beauvoir's feminism' (Moi 1999: vii), but because '[c]ontemporary feminist theory has yet to attempt the radical task of rethinking feminism from a vantage point outside the exhausted categories of identity and difference' (Moi 1999: vii). Although this is a view I do not fully share (excellent work on embodied female subjectivity has been done from a Foucauldian perspective, for example),[2] I am sympathetic to the frustration expressed by both Moi and Kruks with the apparent limitations of postmodern feminism. Feminist philosophy's recent return to existential phenomenology has made it possible to speak again about freedom from oppression for women, and to reconsider concepts like 'experience' without its traditional bedfellow, the autonomous humanist subject, a return that has enabled some of the blind spots of postmodern feminism to come into view.

The modified understanding of Beauvoir's political philosophy collectively undertaken by feminist scholars from the 1980s on is charted by Kruks in the first chapter of *Retrieving Experience*, 'Freedoms that Matter: Subjectivity and Situation in the Work of Beauvoir, Sartre, and Merleau-Ponty'. Beauvoir herself insisted throughout her lifetime that philosophically, she 'adhered completely to *Being and Nothingness* and later to *Critique of Dialectical Reason*' (Sicard 1979: 325, quoted in Kruks 2001: 29), and Sartre never acknowledged that Beauvoir had played any part in the modification of his ideas between these two key volumes of his thought – a modification from the absolutist theory of freedom of consciousness as transcendental in the 1943 book to 'a more nuanced position, in which freedom admits of degree and is socially mediated' (Kruks 2001: 30) in the 1960 one. Sartre claimed instead that it was Merleau-Ponty's 1947 collection of essays *Humanism and Terror* that 'obliged him … to move beyond his earlier individualism, and that taught him about such supraindividual aspects of human existence as history and politics' (Kruks 2001: 32), but it can be demonstrated from Beauvoir's writings, in particular the review of Merleau-Ponty's *Phenomenology of Perception* she wrote for the second issue of *Les Temps modernes* in 1945, that Beauvoir 'had grasped the implications of Merleau-Ponty's thought earlier than Sartre, and better' (Kruks 2001: 32). According to Margaret Simons's 1999 study of Beauvoir's unpublished 1927 diary, Beauvoir may even have started to develop her own philosophy of 'the lived' as early as the late 1920s, a time when she already

---

[2]McLaren (2002).

knew Merleau-Ponty and discussed philosophical ideas with him. Tracing the history of the concept of freedom in French thought over the 30-year period from the 1930s is an enormous and complex undertaking of which I can sketch only the briefest outline here, by drawing on Kruks' pioneering work: what is essential to how I am going to deploy the re-evaluation of freedom that emerged in feminist theory from the 1980s on is simply that the concept was entertained at all, amid the dominance in the academic humanities of post-structuralism, postmodernism and contemporary gender and queer theory. Like Toril Moi in *What Is a Woman?*, Kruks argues in an extremely balanced fashion for the interest of 'bringing back freedom', pointing out that any appeal to the concept must be ambivalent ('Resistance? Perhaps, so long as it is local. [...] But freedom? Surely not! Too much violence, too much silencing of others, has taken place in its name' (Kruks 2001: 28)). She indicates the dangers of appealing to freedom but is also right, I think, when she says that 'that is no reason to abandon freedom as a value' (Kruks 2001: 28).

The importance of freedom as a value, for women and all categories of oppressed humans, begs the question of what *forms* of freedom important to feminist politics and practice are more available to women now than in the mid-twentieth century and are also now being explored and represented by female artists. Sexual freedom has to be primary among these, and is a subject that two of the films already discussed in this book – Catherine Breillat's *Romance* and *Brief Crossing* – seem to me to meditate upon. I shall, therefore, now return to *Romance* and *Brief Crossing* in order to bring out how sexual freedom figures in the episodes of the lives of Marie and Alice we see. This will be followed by a reading of the relevance of freedom to Claire Denis's admired 'encounter sketch' *Vendredi soir/Friday Night* (2002), which is also – and not incidentally – one of a number of films taken up by film critics influenced by the 'phenomenological turn' in film theory inaugurated by Vivian Sobchack and Laura Marks in the 1990s and 2000s.[3] The chapter will close with a reading of Céline Sciamma's recent *Bande de filles/Girlhood* (2014).

Enacting sexual freedom in *Romance* and *Brief Crossing*

A concern with freedom seems to lie at the heart of the films of Breillat's *décalogue* (what I have called 'Breillat's dramas of female subjectivity'). It is implied rather than being broached directly, for instance in her studies of

---

[3]'The Phenomenological Turn' was the title of a one-day film studies event organized at Queen Mary University of London on 25 May 2013.

adolescent femininity *A Real Young Girl*, *Virgin* and *Fat Girl*, in their pervasive atmosphere of confinement, and attempted rebellion against that confinement through underage sex. The languours of Alice's (Charlotte Alexandra) summer vacation with her parents on a rural smallholding in *A Real Young Girl* are if anything exceeded by the pain, mistrust and wild behaviour of Lili (Delphine Zentout) in *Virgin*, while in *Fat Girl*, we see polarized if equally rebellious reactions to the bourgeois sexual morality of their parents' marriage from fifteen-year-old Elena and her misfit younger sister Anaïs. A lack of freedom can also be seen in Fredérique's confinement in heterosexual relations in *Perfect Love!* (1996) and the disability afflicting the autofictional character of Maud in *Abuse of Weakness* (2013). In *Romance*, freedom is explicitly signalled as an issue in gender relations by Marie at her first meeting with Paolo, when she pretends to him that she is married in order, she says, that he should know that she isn't free. ('That way he knows that I'm not free. Because I'm not free' (Breillat 1999a: 34). Marie is in love with Paul rather than married to him, but for her, sex with Paolo will be the equivalent of an extramarital affair.) In addition to the insistent, rebellious speech shown to be characteristic of Breillat's female protagonists in Chapter 5, her characters explore the limits of their relationships with men through their acts, dramatized in *Romance* in the series of spontaneous sexual encounters Marie engages in on her way out of love with Paul.

The theme of 'a woman's sexual odyssey' (Keesey 2009: 119) treated in *Romance* lends itself to a reading in terms of sexual freedom, and it should be remembered that Breillat 'first conceived of the idea for *Romance* and even wrote a synopsis of the film in the late 1970s' (Keesey 2009: 119), in the wake of the radical changes to sexual mores brought about by 1960s sexual liberation and 1970s feminism. Breillat may be seen as picking up the threads of Beauvoir's discussion of sexual freedom in the last chapter of *The Second Sex*, in the pages she devotes there to woman's 'sexual vocation' (Beauvoir 2009: 743–752). A continuity between Beauvoir's and Breillat's approaches to female sexual subjectivity is observed by Liz Constable in an article that focuses particularly on *Romance*, in which Constable maintains that *Romance* 'addresses most explicitly the alienation and estrangement from self that [Breillat] sees as an impediment, social in origin, to young women's explorations of sexual subjectivity and intimacy' (Constable 2004: 2). In the published screenplay to *Romance*, Marie's alienated status at the start of her odyssey is evidenced in the words 'At this moment in her story, Marie exists in her own eyes only as Paul's Woman' (Breillat 1999: 30). Refused all intimacy by Paul, it is only through her encounters with Paolo, Robert and the nameless 'man on the stairs' that Marie will counter the alienated femininity imposed on her by Paul, and begin to construct a sexual subjectivity that allows her intimacy and pleasure.

FIGURE 8.1 *Marie and Paolo have sex and talk*, Romance. *Permission to reproduce granted by Flach Film*

The literary and
the moral // creative
and
critical

It is because Beauvoir is a novelist as well as an essayist, and includes in *The Second Sex* lengthy passages from novels, biographies and other writings that illustrate her arguments about women's condition and unrealized possibilities, that Constable can claim an affinity between Beauvoir's and Breillat's understandings of the importance of images in enabling women to live sex lives unimpeded by society's non-acknowledgement of their desire. According to Constable, Breillat 'is using the filmic medium to refine Simone de Beauvoir's understanding of the constitutive links between the words and images representing women's sexuality....and young women's emerging experiences of sexual subjectivity and erotic intimacy' (Constable 2004: 3). 'Breillat argues cinema could, and should, be formative for young women, and that its images should play a generative role for them as sexual subjects' (Constable 2004: 4). It is because contemporary cinema rarely rises to this challenge that Breillat's scenes and images of consciously lived, free female desire (Marie's visit to the all-night bar where she encounters Paolo, and her explorations of BDSM sex in Robert's apartment) are important for the film's female spectators. For Breillat just as it was for Beauvoir, sexuality is a matter of representation as well as of lived experience (Figure 8.1), an issue shown particularly powerfully in *Romance* in the ritualistic, staged scenes of bondage Marie engages in with Robert. A theatricality acknowledged by Robert ('it's a theatre, you see, there's a rostrum, a stage in fact, I rehearse' (Breillat 1999a: 46–47)) is emphasized in the *mise en scène* of these scenes; dark brown and scarlet are the predominant colours, and Marie adopts highly staged poses she then starts to repeat unthinkingly on her return to Paul's apartment. (When she places her clenched fists to either side of her head in front of him, he recognizes that she is posing without understanding the meaning of her gestures (Breillat 1999a: 63).) Paradoxically, since the poses she adopts are of constriction and confinement (Figure 8.2), Robert's apartment is for Marie a space of freedom and enabling fantasy in which she is guided into an expanded sense of her own subjectivity.

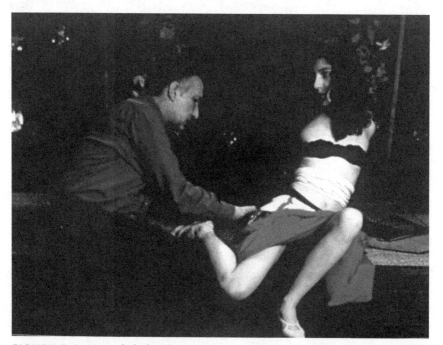

FIGURE 8.2 *Marie feels freedom,* Romance. *Permission to reproduce granted by Flach Film*

It is between the first and second scenes of bondage in Robert's apartment that Marie engages in the freest and riskiest sexual encounter of her odyssey, an offer of oral sex in return for money she accepts because it approaches her quest for 'raw desire' (Breillat 1999a: 57). For Beauvoir too, freedom is always linked to risk, a theme Beauvoir mentions at a number of points in *The Second*

Sex. Although Marie's encounter appears to turn sour when the shady-looking stranger who has approached her shifts from giving Marie oral sex into penetration by force from behind, turning her over violently and refusing to pay her in an explicit verbal denial of the freedom of her desire ('Slut, you have no choice'), it represents the limit point of Marie's odyssey, an act that distresses her but for which she shows no regret. As Constable points out,

> Breillat's films, like Beauvoir's writings, have often stirred indignant, angry responses from viewers and critics on the ground that both portray what critics most frequently designate as emotionally and sexually masochistic female subjects. In order to address these critics' misgivings, we have to ask whether such representations of female desire do not open up unimagined ways of understanding sexual subjectivity and erotic relationality. (Constable 2004: 4)

Marie's encounter with the stranger on the stairs above Paul's apartment ends up seeming closer to rape than to any kind of eroticism, but – like the raw, unemotional first experience of penetrative sex wished for by Anaïs in *Fat Girl* – is only ambivalently experienced by her as such. Breillat's demonstration of the extremity of Marie's desire and her uninhibited exercise of it extends the image repertoire upon which the film's female spectators can call to expand their understanding of their and other women's sexual subjectivity.

A further link between Beauvoir's and Breillat's explorations of freedom seen in *Romance* (and one developed in *Brief Crossing*) is its intersubjective character, which clearly distinguishes the vision of social relations Beauvoir developed in the 1940s from the one Sartre adhered to at the time. As Kruks explains, Beauvoir ended her 1944 essay *Pyrrhus et Cinéas* 'by putting in question [Sartre's] fundamentally conflictual theory of social relations' (Kruks 2001: 35). 'Although freedoms are separate, Beauvoir argues that they are also, paradoxically, instrinsically interdependent...Freedom for Beauvoir, far more than for Sartre at this time, involves a *practical* subjectivity, the ability of each of us to act in the world so that we can take up each other's projects and give them a future meaning', something only feasible in an 'equal social field for action' disallowed by Sartre's theory of mutually hostile competing consciousnesses (Kruks 2001: 35). If subjectivity is intersubjectively constituted for Breillat as it is for Beauvoir, as Constable maintains when she says that 'Breillat points us to the indispensable primacy and temporal priority of the other in the development of female sexual subjectivity' (Constable 2004: 4), and 'implicitly [positions] relationality prior to subjectivity through her emphasis on developing a "vision of oneself"' (Constable 2004: 5), this suggests that Marie's adult subjectivity is formed through the series of very different sexual encounters seen in the film. Intimate exchange is either lacking from most of these or resisted by Marie (when offered by Paolo), but develops alongside the exploration of her sexuality she undertakes under Robert's guidance. Robert becomes a friend as well as a sexual partner, as he and Marie dine together after her visits in an 'intimate and festive' Russian restaurant (Breillat 1999a: 62) whose decor resembles his theatrically designed apartment. This brief scene is perhaps the only one in *Romance* where Marie is evidently having fun: she drinks vodka and observes (in her monologue) that she has become emotionally attached to Robert. Robert and Marie's mutual attachment is confirmed when he takes up Paul's place by Marie's hospital bed at the birth of her son, although he is absent – and there is no place for a father – in the following shot of Marie as newly fulfilled mother, surrounded by flowers.

Since Marie has now become a mother, many forms of freedom are no longer available to her, but freedom has been the touchstone of the sexual odyssey she has undertaken to reach independence and motherhood. We understand that she will bring her joylessly conceived baby up alone, but that her life will not be devoid of intimacy and pleasure as cohabitation and co-parenting with Paul would have been, since the reign of patriarchal masculinity represented by his oppression has given way to an unknown future, and Robert may continue to be a regular sexual partner. A 'queered' or post-patriarchal vision of the family is hinted at by the final images of *Romance*, and this coincides with the 'accomplishment' (Breillat 1999a: 74) of Marie's sexual subjectivity brought about through the exercise of her sexual freedom.

The films of Breillat's *décalogue* focus far more on adolescent and adult women than they do on the subjectivities of the male characters who feature in their dramas, but the parts of Georges Deblaches in *Dirty Like an Angel* (1991) and Thomas in *Brief Crossing* offer substantial roles to male actors Claude Brasseur and Gilles Guillain, and sixteen-year-old Thomas is the only sexually inexperienced male in Breillat's cinema who corresponds to the female virgins Alice, Lili, Elena and Anaïs, which is why Claire Clouzot calls *Brief Crossing* the end of Breillat's 'virginity cycle' (Clouzot 2004: 97, 189). Mark Peranson suggests that although *Brief Crossing* is '[a]s conceptually old-fashioned as *Brief Encounter*', it is 'a perfect companion to *Fat Girl*', because in both films, 'the intimate brief crossing of one's first sexual experience is painted as a tortured introduction to the disappointments of adulthood'.[4]

As my discussion of how the look is deployed in the film in Chapter 4 has already suggested, *Brief Crossing* can be read as a drama of male–

---

[4]Peranson (2001: 17).

female intersubjectivity in which Alice abuses Thomas's trust and exploits his freedom: Alice's greater sexual and social experience means that no 'equal social field for action' of the kind implied by Beauvoir's vision of social relations exists between and around them. In other words, if Thomas's 'project' is the construction of an adult sexual subjectivity for himself, this is not a project Alice takes up and affirms – she takes Thomas's virginity and he thus 'becomes a man', but because contact between them is then broken off, no reciprocity or mutually affirming intersubjective relations are established. It would be possible to extend this reading of *Brief Crossing* as a drama of intersubjectivity to consideration of how Alice's and Thomas's freedoms temporarily mesh and affirm one another (for the duration of their affair), but my argument here will focus rather on Alice's subjectivity, and the implications of how she carefully but unkindly takes advantage of Thomas's inexperience. Like *Romance*, *Brief Crossing* can be viewed as being about a woman's exercise of her freedom, but the type of sexual freedom it focuses on is an adulterous adventure only Alice is aware of until the final moments of the film. Indeed, *Brief Crossing* repays being seen as a deliberate reversal of the typical narrative of adultery between an adult man and an inexperienced younger woman, envisioned by the new, non-monolithic female director's look Breillat refers to in her lecture 'On woman and morality in the cinema; on how her physical appearance is exploited and what her place is in film as *auteur*, as actress or as subject' (Breillat 1999b).[5]

Adultery as a type of sexual freedom is a subject Beauvoir treats along with other aspects of women's situation in the 'Social Life' chapter of the second volume of *The Second Sex*, stating at the outset of her discussion 'Marriage, by frustrating women's erotic satisfaction, denies them the freedom and individuality of their feelings, drives them to adultery by way of a necessary and ironic dialectic' (Beauvoir 2009: 607). This frustration and injustice in the patriarchal institution of marriage is the recurrent theme of the diatribe against men Alice delivers to Thomas in the ferry's bar, his patient endurance of which lends her monologue its force. Although an unintended contradiction slips into Alice's fabricated account of how she has left her husband after eight years together (in the bar she says this happened the previous day, whereas in her cabin later on, the interval has become one of three months), neither Thomas nor the film's viewers have any real reason to doubt her sincerity. However, the postponement of the revelation that Alice has lied about her relationship status until the closing minutes of the film makes it impossible for the viewer

---

[5] 'Because our look is different from men's – it isn't monolithic (a point I shall come back to), and it has the privilege of being new. That women have had few opportunities to exercise this look up to now is an enormous advantage for those women now able to (Breillat 1999b: 10).

to adopt a perspective from which s/he may judge Alice's actions. Considered through the lens of the patriarchal moral code Breillat comments on in 'On woman and morality in the cinema ...', Alice is worthy only of condemnation, both for being unfaithful to the husband she says she has left in France and for lying to Thomas about her circumstances. But since the viewer is not party to the knowledge that Alice's circumstances are not what she says they are, s/he is unable to adopt this perspective except in hindsight. For the duration of the narrative of *Brief Crossing*, Alice's moral status is equal if not superior to Thomas's, by virtue of her age and life experience.

Pertinent here too is Breillat's description of Alice's diatribe against men and marriage as 'a factual lie and true in its essence' (Clouzot 2004: 112), as this clearly goes against any inclination to impose a fixed, 'encoded', moral judgement on her lie. In 'On woman and morality in the cinema ...', Breillat comments that 'The world is so preoccupied by women's morality that I find it laughable/A *morality* that needs guard dogs is not a moral code but an oppression. To have any value at all, a *morality* must be free' (Breillat 1999b: 11).[6] These remarks seem to refer primarily to how sexual acts are depicted on screen and to Breillat's predilection for filming sexual initiation, since she follows them with a declaration of her opposition to censorship, but they may equally well be read as meaning that it is time that cinema put women's moral agency on an equal footing with men's. Since the status of screen women has traditionally been reduced to that of object, and – particularly in the stereotypes of the vamp, the *femme fatale* and the pin-up – to that of the 'object of bad desires', women have been culpabilized by cinema and granted only a debased form of humanity (Breillat 1999b: 11–12). As a low-budget film made for television, *Brief Crossing* does not imitate any genre or art films in which the most stereotyped representations of women are to be found, and de-glamorizes both its lead actors, but by effecting a simple reversal of a classic narrative of intergenerational adultery, it allows Breillat to suggest that it is instructive to look at women's acts without judging them according to the fixed codes of traditional sexual morality. Both the epistemological structuring of the film and Breillat's extra-textual comments on it indicate that it is inappropriate to make any judgement of Alice's actions, and that we should, rather, consider them as they are presented to us, as those of a somewhat cynical and bitter married woman unafraid of seizing the opportunity presented to her. Like Marie in *Romance*, Alice exercises sexual freedom outside of her committed relationship, and gets away with it.

---

[6]It should be noted that although I have here translated the French word *morale* by 'morality', Breillat uses the same word as figures in the title of Beauvoir's *An Ethics of Ambiguity*, the French title of which is 'Pour une morale de l'ambiguité'.

Feeling freedom in Claire Denis's
Vendredi soir/Friday Night

Turning now to *Friday Night*, I shall discuss first how it has gained its reputation of being a 'phenomenological' film, before suggesting a reading of it that extends existing interpretations by relating it to the understanding of freedom rediscovered in Beauvoir's philosophical writings and re-evaluated by Kruks and Moi.

Released after Denis's acclaimed study of interpersonal dynamics among the French Foreign Legion in Djibouti *Beau Travail/Good Work* (1999) and the controversially violent horror thriller *Trouble Every Day* (2001), *Friday Night* seemed to some French critics like a 'little' film that could be summed up as an *exercice de style* or exercise in the adaptation of literature (it is based on the eponymous novel by Emmanuèle Bernheim). For feminist critic Judith Mayne and for Martine Beugnet, author of the influential reassessment of cinema as a medium of the senses *Cinema and Sensation*, however, *Friday Night* confirmed Denis as a major contributor to a new, pan-European or global current of film-making privileging rhythm, atmosphere, touch and bodily experience over conventional story-telling and cinematography. Both book and film follow the actions of a woman, Laure, the night before she gives up her Paris apartment in order to move in with her partner, François, who never appears in the film. Forgetting, as she gets into her car to drive to the home of some friends for supper, that Paris is gridlocked with traffic because of a major public transport strike (the setting of Bernheim's novel was an actual such strike that paralyzed Paris during the winter of 1995), Laure is caught up in the lines of cars and inches through them until, following a pragmatic suggestion by the city authorities she has heard on the radio, she gives a lift to a man she does not know, Jean. After making acquaintance almost wordlessly for a while, Laure follows Jean into a bar and then to a hotel room, where they make love. They then go and eat pizza nearby, and return to the hotel for the night. As she leaves the hotel in the morning, Laure runs through the streets back to her car, smiling to herself.

Mayne's reading of *Friday Night* begins by pointing out that the film 'represent[s] a departure for Denis' (Mayne 2005: 117) 'in that it is concerned exclusively with the perceptions of a female protagonist' (Mayne 2005: 118). Beugnet does not explore Laure's femininity, but emphasizes that one of the main difficulties Denis had to deal with in transposing novel to screen was 'the subjectivity built into the text', an aspect Mayne considers as 'the implications of free indirect style for a female protagonist'. (Free indirect style is the mode of narration that allows point of view to move in and out of the minds of characters; '[t]he novel is both inside and outside Laure's consciousness at the same time; she is observed, but she is also the subjective center of the novel' (Mayne 2005: 121).) Beugnet sums up how *Friday Night* skilfully recreates this prevalence of subjectivity, in cinematic rather than literary mode, as follows:

> It is in the singular and evocative description of space and time, and in the way it inscribes the characters within their environment both as physical presence and as observers/perceivers that the film recreates the subjective dimension. (Beugnet 2004: 185)

Although Mayne's reading of Laure's 'transitional' state on this particular Friday evening brings out fully the new autonomy of sensibility she gains from her enclosed, protected car journey through Paris and from her meeting with Jean, and Beugnet's close analysis of Denis's use of dissolves, travelling shots of varying speeds, and extreme close-ups on skin and textured clothing to create a dreamy, timeless Paris and an intimate erotic encounter demonstrate compellingly how *Friday Night* conveys subjectivity as well as touch and atmosphere, neither critic explicitly refers to a phenomenological approach to desire and lived experience. The commentator who does this is Elizabeth Newton, in an analysis suggesting that the film 'enacts a phenomenological reduction, a bracketing out of the usual conditions of its protagonist's existence' (Newton 2008: 17). Newton argues that *Friday Night* as a whole suspends habitual and cultural modes of understanding in the same way that a phenomenological reduction places acculturated existence into parentheses in order to attempt to 'return to the things themselves' (Merleau-Ponty 1962: ix, in Newton 2008: 21). The film quite literally covers an out-of-the-ordinary, transitional night in Laure's life, in that she is between apartments, stuck in a traffic jam and enclosed in her car; the suspended slice of time and space reproduced is perfectly suited to a focus on the non-epistemological, sensory experience of phenomena. Newton's reading also claims to account for a few blatantly anti-realistic moments of Denis's film that have puzzled or frustrated other critics, such as the inexplicable way a silver letter 'S' dances across Laure's field of vision and 'wiggles its way to the end of the silver "16 valve" sign on the back of the [Volvo car waiting in front of hers], so that it reads "16 valves"' (Newton 2008: 24). A Merleau-Pontyan reading of these imaginary visions can account for them because a phenomenological approach to lived experience extends to all perceptions, real or imaginary, and imagined phenomena have equivalent experiential value to physically present ones.

Like Mayne and Beugnet, Newton agrees that the film 'presents the embodied perspective of a female character' (Newton 2008: 25), although not exclusively so, and suggests that the absence of a 'controlling gaze of a male character' (Newton 2008: 26) discourages any tendency on the part of the viewer to objectify Laure's body or particular parts of it. This is certainly true of the scenes of love-making at the hotel, in which the parts of Jean's and Laure's bodies filmed are more often clothed than naked, Laure's torso and upper body are hardly seen (although her head, face and hair are repeatedly returned to), and the camera generally prefers Jean's burly frame to Laure's slighter one. Despite the eroticism created by the close pursuit by Agnès Godard's camerawork of the rhythm of the couple's movements, the atmosphere created is as much one of affection and mutual comfort as of erotic desire, Laure frequently burying her head in the crook of Jean's shoulder as if asking for protection, which he smilingly provides.

Surprisingly, however, neither Newton, nor Beugnet or Mayne link the asymmetrical perspective of *Friday Night* constituted by the prevalent perspective of an embodied female character to the admittedly slender plot shared by film and novel, and particularly, to Laure's behaviour in the film's final sequence. I suggest that it is this affirmation at the level of narrative that makes a reading involving freedom possible. An anxious sense of freedom on Laure's part is detectable in a number of scenes of the film where she is not protected by the shelter of her own flat, car, the hotel or the restaurant: Mayne draws attention to Laure's 'anxiety-ridden state' as she leaves her flat, and how she is 'terrified' when a man knocks at the car window (probably in search of a lift like Jean a little later, though Laure does not realize this at this point) (Mayne 2005: 118, 119). On leaving the car to phone her friends from a call box to tell them she will not make it for dinner, Laure is horrified to find the car gone on her return, realizes she may have been foolish to have left its keys with a man she hardly knows, and (when Jean returns) is even reproached by him for so doing. If anxiety has the upper hand over freedom at these moments of *Friday Night*, however, it seems gradually to give way to an enquiring sense of freedom on Laure's part: when Jean walks away from the car after scaring her by taking the wheel to extricate them from the traffic by reversing at high speed (it is not clear entirely how he manages this, though the manoeuvre certainly brings them to a much quieter, less commercial and less well-lit district of Paris), she hesitates only momentarily before getting out of the car and wandering through back streets to find him again. She walks slowly, and yet a sense of purpose has crept into her movements: she has decided she wants to spend the night with Jean, and the anxiety of her transitional situation and of the uneasy mutual registering of desire that has gone on in the traffic jam has been replaced by a measured yet apparently contented sense of freedom. This continues in the café where she finds Jean, in the hotel they repair to and in the pizza restaurant, where the couple communicate almost wordlessly through looks and smiles.

One of few comments on freedom as an atmosphere attaching to the sensory and sense-led experience Denis and Agnès Godard convey in *Friday Night* occurs in a review for the French newspaper *L'Humanité* titled 'A night of freedom', which concludes 'the way in which formal constraint produces a lovely breath of freedom has rarely been so well felt'.[7] *Friday Night's* atmosphere of freedom can certainly be argued to attach to Jean as well as to Laure, but she is undeniably the film's principal character, and by observing anxiety and freedom just in Laure as she leaves the hotel at dawn to return to her moving day (Jean is still asleep), the final sequence of the film suggests that these existential sentiments pertain more to her female subjectivity than to Jean's. Four or five tracking shots of Laure jogging worriedly along pavements give way to an open shot of a junction where she runs out into the road and, as she rounds the corner, breaks into a smile – of relief, possibly, but of freedom, certainly; no other sentiment can account for Denis's decision to cut short the action of Bernheim's novel before Laure reaches her car, the ambivalent 'vehicle' of freedom in the narrative. If Laure can be said to have chosen her life with François over seeing Jean again, it is a choice indistinguishable from the same bodily desire that led her to the hotel in the first place. This is not a Sartrean freedom of consciousness in spite of situation, but a physical, bodily freedom of movement 'chosen' as it is enacted, felt as it is lived.

Melancholy freedom in Céline Sciamma's *Girlhood*

Céline Sciamma, whose third feature *Girlhood* was first seen at the 2014 Cannes film festival and was released internationally the same autumn, has been one of the most talked-about young French directors of recent years. Her début feature *Waterlilies/Naissance des pieuvres* (2007) focused on the lives of adolescent girls in a Paris suburb not far from the *cité* (inner-city housing estate) featured in *Girlhood*, and her second film *Tomboy* (2011) employed a highly anti-realist aesthetic in order to zoom in on the transgender desires of 10-year-old Zoé/Mickaël, who successfully passes as a boy for some time among the new friends she makes when her parents move house. Sciamma has referred to her three features to date as a loosely conceived trilogy about girls of different ages, but *Girlhood* stands out by being about young black women (evidently the majority in the *cité* they inhabit, although a mixture of skin colours is visible whenever large groups are filmed), by whose dress

---

[7] 'M.G', in *L'Humanité* 11/09/02.

styles and public behaviour Sciamma became fascinated, leading her to audition tens of young hopefuls before finding the foursome on whom her film focuses, Marième/Vic (Karidja Touré), Lady (Assa Sylla), Adiatou (Lindsay Karamoh) and Fily (Mariétou Touré).

As Despoina Mantziari observes in a short article in the women's cinema blog 'Auteuse Theory', *Girlhood* bears comparison with Arnold's *Fish Tank*, as main protagonist Vic drops out of school after repeating the year and failing to be admitted to the year above – although Vic lies to her mother (who works as a cleaner and only makes two brief appearances in the film) about this to avoid questions about how she is spending her time.[8] Like Mia, Vic is just turning 16, but it is not on account of conflict between mother and daughters (she has two younger sisters) that Vic's family is dysfunctional, but due to the punitive regime run by her sole and elder brother Djibril (Cyril Mendy), a friend of the boy with whom Vic engages in her first sexual relationship, Ismaël (Idrissa Diabaté). Through the men and boys he knows in the neighbourhood, Djibril polices Vic's every public action as well as the domestic space they share, her only solace provided by the affection between her and sister Bébé (Simina Soumaré), and by the bond both sisters have with tiny Mini (Chance N'Guessan), apart from her meetings with Ismaël and her membership of the girl gang. She and Lady, Adiatou and Fily spend most of their time together, engaging in casual shoplifting, intimidating other girls into giving them money and booking hotel rooms for the night where they can eat, sleep and party together away from their families. *Girlhood*'s 'set piece' is a scene that takes place one such evening when the four girls lip-synch, sing the lyrics of and dance to Rihanna's 'Diamonds ~~in the Sky~~': the camera caresses their glossy black hair and glowing skin as they move between and around one another in the limited space available in the hotel's double room, capturing their exhilaration and the sense of shared pleasure and solidarity that performing to music creates.

That *Girlhood* is partly about freedom is asserted, in the face of much of the film's action, by its final scene, in which Vic returns to her family's tower block after weeks away working for drug dealer Abou (Djibril Gueye), a period during which she no longer sees Lady, Adiatou and Fily. She buzzes for entry but is unable to reply to the female voice that replies, and after grasping the door's handle with the intention of opening it, lets it close again, and moves away, breaking into sobs. It is a sunny, breezy morning, and vistas of Paris can be seen on all sides of the *cité*: the camera zooms slowly towards one of these,

---

[8]Despoina Mantziari, "Solide mais pas Solitaire': Female Solidarity and Feminist Empowerment in *Girlhood* (*Bande de filles*, Céline Sciamma, 2014), 24/6/15 at www.auteusetheory.blogspot.co.uk (accessed 15 December 2015).

excluding Vic from the frame as it does so. She then moves decisively back into the frame from the right-hand side, and almost as quickly out again to the left, evidently resolved to overcome emotion and move on, though to what she may not know. Since she moves from right to left against the conventional direction of 'progress', as in the symbolically employed tracking shots of Agnès Varda's *Vagabond* (1985) and the memorable last train-borne tracking shot of Michael Haneke's *Le Temps du loup/The Time of the Wolf* (2002), her movement does not suggest hope or optimism, but it does imply that she is choosing freedom of action over stasis and predictable confinement. Only a few weeks previously she opted for sexual freedom in just the same manner, when, buoyed up by winning a street fight with a girl from another gang who had previously 'wasted' Lady (an act that honoured the suggestion of *Victory* in her gang name and restored her group's credibility), she arrived at Ismaël's family home while he was sleeping, and ordered him to undress in readiness for sex, only removing her own clothes afterwards. Grasping sexual freedom in this manner earns her the beating from Djibril that leads her to leave home and work for Abou, as to Djibril and many other men of her acquaintance, female sexual freedom outside marriage is completely beyond the pale, the behaviour of a whore [*pute* or *salope*]. Tellingly, Vic then becomes completely alienated from her femaleness during the weeks she works for Abou, binding her breasts to conceal them in the manner of Brandon Teena in Kimberley Peirce's *Boys Don't Cry* (1999), and exchanging her ultra-feminine red dress, high heels and peroxide blonde wig for a boy's slacks and jogging top as soon as she exits from the parties to which she delivers Abou's customers' drugs. Despite exercising sexual freedom by sleeping with Ismaël, there is no 'space' to continue doing so while she is living at home, and although the sweet-natured Ismaël offers to marry her in order to provide her with another one, Vic does not consider herself suited to accepting the offer, as marriage and children do not feature among her life plans.

That Vic's quest for a free life is more tenacious than many girls of her age is suggested by the rejection of drug dealing as an activity by Lady, Adiatou and Fily when Vic meets them in a hotel room before she leaves home. Dynamics in the girl gang shift after Vic wins the fight Lady lost, with Lady no longer the leader (although Vic does not assume the role either). The dilemma Vic faces about where to live in fact points to the complete lack of space for female subjectivity(ies) in the community she comes from, but although *Girlhood* repeatedly points out the masculine coding of her more aggressive and determined behaviour – she shares a single moment of good-humoured exchange with Djibril after he hears about her winning the fight, and her cross-dressing while working for Abou can be read as a denial of the gender coding observed by his employees (girls deliver and men drive or organize) as well as alienation from her own, female body – the film also gives ample screen time to how girls are able to live their bodies when in all-female company. The most eloquent expression of this, apart from the nights the foursome spend together in hotels (in these scenes, the camera moves steadily across their sleeping bodies to show how much more contented and at peace the girls are as a group than when alone or in mixed company) is probably the highly televisual sequence of a game of American football that opens the film. Here the girls are every bit as protected as in the men's game, their faces mostly obscured by the guards attached to their helmets and their shoulders and legs padded, but the bodies lining up, breaking loose, passing and colliding with one another are unmistakably female in form, and the high spirits the game gives rise to seem enacted differently from the running and punching of the air familiar from men's sports: as the game finishes and the girls walk home as a group, they form a bonded mass inspired and enlivened by their collectivity. As they enter the *cité* their continuous hubbub of chatter diminishes, however, and they fall silent as they pass men and boys congregated in the shadows, a dramatic introduction to the incompatibility of women's self-expression and *cité* territory. Sciamma often films the gang walking along the concrete walkways of the *cité* or through Paris shopping centres in horizontal formation that emphasizes their solidarity, square on from the front or the rear, and the female body is self-consciously framed in a way that the male body is not: apart from during the American football match athleticism is not as much in evidence as in the films discussed in Chapter 3, but Vic and Lady move with a fluid grace that fills the frame, especially as Sciamma uses long shots extremely sparingly throughout the film, preferring medium shots and close-ups that isolate a girl's head and upper torso from any other objects around her. In one remarkable scene shot on the esplanade at La Défense, whose huge arch has become a landmark of 'suburban' Paris since it was constructed in the Mitterrand era, girls display their hip hop dancing in pairs or small groups, and Sciamma's camera focuses on the hips and pelvis of each girl in turn in a manner that emphasizes strength and flexibility rather than desirability: the girls' bellies are not bared, and they dance athletically, for their own pleasure rather than that of others. Lady and Vic are cheered when they add deftly co-ordinated hand movements to their dancing, although this brief vision of sunlit female camaraderie is broken up moments later when Vic spots her sister Bébé out intimidating other girls in behaviour resembling her own, slaps her, and is reminded by Bébé that this disciplinary attitude exactly matches Djibril's surveillance of their movements and action outside the family home.

The most striking element of *Girlhood*'s cinematography, however, must be the way Sciamma employs colour to create a palette dominated by black and blue – with blue connoting melancholy and freedom, and possibly also a meditativeness absent from the film's dialogue but palpable in the many scenes of silent, fluid physical movement. The dress styles of the girls that Sciamma says initially drew her to investigate their lives feature blue denim and black leather heavily, and Vic wears blue sweatshirts and tops to the virtual exclusion of brighter colours (except when clad in the figure-hugging red dress and blonde wig she dons to deliver drugs, and removes as soon as she is back in the car with Abou's driver). Almost every wall in Vic's family's flat is a shade of blue or turquoise, as is the bedding on her and Bébé's beds. On at least two occasions Sciamma transmutes the background against which Vic moves into a surface reminiscent of an abstract blue painting – a lift door opens and closes again so that the line where the doors meet exactly bisects the frame vertically, and the half-landing on one of the *cité*'s concrete staircases where she and Ismaël first kiss is tiled in small, turquoise hexagonal tiles, blue changing to black as the timed lighting goes out, then returning to blue as it is switched on again from elsewhere on the staircase. Blue light shows off black skin and hair to its greatest advantage, which Sciamma exploits fully when the girls sing and dance to Rihanna's 'Diamonds in the Sky' (when Vic is clad in a royal blue dress), without it being evident where the source of this blue light is. *Girlhood* may or may not be a realistic evocation of adolescent life in one of Paris's *banlieues*, but its highly stylized cinematography contrasts utterly with the camerawork and aesthetics of a film like *Fish Tank*, and probably excludes it from the French film genre called *cinéma de banlieue*, unless its stylization is considered to be as dramatically integrated and effective as in a classic of the genre like Mathieu Kassovitz's *La Haine* (1995). Sciamma's film was released only months after Richard Linklater's instant modern classic *Boyhood* (2014), and the English translation of its less-generic French title *Bande de filles* into *Girlhood* (why not *Girl Gang*?) may have been influenced by this proximity, but whereas Linklater's admirable film is really about the entire family of its chief character Mason (Ellar Coltrane), *Girlhood* gives pride of place to Vic and her friends, visually and dramatically, and uses colour, the memorable electronic music of Para One, and stylized cinematography in order to take us into the uncertain world of young black women living in the Paris suburbs. Their futures are entirely unknown, but they inhabit their world with conviction, determination and an unmistakable awareness of the freedom that is theirs to live out.

In this final chapter I began by exploring how an understanding of freedom distinct from Sartre's employment of the concept was rediscovered in Beauvoir's philosophical writings from the 1980s onwards, and exploited by Kruks and Moi in feminist writings that sought to theorize the body, subjectivity and freedom because they had become disenchanted with postmodern feminism's preoccupation with identity and difference, and had 'come to the conclusion that no amount of rethinking of the concepts of sex and gender' (Moi 1999: 4) – as undertaken by contemporary gender and queer theory – could address the *value* of the notion of freedom for women and feminism. Suggesting that sexual freedom is one form of freedom far more available to twenty-first-century women than it was to those of Beauvoir's generation, I examined the sexual freedom exercised by Marie of *Romance* and Alice of *Brief Crossing*, and then the strikingly sensory, sensual feelings of freedom experienced by Laure in Denis's *Friday Night*. In the reading of Sciamma's *Girlhood* that concluded the chapter, I emphasized that it is freedom of movement and action and the powerfully embodied female solidarity of Vic and her friends that gives them the means to combat the patriarchal oppression rife in their Parisian *banlieue*, a struggle conveyed by Sciamma in a stylized 'black and blue' aesthetic of melancholy. Embodied female subjectivities best accounted for by feminist phenomenology have been just as much in evidence in this chapter's readings as in Chapters 3–7, a set of readings I shall now bring together in a brief conclusion, integrating them with the feminist philosophical framework set out in Chapters 1 and 2 as I do so.

Conclusion

Relationality in narrative: Female subjectivity in formation in women's cinema

In Irigaray's critique of the polarization of sexual difference in the philosophy of Levinas in 'Questions to Emmanuel Levinas', she insists that the feminine must be apprehended 'in relation to itself', a point reiterated in different terms by Elena del Rio in her reading of Sally Potter's *Thriller*, when she states that a feminist phenomenological approach to film must start from and focus on screen women as the subjects of their own experience and desire, and differently again by Catherine Breillat when she specifies that sex is the 'subject' rather than the 'object' of her film-making. Approaching screen women *as* subjects entails allowing that approach to be made without the mediation of phallic desire involved in an intra- or extra-diegetic male look, to which the female authorship of all the films I have discussed contributes (without in any way guaranteeing it). Apprehending female subjectivity 'in relation to itself' demands that we conceive of it as relational *from the start*, and sends us back to Irigaray's 'labial feminism', her insistence that female identity is never self-identified, but 'always already two', as figured by the oral/vaginal lips that gave the title to *This Sex Which Is Not One*. It is also significantly in tune with the philosophy of ambiguity set out in Beauvoir's *An Ethics of Ambiguity*, although Beauvoir's book is concerned with 'ambiguous', non-self-identified subjectivity in general rather than only with that of women.

The non-individual, ethical structure of female subjectivity insisted on by Irigaray and implicit in Battersby's privileging of natality has been evident throughout the films discussed in Chapters 3–8 of this book: intimate female friendship entailing bodily closeness and on which agency sometimes

ambi → 'both'

depends is shown in *Morvern Callar* and *Girlhood*, while the wordless dance up and down the sitting room in the penultimate scene of *Fish Tank* dramatizes an unexpected ethical bond between Mia, her mother Joanne and her sister Tyler. With Claire Denis's *White Material*, it was collective creation by women only (Denis, co-writer Marie NDiaye and star Isabelle Huppert) that produced the character of Maria Vial. Although Maria is filmed in a manner that sometimes makes her appear fragile, and dissolves into a desperately emotional state as her world disintegrates around her, her violent and rationally explicable confrontation with patriarchy shows her agency to be undiminished, while the protagonists of *Morvern Callar*, *Girlhood* and *Fish Tank* win their struggles for freedom, however ambivalent a condition this looks like turning out to be.

I began this book by setting out the thinking of several important women philosophers (Beauvoir, Irigaray, Battersby) on the issue of female subjectivity, drawing too on Foucault's critical and anti-universalist ethics to produce a new 'theory' (an original synthesis of existing thought) of ethical and embodied female subjectivity, with which the first chapter concluded. Then, while detailing how psychoanalytic feminist film theory, now practised considerably less than in its heyday of the 1970s and 1980s while not being entirely obsolete, failed to offer an account of female subjectivity that would 'stick' and be of real utility to the huge amount of writing about filmic gender identities ongoing in film studies and other disciplines, I suggested that a strand of feminist film-philosophical writing is now extant that is better placed to remedy this state of affairs than feminist psychoanalytic film theory was, proposing that Sobchack, Studlar and contemporary critics Constable, Bainbridge, Bolton and Chamarette have published this strand's most significant works to date. In the chapters following the introductory two, I have offered analytically descriptive readings of women's embodied movement, looking, speaking, performance and desiring action in a range of films directed by women. The final chapter, on freedom, did not affirm its title in as thoroughgoing a manner as the preceding chapters, since it approached freedom as a value and a praxis rather than as a foundational concept, but it did maintain that women's sexual freedom has been a major theme and narrative element of films directed by Catherine Breillat and Claire Denis in the 2000s.

In her recent book *What if I Had Been the Hero: Investigating Women's Cinema*, Sue Thornham considers what might result from a substitution of women for the 'heroes' of patriarchally structured narratives such as thrillers and classic crime dramas, referring as she does so to feminist critics Patricia Mellencamp and Laleen Jayamanne, who have pondered the issue of what becomes of hero(in)ism when women are the subjects of film narratives.

Hero(in)ism, she concludes, depends on the transgression of 'some dominant narrative codes, and the psychoanalytic structures that they reproduce' (Thornham 2012: 12). I have consciously avoided psychoanalytic accounts of narrative in this book, because of the Oedipal structures of subjectivity (male and female) they almost always imply, and have attempted to keep desiring subjectivity separate from questions of narrative 'progress' or closure. A remarkable degree of openness characterizes the conclusions of most of the films I have discussed: it is true that a degree of resolution of the female protagonist's trauma occurs in *Red Road*, but in the one film that presents a kind of heterosexual romance, *No Sex Last Night*, the highly ironic and performative presentation of Calle and Shephard's drive across the United States and the breakdown of their brief marriage at the end of the film undoes the closure temporarily attained in their drive-in Las Vegas wedding. *Morvern Callar* closes on an out-of-time sequence that privileges sensory experience over the driven, escapist mode of travel Morvern engages in during the film, and *Fish Tank*'s Mia quits the family home definitively, heading west with a boy who is not any kind of romantic partner. The desire of women like Morvern and Mia is not end-directed or concerned with any identifiable kind of progress; it is an ethical desire that manifests itself either in aggression and violence or as a quest to live free of energy-sapping ordinariness and dysfunctional family relationships. I discussed the sexual freedom narrativized in Breillat's *Romance* and *Brief Crossing* and Denis's *Friday Night* in Chapter 8, but a freedom that is not solely or particularly sexual is also explored by Mia, Morvern and Marième/Vic of *Girlhood*, while Violetta, like Mia, gains release from a relationship with her abusive mother at the end of *My Little Princess*. In the films discussed in Chapter 5, a kind of 'free speech' seems to be being explored by Breillat's protagonists (particularly Solange of *Nocturnal Uproar*), one I have suggested might fruitfully be considered in relation to the practice of *parrhesia* explored alongside other practices of freedom in Foucault's late writings on ethics.

If its ethical 'two-ness' brings the approach to female subjectivity formulated in Chapter 1 within reach of some recent considerations of ethics and film, as I suggested there, it is also this ethicality of female subjectivity I want to emphasize to conclude the book, in order to argue not only that female subjectivity accommodates the recent and contemporary turn to ethics better than the autonomous masculine humanist subject of modernity, but that we are at a historical juncture at which it makes sense to see female subjectivity as in a crucible of formation. (I hope, perhaps obviously, that this book's readings of films directed by women can contribute significantly to a process of formation that is already underway.) Just like the films in which they are dramatized, however, the female subjectivities that feature in these

— hence collaging. fragmenting here

pages are not linear or teleological in form: instead, the open, inconclusive narratives of the films imply that the ethical female subjectivity at work in and around them (because it features in their collaborative creation as well as in their narratives) is *in formation* – the kind of self-formation, perhaps, that is suggested by Foucault's characterization of ethics as a practice of freedom. Contemporary women's cinema may be considered as a discursive entity of the type Foucauldian criticism has often profitably considered, since even if it is rarely anti-humanist, it is most certainly historically specific, having expanded considerably (if not always steadily) since its birth as a cultural category in the 1970s. This book has not attempted to offer a Foucauldian-style genealogy of women's cinema to the same extent as it has performed one of female subjectivity in feminist philosophy, but one term deriving from genealogical studies can, I think, usefully describe the current condition of ethical female subjectivity *in* women's cinema – *entstehend*, or 'emergent' (from *Entstehung* or 'emergence', the second aspect of genealogy after *Herkunft* or 'descent' (McLaren 2002: 85)). Genealogy is 'centrally concerned with the body' as 'the site of constestation and struggle' (McLaren 2002: 85), and women's embodied subjectivity can be seen in contestatory and struggling as well as desiring and haptic mode in many of the films I have discussed. No further conclusions can yet be drawn.

Bibliography

Ahmed, Sara, *Queer Phenomenology: Orientations, Object Others*, Durham, NC: Duke University Press, 2006.

Althusser, Louis, 'Ideology and Ideological State Apparatuses', in *Lenin and Philosophy and Other Essays*, trans. Ben Brewster, New York and London: Monthly Review Press, 1971.

Arp, Kristana, 'The Joys of Disclosure: Simone de Beauvoir and the Phenomenological Tradition', *Analecta Husserliana* LXXXVIII (2005), 393–406.

Austin, J. L., *How to Do Things with Words*, Oxford: Clarendon Press, 1962.

Badiou, Alain, *Ethics: An Essay on the Understanding of Evil*, trans. Peter Hallward, London and New York: Verso, 2001.

Bainbridge, Caroline, *A Feminine Cinematics: Luce Irigaray, Women and Film*, Basingstoke and New York: Palgrave Macmillan, 2007.

Barker, Jennifer, *The Tactile Eye: Touch and the Cinematic Experience*, University of California Press, 2009.

Battersby, Christine, *The Phenomenal Woman. Feminist Metaphysics and the Patterns of Identity*, Cambridge, UK: Polity Press, 1998.

Battersby, Christine, 'Singularity and the Female Self: Encountering the Other', *Women: A Cultural Review* 22: 2–3 (2011), 125–42.

Baudrillard, Jean, 'Please Follow Me', in Sophie Calle ed., *Suite Venitienne*, Paris: Editions de l'Etoile, 1983, 81–93.

de Beauvoir, Simone, *Brigitte Bardot and the Lolita Syndrome*, London: New English Library, 1962.

de Beauvoir, Simone, *The Ethics of Ambiguity*, trans. Bernard Frechtman, Kindle Edition from Citadel Press Books, 2nd edn, 1976 (first published 1948).

de Beauvoir, Simone, *Philosophical Writings*, ed. Margaret A. Simons with Marybeth Timmerman and Marybeth Mader, Urbana: University of Illinois Press, 2004.

de Beauvoir, Simone, *The Second Sex*, trans. and ed. H. M. Parshley, London: Pan Books Ltd, 1988.

de Beauvoir, Simone, *The Second Sex*, trans. Constance Borde and Sheila Malovany-Chevallier, London: Jonathan Cape, 2009.

Bell, Melanie and Williams, Melanie eds, *British Women's Cinema*, London: Routledge, 2010.

Bergoffen, Debra, *The Philosophy of Simone de Beauvoir: Gendered Phenomenologies*, Erotic Generosities, Albany: State University of New York Press, 1997.

Beugnet, Martine, *Claire Denis*, Manchester: Manchester University Press, 2004.

Beugnet, Martine, 'Close-up Vision: Remapping the Body in the Work of Contemporary French Filmmakers', in Gill Rye and Carrie Tarr eds, *Focalizing the Body in Contemporary Women's Writing and Filmmaking in France*, *Nottingham French Studies*, 45: 3 (September 2006), 24–38.

Beugnet, Martine, *Cinema of Sensation: French Film and the Art of Transgression*, Edinburgh: Edinburgh University Press, 2007.

Bolton, Lucy, *Film and Female Consciousness: Irigaray, Cinema and Thinking Women*, Basingstoke and New York: Palgrave Macmillan, 2011.

Boothroyd, Dave, *Ethical Subjects in Contemporary Culture*, Edinburgh: Edinburgh University Press, 2013.

Bordwell, David and Caroll, Noël eds, *Post-Theory: Reconstructing Film Studies*, London and Madison, WI: The University of Wisconsin, 1996.

Boulé, Jean-Pierre and Tidd, Ursula, *Existentialism and Contemporary Cinema: A Beauvoirean Perspective*, New York and Oxford: Berghahn Books, 2012.

Braidotti, Rosi, *Nomadic Subjects: Embodiment and Sexual Difference in Contemporary Feminist Theory*, New York and Chichester, West Sussex: Columbia University Press, 1994.

Breillat, Catherine, 'De la femme et la morale au cinema, de l'exploitation de son aspect physique, de sa place dans le cinéma: comme auteur, comme actrice, ou comme sujet', in Breillat 1999a, 1999b, 8–20.

Breillat, Catherine, *Corps amoureux: entretiens avec Claire Vassé*, Paris: Editions Denoël, 2006.

Brennan, Teresa ed., *Between Feminism and Psychoanalysis*, London and New York: Routledge, 1989.

Butler, Alison, *Women's Cinema. The Contested Screen*, London: Wallflower Press, 2002.

Butler, Judith, 'Sex and Gender in Simone de Beauvoir's *Second Sex*', *Yale French Studies* 72 (1986), 35–49.

Butler, Judith, 'Sexual Ideology and Phenomenological Description: A Feminist Critique of Merleau-Ponty's *Phenomenology of Perception*', in Jeffner Allen and Iris Marion Young eds, *The Thinking Muse: Feminism in Modern French Philosophy*, Indiana University Press, 1989, 85–100.

Butler, Judith, *Gender Trouble: Feminism and the Subversion of Identity*, London and New York: Routledge, 1990.

Butler, Judith, *Bodies that matter: on the discursive limits of "sex"*, London and New York: Routledge, 1993.

Butler, Judith, 'Variations on Sex and Gender: Beauvoir, Wittig and Foucault', first published in Seyla Benhabib and Drucilla Cornell eds, *Feminism as Critique: Essays on the Politics of Gender in Late-Capitalist Societies*, Cambridge: Polity Press, 1987, 128–42, reprinted in Sara Salih with Judith Butler eds, *The Judith Butler Reader*, Oxford: Blackwell Publishing, 2004, 21–38.

Butler, Judith, *Giving an Account of Oneself*, New York: Fordham University Press, 2005.

Butler, Judith, 'Sexual Difference as a Question of Ethics: Alterities of the Flesh in Irigaray and Merleau-Ponty', originally written 1990 and published in Laura Doyle ed., *Bodies of Resistance: New Phenomenologies of Politics, Agency, Culture*, Evanston, IL: Northwestern University Press, 2001, then in Dorothea Olkowski and Gail Weiss eds, *Feminist Interpretations of Merleau-Ponty*, The Pennsylvania State University Press, 2006, 107–26.

Butler, Judith, *Frames of War: When Is Life Grievable?* London and New York, Verso, 2009.

Carman, Taylor, *Merleau-Ponty*, London and New York: Routledge, 2008.

Carroll, Noël, *Mystifying Movies: Fads and Fallacies in Contemporary Film Theory*, New York: Columbia University Press, 1988.

Chamarette, Jenny, *Phenomenology and the Future of Film: Rethinking Subjectivity beyond French Cinema*, Basingstoke and New York: Palgrave Macmillan, 2012.

Chamarette, Jenny, 'Embodied Worlds and Situated Bodies: Feminism, Phenomenology, Film Theory', *Signs: Journal of Women and Society*, 40: 2 (2014) 289–95.

Chamarette, Jenny, 'Embodying Spectatorship: From Phenomenology to Sensation', in E. Ann Kaplan, Patrice Petro, Dijana Jelača, and Kristin Hole eds, *The Routledge Companion to Cinema and Gender*. London: Routledge, 2016 (forthcoming).

Chaudhuri, Shohini, *Feminist Film Theorists. Laura Mulvey, Kaja Silverman, Teresa de Lauretis, Barbara Creed*, London and New York: Routledge, 2006.

Choi, Jinhee and Frey, Matthias, eds, *Cine-Ethics: Ethical Dimensions of Film Theory, Practice, and Spectatorship*, London and New York: Routledge, 2014.

Cixous, Hélène, 'The Laugh of the Medusa', in E. Marks and I. de Courtviron eds, *New French Feminisms: An Anthology*. Brighton: The Harvester Press Ltd, 1981, 245–64.

Clouzot, Claire, *Catherine Breillat: Indécence et Pureté*, Paris: Editions Cahiers du cinema, 2004.

Clover, Carol, *Men, Women and Chainsaws: Gender in the Modern Horror Film*, Princeton: Princeton University Press, 1992.

Constable, Catherine, *Thinking in Images: Film Theory, Feminist Philosophy and Marlene Dietrich*, Basingstoke: Palgrave Macmillan, 2005.

Constable, Liz, 'Unbecoming Sexual Desires for Women Becoming Sexual Subjects: Simone de Beauvoir (1949) and Catherine Breillat (1999)', *MLN* 119: 4 (2004), 672–95.

Cooper, Sarah, *Relating to Queer Theory: Rereading Sexual Self-Definition with Irigaray, Kristeva, Wittig and Cixous*, Bern and Oxford: Peter Lang, 2000.

Cooper, Sarah, *Selfless Cinema? Ethics and French Documentary*, Oxford: Modern Humanities Research Association and W.S.Maney & Son Ltd., 2006.

Corrigan, Timothy, 'The Commerce of Auteurism' in *A Cinema without Walls: Movies and Culture after Vietnam*, London: Routledge, 1991.

Creed, Barbara, *The Monstrous Feminine: Film, Feminism, Psychoanalysis*, London and New York: Routledge, 1993.

Del Rio, E., 'Rethinking Feminist Film Theory: Counter-Narcissistic Performance in Sally Potter's *Thriller*', *Quarterly Review of Film and Video* 21: 1 (2003), 11–24.

Diamond, Irene and Quinby, Lee eds, *Feminism and Foucault: Reflections on Resistance*, Boston: Northeastern University Press, 1988.

Doane, Mary Ann, 'Remembering Women: Psychical and Historical Constructions in Film Theory', in E. Ann Kaplan ed., *Psychoanalysis and Cinema*, London and New York: Routledge, 1990.

Doane, Mary Ann, 'Film and the Masquerade: Theorizing the Female Spectator', in Sue Thornham ed. *Feminist Film Theory: A Reader*, Edinburgh: Edinburgh University Press, 1999, 131–45.

Dobson, Julia, *Negotiating the auteur: Dominique Cabrera, Noémie Lvovsky, Laetitia Masson and Marion Vernoux*, Manchester: Manchester University Press, 2012.

Downing, Lisa, *The Cambridge Introduction to Michel Foucault*, Cambridge: Cambridge University Press, 2008.

Downing, Lisa and Saxton, Libby, *Film and Ethics: Foreclosed Encounters*, London and New York: Routledge, 2009.

Foucault, Michel, 'Discourse and Truth: the Problematization of Parrhesia', at http://foucault.info/documents/parrhesia. Text edited by Joseph Pearson 1999 and re-edited 2006, adapted for the web as a digital archive by Foucault.info in 1999.

Foucault, Michel, 'Docile Bodies' and 'The Means of Correct Training', in Paul Rabinow ed., *The Foucault Reader*, London: Penguin, 1971, 179–205.

Foucault, Michel, *Discipline and Punish: The Birth of the Prison*, London: Vintage Books, 1977.

Foucault, Michel, *Foucault Live: Collected Interviews 1961–1984*, ed. by Sylvère Lotringer, New York: Semiotext, 1989, 1996.

Fowler, Catherine, *Sally Potter*. Urbana and Chicago: University of Illinois Press, 2009.

Fraser, Nancy and Bartky, Sandra Lee eds, *Revaluing French Feminism: Critical Essays on Difference, Agency and Culture*, Bloomington and Indianapolis: Indiana University Press, 1992.

Fulbrook, Kate and Fulbrook, Edward, *Simone de Beauvoir and Jean-Paul Sartre: The Remaking of a Twentieth-Century Legend*, Hemel Hempstead: Harvester Wheatsheaf, 1993 OR New York: Basic Books, 1994.

Gatens, Moira, *Feminism and Philosophy. Perspectives on Difference and Equality*, Cambridge, UK: Polity Press, 1991.

Grant, Catherine, 'Secret Agents: Feminist Theories of Women's Film Authorship', in *Feminist Theory* 2:1 (April 2001) 113–30, or at www.catherinegrant. wordpress.com/secret_agents.

Gratton, Johnie and Michael Sheringham, *The Art of the Project: Projects and Experiments in Modern French Culture*, New York and Oxford: Berghahn Books, 2005.

Green, Laura, 'A 'Fleshy Metaphysics': Irigaray and Battersby on Female Subjectivity', *Women: A Cultural Review* 22: 2–3 (2011), 143–54.

Harper, Sue, *Women in British Cinema: Mad, Bad and Dangerous to Know*, London: Bloomsbury, 2000.

Heidegger, Martin, *Basic Writings*, New York: HarperCollins Publishers, 1977.

Heinamaa, Sara, 'What Is a Woman? Butler and Beauvoir on the Foundations of the Sexual Difference', *Hypatia* 12: 1 (1997), 20–39.

Ince, Kate ed., *Five Directors: Auteurism from Assayas to Ozon*, Manchester: Manchester University Press, 2008.

Ince, Kate ed., 'Introduction: Women's Film-Making in France 2000–2010', *Studies in European Cinema* 10: 1 (2013), 3–10.

Irigaray, Luce, *Speculum. De l'autre femme*, Paris: Les Editions de Minuit, 1974.

Irigaray, Luce, 'This Sex Which Is Not One', in E. Marks and I. de Courtivron eds, *New French Feminisms: An Anthology*. Brighton: The Harvester Press Ltd, 1981, 99–106.

Irigaray, Luce, *Speculum of the Other Woman*, trans. Gillian C. Gill, Ithaca, NY: Cornell University Press, 1985.

Irigaray, Luce, 'The Forgotten Mystery of Female Genealogies/Le mystère oublié des genealogies féminines', in *Le Temps de la Différence*, Paris: Librairie Générale Française, 1989, 101–23.

Irigaray, Luce, 'Questions to Emmanuel Levinas', in Margaret Whitford ed., *The Irigaray Reader*, Oxford: Blackwell, 1991a, 178–89.

Irigaray, Luce, 'Questions', in Margaret Whitford ed., *The Irigaray Reader*, Oxford: Blackwell, 1991b, 133–39.

Irigaray, Luce, *Marine Lover of Friedrich Nietzsche*, trans. Gillian C. Gill, New York: Columbia University Press, 1991c.

Irigaray, Luce, *Elemental Passions*, trans. Joanne Collie and Judith Still, London: Routledge, 1992.

Irigaray, Luce, *An Ethics of Sexual Difference*, trans. Carolyn Burke and Gillian C. Gill, Ithaca, NY: Cornell University Press, 1993a.

Irigaray, Luce, 'The Fecundity of the Caress', in *An Ethics of Sexual Difference*, trans. Carolyn Burke and Gillian C. Gill, Ithaca, NY: Cornell University Press, 1993b, 185–217.

Irigaray, Luce, *I Love to You: Sketch for a Possible Felicity within History*, trans. Alison Martin, London: Routledge, 1996.

Irigaray, Luce, *To Be Two*, trans. Monique M. Rhodes and Marco F. Cocito Monoc, London: Athlone Press, 2000a.

Irigaray, Luce, *Democracy Begins between Two*, trans. Kirsteen Anderson, London: Athlone Press, 2000b.

Irigaray, Luce, *Dialogues. Around Her Work*, special issue of *Paragraph* 25: 3 (2002).

Irigaray, Luce, *Luce Irigaray: Key Writings*, London and New York: Continuum, 2004.

Irigaray, Luce, *Conversations: Luce Irigaray*, London and New York: Continuum, 2008a.

Irigaray, Luce, *Luce Irigaray. Teaching*, London and New York: Continuum, 2008b.

Johnston, Claire, 'Women's cinema as counter-cinema', in Sue Thornham ed. *Feminist Film Theory: A Reader*, Edinburgh: Edinburgh University Press, 1999, 31–40.

Jones, Rachel, *Irigaray. Towards a Sexuate Philosophy*, Cambridge, UK and Malden, MA: Polity Press, 2011.

Keane, Marian E., 'A Closer Look at Scopophilia: Mulvey, Hitchcock and *Vertigo*' in Marshall Deutelbaum and Leland Poague eds, *The Hitchcock Reader*, Oxford: Wiley Blackwell, 2nd edn, 2009, 231–48.

Keesey, Douglas, *Catherine Breillat*, Manchester: Manchester University Press, 2009.

Kruks, Sonia, *Situation and Human Existence: Freedom, Subjectivity and Society*, London: Unwin Hyman, 1990.

Kruks, Sonia, 'Gender and Subjectivity: Simone de Beauvoir and Contemporary Feminism', *Signs* 18: 1 (1992), 89–110.

Kruks, Sonia, *Retrieving Experience: Subjectivity and Recognition in Feminist Politics*, Ithaca, NY: Cornell University Press, 2001.

De Lauretis, Teresa, *Alice Doesn't: Feminism, Semiotics, Cinema*, London: Macmillan, 1984.

De Lauretis, Teresa, *Technologies of Gender*, London and Basingstoke: Macmillan, 1987.

De Lauretis, Teresa, 'Feminist Genealogies: A Personal Itinerary', *Women's Studies International Forum* 16: 4 (1993), 393–403.

Lorraine, Tamsin, *Irigaray and Deleuze: Experiments in Visceral Philosophy*, Ithaca, NY and London: Cornell University Press, 1999.

Marks, Laura U., *The Skin of the Film: Intercultural Cinema, Embodiment and the Senses*, Durham, NC: Duke University Press, 2000.

Marks, Laura U., *Touch: Sensuous Theory and Multisensory Media*, Minneapolis and London: University of Minnesota Press, 2003.

Martin, Angela, 'Refocusing Authorship in Women's Filmmaking', in B.K. Grant ed., *Auteurs and Authorship: A Film Reader*, Oxford: Blackwell Publishing, 2008, 127–34.

Martin, Luther H., Gutman, Huck and Hutton, Patrick H. eds, *Technologies of the Self: A Seminar with Michel Foucault*, London: Tavistock, 1988.

Martin, Marcel and Nacache, Jacqueline, 'Agnès Varda – Profession: documenteuse', *La Revue du cinéma* 436 (March 1988), 53–8.

Martin-Jones, David, ed. 'Film-Philosophy and a World of Cinemas', *Film-Philosophy* 20:1 (2016), 6–194, at www.euppublishing.com/toc/film/20/1.

Maule, Rosanna, *Beyond Auteurism. New Directions in Authorial Film Practices in France, Italy and Spain since the 1980s*, Bristol and Chicago: Intellect Books, 2008.

Mayer, Sophie, *The Cinema of Sally Potter: A Politics of Love*, London: Wallflower Press, 2009.

Mayne, Judith, *The Woman at the Keyhole. Feminism and Women's Cinema*, Bloomington and Indianapolis: Indiana University Press, 1990.

Mayne, Judith, *Cinema and Spectatorship*, London and New York: Routledge, 1993.

Mayne, Judith, *Directed by Dorothy Arzner*, Bloomington: Indiana University Press, 1994.

Mayne, Judith, *Claire Denis*, Urbana and Chicago: University of Illinois Press, 2005.

Mazierska, Eva and Rascaroli, Laura, *Crossing New Europe: Postmodern Travel and the European Road Movie*, London and New York: Wallflower Press, 2006.

McCabe, Janet, *Feminist Film Studies: Writing the Woman into Cinema*, London: Wallflower Press, 2004.

McGowan, Todd, *The Real Gaze: Film Theory after Lacan*, Albany State University of New York Press, 2007.

McHugh, Kathleen and Sobchack, Vivian eds, 'Beyond the Gaze: Recent Approaches to Film Feminisms', *Signs* 30: 1 (2004), 1205–489.

McLaren, Margaret A., *Feminism, Foucault and Embodied Subjectivity* Albany: State University of New York Press, 2002.

McNay, Lois, *Foucault and Feminism: Power, Gender and the Self*, Cambridge: Polity Press, 1992.

Merleau-Ponty, Maurice, 'The Philosopher and His Shadow', in *Signs*, trans. with an introduction by Richard C McCleary, Evanston: Northwestern University Press, 1964a, 159–81.

Merleau-Ponty, Maurice, 'The Child's Relations with Others', trans. William Cobb in *The Primacy of Perception*, Northwestern University Press, 1964b, 96–155.

Merleau-Ponty, Maurice, *Phenomenology of Perception*, trans. Colin Smith, London and New York: Routledge, 2002.

Metz, Christian, *The Imaginary Signifier: Psychoanalysis and Cinema*, trans. Celia Britton, Annwyl Williams, Ben Brewster, and Alfred Guzzetti, Bloomington: Indiana University Press, 1982.

Michaud, Jean and Bellour, Raymond, 'Agnès Varda de A à Z', *Cinéma* 61: 60 (1961), 3–20.

Moi, Toril, *Simone de Beauvoir. The Making of an Intellectual Woman*, Oxford: Blackwell, 1994.

Moi, Toril, *What Is a Woman? And Other Essays*, Oxford: Oxford University Press, 1999.

Mulvey, Laura, 'Visual Pleasure and Narrative Cinema', *Visual and Other Pleasures*, Indiana: Bloomington University Press, 1989a, 14–26.

Mulvey, Laura, 'Afterthoughts on "Visual Pleasure and Narrative Cinema" inspired by King Vidor's *Duel in the Sun*', *Visual and Other Pleasures*, Indiana: Bloomington University Press, 1989b, 29–38.

Mulvey, Laura, *Death 24 x a Second*, London: Reaktion Books, 2006.

Osborne, Peter, 'Gender as Performance: An Interview with Judith Butler,' *Radical Philosophy* 67 (1994), 32–9.

Penley, Constance, *The Future of an Illusion: Film, Feminism, and Psychoanalysis*, London: Routledge, 1989.

Prédal, René, 'Agnès Varda, une oeuvre en marge du cinema français', in Michel Estève ed. *Agnès Varda, Etudes cinématographiques, 179–186*, Paris: Editions Minard, 1991, 13–39.

Ramazanoglu, Caroline ed., *Up against Foucault: Explorations of Some Tensions between Foucault and Feminism*, London: Routledge, 1993.

Riggs, Larry W., 'Trouble in the Empire of the Gaze: Woman, Scopophilia and Power in Several Seventeenth-Century Works', *Literature Interpretation Theory* 8: 2 (1997), 123–33.

Ruby Rich, B. *Chick Flicks: Theories and Memories of the Feminist Film Movement*, Durham: Duke University Press, 1998.

Ruby Rich, B. 'The Crisis of Naming in Feminist Criticism', in Sue Thornham, ed., *Feminist Film Theory: A Reader*, Edinburgh: Edinburgh University Press, 1999, 41–7.

Ruti, Mari, *Between Levinas and Lacan: Self, Other, Ethics*, London and New York: Bloomsbury Academic, 2015.

Sawicki, Jane, *Disciplining Foucault: Feminism, Power and the Body*, London: Routledge, 1991.

Sellier, Geneviève, *Masculine Singular: French New Wave Cinema*, trans. Kristin Ross, Durham, NC: Duke University Press, 2008.

Silverman, Kaja, 'The Female Authorial Voice', *The Acoustic Mirror: The Female Voice in Psychoanalysis and Cinema*, Indiana University Press, 1988, 187–234.

Simons, Margaret, *Beauvoir and the Second Sex: Feminism, Race and the Origins of Existentialism*, Lanham, Maryland and Oxford: Rowman & Littlefield Publishers, Inc., 1999.

Sinnerbrink, Robert, *New Philosophies of Film: Thinking Images*, London: Bloomsbury, 2011.

Sobchack, Vivian, *The Address of the Eye: A Phenomenology of Film Experience*, Princeton, NJ: Princeton University Press, 1992.

Stacey, Jackie, 'Desperately Seeking Difference', *Screen* 28: 1 (Winter 1987), 48–61.

Studlar, Gaylyn, 'Reconciling Feminism and Phenomenology: Notes on Problems and Possibiltiies, Texts and Contexts' *Quarterly Review of Film and Video* 12: 3 (1990), 69–78.

Tarr, Carrie, 'Introduction: Women's Film-Making in France 2000–2010' *Studies in French Cinema* 12: 3 (2012), 189–200.

Tarr, Carrie and Rollet, Brigitte, *Cinema and the Second Sex*, London: Continuum Books, 2001.

Thornham, Sue ed., *Feminist Film Theory: A Reader*, Edinburgh: Edinburgh University Press, 1999, 31–40.

Thornham, Sue ed., *What If I Had Been the Hero? Investigating Women's Cinema*, Basingstoke and New York: Palgrave Macmillan, 2012.

Varda, Agnès, 'Autour et alentour de Daguerréotypes', *Cinéma* 204 (1975), 39–53.

Vintges, Karen, *Philosophy as Passion: The Thinking of Simone de Beauvoir*, Bloomington: Indiana University Press, 1996.

Wheatley, Catherine, *Michael Haneke's Cinema: The Ethic of the Image*, New York and Oxford: Berghahn Books, 2009.

Whitford, Margaret, *Luce Irigaray: Philosophy in the Feminine*, London and New York: Routledge, 1991.

Woolf, Virginia, *Orlando: A Biography*, Oxford: Blackwell, 1998.

Woolf, Virginia, *Mrs Dalloway*, London: Penguin, 2012.

Young, Iris Marion, 'Throwing Like a Girl: A Phenomenology of Feminine Body Comportment, Motility and Spatiality', in Jeffner Allen and Iris Marion Young eds, *The Thinking Muse: Feminism in Modern French Philosophy*, Bloomington: Indiana University Press, 1989, 51–70.

Young, Iris Marion, *On Female Body Experience*, Oxford: Oxford University Press, 2005.

Žižek, Slavoj, 'Neighbours and Other Monsters: A Plea for Ethical Violence', in Slavoj Žižek, Eric L. Santner and Kenneth Reinhardt eds, *The Neighbour: Three Enquiries in Political Theology*, with a new Preface, Chicago: University of Chicago Press, 2nd edn 2013, 134–90.

Bande de filles/Girlhood

Mantziari, Despoina, "Solide mais pas Solitaire': Female Solidarity and Feminist Empowerment in *Girlhood* (*Bande de filles*, Céline Sciamma, 2014), 24/6/15 at www.auteusetheory.blogspot.co.uk.

Brève Traversée/Brief Crossing

Peranson, Mark, 'Gentler, not Kinder: *Brève Traverseé*', report from the Thessaloniki film festival, *CinémaScope* 9 (2001), 17.

Fish Tank
Budt, Karin Luisa, 'Festivals: Cannes 2009: Andrea Arnold's *Fish Tank* Makes the Most Waves', *Film Criticism* 33: 3 (2009), 67–71.
Mullen, Lisa, 'Estate of the Mind', *Sight and Sound* 19: 10 (2009), 16–19.

Les Glaneurs et la glaneuse/The Gleaners and I
Rosello, Mireille, 'Agnès Varda's *Les Glaneurs et la glaneuse*: Portrait of the Artist as an Old Lady', *Studies in French Cinema* 1: 1 (2001), 29–36.

Les Plages d'Agnès/The Beaches of Agnes
Bellour, Raymond, 'Varda ou l'art contemporain: Note sur *Les Plages d'Agnès*. *Trafic* 69 (2009), 16–19.
Romney, Jonathan, 'A Life through a Lens', *Sight and Sound* 19: 10 (2009), 46–7.

Morvern Callar
Darke, Chris, 'Has Anyone Seen This Girl?' *Vertigo* 2: 4 (2003), 16–17.
Elsey, Eileen, Interview with Lynne Ramsay about *Morvern Callar, Vertigo* 2: 4 (2003), 14–15.
Pride, Ray, 'Sound and Vision: Lynne Ramsay on *Morvern Callar*', *CinemaScope* 13 (2002), 5–8.
Smith, B., 'On the Brink of the New', *Inside Film* 48 (2002), 22, 24, 26.
Williams, Linda Ruth, 'Escape Artist', *Sight and Sound* 12: 10 (2002), 22–5.

Mrs Dalloway
Bell, Vereen M., 'Misreading Mrs Dalloway', *The Sewanee Review* 114: 1 (2006), 93–111.
Hankins, Leslie Kathleen, '"Colour Burning on a Framework of Steel": Virginia Woolf, Marleen Gorris, Eileen Atkins and *Mrs Dalloway(s)*', *Women's Studies* 28: 4 (1999), 367–77.
Kaufman, Debra, 'Production Slate: The Two Faces of Mrs Dalloway', *American Cinematographer* 79: 2 (1998), 20–4.
Kendrick, Walter, 'The Unfilmable', in *Salmagundi* 121/122 (Winter/Spring 1999), 47–62.

My Little Princess
Jean-Marc Lalanne in *Les Inrockuptibles* 29/6/11.
Jacques Mandelbaum in *Le Monde* 29/6/11.
Les Inrockuptibles 14/07/10.
Les Inrockuptibles 18/05/11.
Le Figaro 29/6/11.
Le Canard enchaîné 29/6/11.
Les Echos 29/6/11.
Télérama 29/06/11.

Tapage nocturne/Nocturnal Uproar
Babert, Caroline, '*Tapage nocturne*: le malaise d'une jeune marginale', in *Le Matin* 26/09/79.
Delila Hervé in *Libération*, 26/09/79.
Devarrieux, Claire, '*Tapage nocturne*. Des cris, des cris..', *France-Soir* 08/10/79.

Fieschi, Jacques, 'Tapage nocturne', *Cinématographe* 51 (1979), 47.
Marmin, Michel, 'Lamentations narcissiques', *Le Figaro* 01/10/79.

No Sex Last Night
Cooke, Lynne, 'Doubleblind', Interview with Sophie Calle and Greg Shephard, *Art Monthly* 163 (1993), 3–7.
Ince, Kate, 'Games with the Gaze: Sophie Calle's Postmodern Phototextuality', in Johnnie Gratton and Michael Sheringham eds, *The Art of the Project: Projects and Experiments in Modern French Culture*, New York and Oxford: Berghahn Books, 2005, 111–22.

Orlando
Degli-Esposti, C., 'Sally Potter's *Orlando* and the Neo-Baroque Scopic Regime', *Cinema Journal* 36: 1 (1996), 75–93.
Garrett, Roberta, 'Costume Drama and Counter Memory: Sally Potter's *Orlando*', in J. Dowson and S. Earnshaw eds, *Postmodern Subjects/Postmodern Texts*, Amsterdam and Atlanta: Rodopi, 1995, 89–99.
Imre, Aniko, 'Twin Pleasures of Feminism: *Orlando* Meets *My Twentieth Century*', *Camera Obscura* 18: 54 (2003), 176–211.
Mayer, Sophie, *The Cinema of Sally Potter: A Politics of Love*. London and New York: Wallflower Press, 2009.
Mellencamp, Patricia, 'What Virginia Woolf Did Tell Sally Potter', *A Fine Romance – Five Ages of Film Feminism*. Philadelphia, PA: Temple University Press, 1995, 281–88.
Pidduck, Joanne, 'Travels with Sally Potter's *Orlando*: Gender, Narrative, Movement', *Screen* 38: 2 (1997), 172–89.

Red Road
Lake, Jessica, '*Red Road* (2006) and Emerging Narratives of "Sub-Veillance"', *Continuum: Journal of Media and Cultural Studies* 24: 2 (2010), 131–40.
Pisters, Patricia, 'The Neurothriller', *New Review of Film and Television Studies* 12: 2 (2014), 83–93.

Romance
Breillat, Catherine, *Romance: Scenario*, Paris: Editions Cahiers du cinema, 1999a.
Breillat, Catherine, Interview with Linda Ruth Williams, *Sight and Sound* 9: 10 (1999), 13–14.
Breillat, Catherine and Denis, Claire, 'Le ravissement de Marie: Dialogue entre Catherine Breillat et Claire Denis', *Cahiers du cinema* 534 (1999), 42–5.
Brinkema, Eugénie, 'Celluloid is Sticky: Sex, Death, Materiality, Metaphysics (in some films by Catherine Breillat)', *Women: A Cultural Review* 17: 2 (2006), 147–70.
Felperlin, Leslie, 'The Edge of the Razor', *Sight and Sound* 9: 10 (1999), 12–13.
Jousse, Thierry, 'Les mystères de l'organisme', *Cahiers du cinema* 534 (1999), 40–41.

Sex Is Comedy
Frappat, Hélène and Lalanne, Jean-Marc, 'Breillat Parillaud: Auto-Frictions', *Cahiers du cinéma* 568 (2002), 34–7 and 38–99.

The Tango Lesson

Fischer, Lucy, '"Dancing through the Minefield": Passion, Pedagogy, Politics and Production in *The Tango Lesson*', *Cinema Journal* 43: 3 (2004), 42–58.

Guano, Emmanula, 'She Looks at Him with the Eyes of a Camera: Female Visual Pleasures and the Polemic with Fetishism in Sally Potter's *Tango Lesson*', *Third Text* 18: 5 (2004), 461–74.

Potter, Sally, 'Bruises and Blisters', *Sight and Sound*, LFF supplement (1997), 4–7.

White Material

Andrew Asibong, 'Claire Denis's Flickering Spaces of Hospitality', *L'Esprit Createur* 51: 1 (Spring 2011), 154–67.

Les Inrockuptibles 18/08/09.

Les Echos 24/03/10.

Les Inrockuptibles 24/03/10.

Marianne 20/03/10.

Télérama 24/03/10.

Pourquoi (pas) le Brésil?/Why (Not) Brazil?

Audé, Françoise, Eisenreich, P. and Martinez, D., 'Entretien, Laetitia Masson. J'ai un côté rock'n'roll', *Positif* 523 (2004), 15–18.

Masson,'La Libre Interview',at http://letelelibre.fr/index.php/2007/12/lalibreinterview-de-laetitia-masson/.

Romney, Jonathan, 'French Exceptions', *Sight and Sound* 18: 5 (2008), 42–44.

Journal du dimanche 19/09/04.

Le Figaroscope 15/9/04.

France-soir 15/9/04.

Vendredi soir/Friday Night

Newton, Elizabeth, 'The Phenomenology of Desire: Claire Denis's *Vendredi soir* (2002)', *Studies in French Cinema* 8: 1 (2008), 17–28.

'M.G', in *L'Humanité* 11/09/02.

Filmography

Primary sources

Bande de filles/Girlhood, directed by Céline Sciamma, 2014, France: StudioCanal, 2015, DVD.

Brève Traversée/Brief Crossing, directed by Catherine Breillat, 2001, UK: Second Sight Films, 2006, DVD.

Fish Tank, directed by Andrea Arnold, 2009, London: Artificial Eye, 2010, DVD.

Les Glaneurs et la glaneuse/The Gleaners and I, directed by Agnès Varda, 2000, London: Artificial Eye, 2011, DVD.

Les Plages d'Agnès/The Beaches of Agnes, directed by Agnès Varda, 2008, London: Artificial Eye, 2008, DVD.

Morvern Callar, directed by Lynne Ramsay, 2002, London: Momentum Pictures, 2003, DVD.

Mrs Dalloway, directed by Marleen Gorris, 1997, London: Artificial Eye, 1998, VHS.

My Little Princess, directed by Eva Ionesco, 2011, Paris: blaq out, 2011, DVD.

No Sex Last Night, directed by Sophie Calle and Greg Shephard, 1995, Paris: FNAC/Cinéma Portugais, VHS.

Orlando, directed by Sally Potter, 1992, London: Artificial Eye, 1997, DVD.

Pourquoi (pas) le Brésil?/Why (Not) Brazil?, directed by Laetitia Masson, 2004, Paris: blaq out, 2005, DVD.

Red Road, directed by Andrea Arnold, 2005, London: Verve Pictures, 2007, DVD.

Romance, directed by Catherine Breillat, 1999, London: blue Light, 2000, DVD.

Sex Is Comedy, directed by Catherine Breillat, 2002, Paris: Editions Montparnasse, 2003, DVD.

Tapage nocturne/Nocturnal Uproar, directed by Catherine Breillat, 1979. No longer issued on VHS or DVD.

The Tango Lesson, directed by Sally Potter, 1997, Netherlands: Home Screen, 1997, DVD.

Vendredi soir/Friday Night, directed by Claire Denis, 2002, France: Tartan DVD, 2002.

White Material, directed by Claire Denis, 2009, London: Artificial Eye, 2010, DVD.

Secondary sources

Abus de faiblesse, directed by Catherine Breillat, 2013.

A ma soeur!, directed by Catherine Breillat, 2001.

Anatomie de l'enfer, directed by Catherine Breillat, 2004.

And Life Goes On, directed by Abbas Kiarostami, 1992.

Antonia's Line, directed by Marleen Gorris, 1995.

Baise-moi, directed by Virginie Despentes and Coralie Trinh-Thi, 2000.

Barbe bleue, directed by Catherine Breillat, 2009.

Beau Travail, directed by Claire Denis, 1998.

Boyhood, directed by Richard Linklater, 2014.

Boys Don't Cry, directed by Kimberley Peirce, 1999.

Cléo de 5 à 7, directed by Agnès Varda, 1961.

Daguerréotypes, directed by Agnès Varda, 1975.

Daughters of the Dust, directed by Julie Dash, 1991.

Dog, directed by Andrea Arnold, 2001.

Donkeys, directed by Mary McKinnon, 2010.

8 Femmes, directed by François Ozon, 2002.

Empire of the Senses, directed by Nagisa Ôshima, 1976.

Gouttes d'eau sur pierres brûlantes, directed by François Ozon, 2000.

Jacquot de Nantes, directed by Agnès Varda, 1991.

Jane B. by Agnès V., directed by Agnès Varda, 1988.

Kung-Fu Master, directed by Agnès Varda, 1988.

La belle endormie, directed by Catherine Breillat, 2010.

La Haine, directed by Matthieu Kassovitz, 1995.

L'Intrus, directed by Claire Denis, 2004.

La Jetée, directed by Chris Marker, 1962.

Le Locataire, directed by Roman Polanski, 1976.

La Nuit américaine, directed by François Truffaut, 1973.

Le Repentie, directed by Laetitia Masson, 2002.

Les Salauds, directed by Claire Denis, 2013.

Le Temps du loup, directed by Michael Haneke, 2005.

Le Temps qui reste, directed by François Ozon, 2005.

Maladolescenza, directed by Pier Giuseppe Murgia, 1977.

Milk, directed by Andrea Arnold, 1998.

Naissance des pieuvres, directed by Céline Sciamma, 2007.

Nikita, directed by Luc Besson, 1990.

Parfait Amour!, directed by Catherine Breillat, 1996

Rage, directed by Sally Potter, 2009.

Ratcatcher, directed by Lynne Ramsay, 1999.

Sale comme un ange, directed by Catherine Breillat, 1991.

Sans toit ni loi, directed by Agnès Varda, 1985.

S'en fout la mort, directed by Claire Denis, 1990.

Sous le sable, directed by François Ozon, 2000.

The Gold Diggers, directed by Sally Potter, 1983.

The Hours, directed by Stephen Daldry, 2002.

The London Story, directed by Sally Potter, 1986.

The Piano, directed by Jane Campion, 1993.

36 fillette, directed by Catherine Breillat, 1988.

Thriller, directed by Sally Potter, 1979.

Through the Olive Trees, directed by Abbas Kiarostami, 1994.

Tomboy, directed by Céline Sciamma, 2011.

Trouble Every Day, directed by Claire Denis, 2001.

Une vieille maîtresse, directed by Catherine Breillat, 2007.

Une vraie jeune fille, directed by Catherine Breillat, 1976.

Vertigo, directed by Alfred Hitchcock, 1958.

Index

Note: The letter 'n' following locators refers to notes